W9-BLZ-385

DIEFENBAKER: LEADERSHIP GAINED 1956–62

PETER STURSBERG

Diefenbaker: Leadership gained 1956-62

UNIVERSITY OF TORONTO PRESS

TORONTO AND BUFFALO

F
1034.3
.D5
S 8x

Contents

ACKNOWLEDGMENTS vii

INTRODUCTION ix

1
Leadership gained 3

2
The road to the Coliseum 23

3
The turning point 35

4
Leadership exercised 61

5
The Liberals commit suicide 81

6
Too great a triumph 91

7
Vision and reality 107

8
From Saskatchewan to China 127

9
Public and official relations 141

10
For Commonwealth and trade 161

11
'Stuff' and cabinet meetings 175

12
Diefenbaker and French Canada 191

13
The wrong and the rights 209

14
The Coyne catastrophe 229

15
The disaster of an election devaluation 251

INDEX 273

Acknowledgments

In writing this book, I am indebted to many persons, but most of all to Leo La Clare, the head of the historical sound recording section of the Public Archives of Canada, who seized on my project of recording the memoirs of the Diefenbaker era when it was at a tentative stage and helped push it to completion. He turned out to be a delightful travelling companion and a shrewd adviser as we journeyed across the country to interview the surviving cabinet ministers and other associates of the thirteenth prime minister. It is a tribute to the far-sightedness of Dr W.I. Smith, the dominion archivist, that the Public Archives should have gone beyond the bounds of collecting and preserving our history and undertaken the exceptional task of going out and getting or 'creating' it.

From the beginning, Mr Marsh Jeanneret, director of the University of Toronto Press, lent his support. Ian Montagnes, general editor of the Press, had had experience in transposing the spoken word to the printed page and gave me invaluable advice as to structure and format. It was a pleasure to work with Patricia Lagacé on the editing.

I wish to thank B.T. Richardson, who was Mr Diefenbaker's last executive assistant when he was prime minister and is his literary executor, for his encouragement, and Keith Martin, Mr Diefenbaker's present executive assistant, for his help.

Before the Public Archives became involved, Dr Arthur E. Blanchette, director of the historical division, Department of External Affairs, was of the greatest assistance. It was he who got the first tapes transcribed. This is the hardest job in any so-called oral history, and it takes a special skill.

Louise Marshall transcribed the first half-dozen of the two-to-four hour interviews. When the Public Archives became involved, Mrs Sylvia Carrière did fully half of the transcripts, and Mrs Bonnie McConnell and Miss Wendy Halcro the rest. Mrs Marlene Pratt, Mr La Clare's secretary, retyped many of the interviews. Leo La Clare himself cut up the transcripts and arranged the excerpts according to the chapter heads. Publication of this volume was assisted by the Canada Council and the Ontario Arts Council under their block grant programs.

A complete list of the interviews and the transcripts, which are the raw material of this book, will be included at the end of the second volume.

Introduction

This is the first volume of a history of the Diefenbaker era, as told by men and women who were for the most part directly involved in its making. It is different from some examples of the new approach called 'oral history' in that those who are quoted are identified. They are the main characters in the play of events, not anonymous members of the crowd. They include: Donald Fleming, the former finance minister, giving his version of the embittered struggle with James Coyne, governor of the Bank of Canada; Alvin Hamilton describing the big breakthrough of the wheat deal with China; and Allister Grosart talking of what he did to produce the greatest parliamentary majority in Canadian history. But most of all the book is about John George Diefenbaker – the upstart, the crusader, the orator, the renegade, the Chief, the folk hero – and the way he was regarded by the many who loved and admired him and the few who feared and hated him.

It is called oral history because it is the result of recorded interviews and discussions I had with some forty people. However, the term has an electronic connotation, as if oral history had something to do with a radio or television documentary. That is why I prefer to call this approach 'living history.' It is fresh and vital and as compelling as if in your own living room you were hearing Mike Starr recall his adventures in becoming the first minister of Ukrainian descent, or Pierre Sévigny frankly recount how he tricked Diefenbaker into winning the support of Premier Maurice Duplessis and the powerful Union Nationale party in Quebec.

The actual words spoken in the recorded interviews are reproduced. The transcripts have been edited only to abridge and adapt the spoken word to print. Some of the transcripts had to be edited more than others, but every precaution was taken not to change the meaning or the intent of what was said, or to remove words from their context. As often happens in conversation, and even in sworn testimony, occasional mistakes were made in facts, dates, and places. For instance, where was Diefenbaker when he learned about the devaluation of the dollar during the 1962 election campaign? He told me that he was in Grandby, Quebec, but Roy Faibish, who accompanied him on that campaign, said he was in Chicoutimi.

In most cases facts can be checked, and, wherever possible, in fairness to both reader and speaker matters of detail have been corrected. Different participants, however, may give different interpretations of the same event; this is bound to happen, especially if it is a controversial matter. Living or oral history brings out the fact there is no simple explanation, no single truth. In such instances the varying views of the participants have not been touched, nor has any attempt been made at assessment or judgment. That is left to the reader.

Another feature of a history based on personal interviews is that it discloses emotions and human qualities – the prickly partisanship of Jack Pickersgill; the indignation of Ellen Fairclough, the first woman cabinet minister, when she denied that she had ever cried at a cabinet meeting, as a colleague had said; the portentous sadness of the economic adviser, Merril Menzies, in the face of the overwhelming opposition to his expansionist policies; the soldierly loyalty of Gordon Churchill. From what they say, John Diefenbaker emerges.

However, there are some aspects of his character and the times that the interviews which follow do not adequately reveal. There is particularly his humour, which the printed word seems to dull. Gowan Guest, who was his executive assistant, told me: 'There literally wasn't a day in the whole two and a half years that I worked with him that there wasn't a belly laugh about something.' Guest also said that Diefenbaker, as prime minister, was not obsessed with power; he was very conscious of his office but had no desire to move people around because of it, and so turned down the pleas of some of his ministers to shuffle top officials. James Nelson spoke of Diefenbaker's stamina and vigour. He recalled that, shortly after his appointment as the first press secretary to a Canadian prime minister, there was a lost weekend of flying back and forth across the continent, to Banff where the prime minister addressed the Canadian Bar Association, then, through the night to Dartmouth University where he received a degree, and on to Quebec City for another ceremony before returning to Ottawa. The reason Diefenbaker was not completely exhausted after so arduous a trip was his ability to sleep at will, sitting up in a plane or automobile. It is sometimes forgotten that he was the first jet-age prime minister (although that continent-crossing-and-recrossing flight was made in the noisy propeller-driven North Star), and yet he liked to campaign by train.

The portable tape recorder has made possible living, or oral, history. (There are some zealots who insist on calling it aural history, which seems to make it more than ever akin to radio.) Portability is a relative and recent phenomenon, as I well know. The first tape recording I made was when I was the CBC correspondent at the United Nations in the early fifties, and the first portable tape recording machine that I saw was the bulky old Webcor. It was almost as heavy as one of the two large black suitcases which contained the so-called portable recording equipment which we had during the Second World War. The Canadian Broadcasting Corporation provided its war correspondents in Europe with the very latest electronic gear, which was a high fidelity disc recording machine that was portable only to the extent that it could be carried around on a jeep; it was run off the jeep's battery as it had no power source of its own, and the jeep's engine had to be kept running to provide it with enough charge so that we could capture the sounds of battle.

The latest generation of tape recorders is so small that it fits into a purse; it is about the size of a notebook and not much heavier, and newspaper reporters have taken to carrying it around and using it to record interviews and announcements. The tape recorder saves a lot of scribbling and is much more accurate. However, the use they make of it as a notebook is very different from the use of portable tape recorders by electronic journalists. Generally speaking, the correspondents of radio and television 'publish' excerpts of the actual spoken words from the tapes they take, while the newspaper correspondents report on what was said. This is the difference between a documentary film, for which episodes have been recreated and even re-enacted, and cinéma vérité, which is like being there at the time and listening to those who made history explain what they did and what they did not do. What a thrill it would be if we could hear the reminiscences of the Fathers of Confederation, as they recalled the events of a century ago, and have them printed so we could read them. And what a revelation it would probably be!

My first venture into oral history (it wasn't called that then) was in the late fifties and early sixties. The hour-long or longer interviews-in-depth were done primarily for the CBC archives, although it was intended that they could be used as raw material for programs. At the prompting of Dan McArthur, the corporation's former chief news editor, I recorded the memoirs of veterans of the First World War, including those of General A.G.L. McNaughton, and General Sir Richard Turner, who commanded the Canadian Corps before Sir Arthur Currie. Unfortunately, Sir Richard was past his prime when I talked to him. I also taped interviews with such people as former Prime Minister Louis St Laurent, Senator Chubby Power, and Vilhjalmar Steffanson: those three and half hours of reminiscences by the Arctic explorer amounted to his last public words, for he suffered a fatal stroke a few days later. I also did a series on the pioneers of broadcasting in which Alphonse Ouimet, then president of the CBC, described how the gap between his front teeth was used as a test pattern for the first television camera, which he invented in the early thirties.

Shortly after the 1967 Conservative leadership convention, I began recording Mr Diefenbaker's memoirs. I remember that we had the first hour-and-a-half long sessions at Stornoway, the official residence of the leader of the opposition in Ottawa. By the early seventies, Mr Diefenbaker seemed not to want to continue. We had had a half-dozen sessions where he had dealt fairly fully with the early days in Saskatchewan, his struggle to become leader, the formation of the first Conservative government in twenty-two years, and had reached the historic 1958 majority, when he said that he wanted to consult his papers before going on. Although he never closed the door, he kept putting me off. By then, McArthur was dead and the CBC had no funds for oral history. For a time I gave up.

Then I had lunch with Senator Eugene Forsey, who entertained me with stories about Mr Diefenbaker. I felt the stories were so good that they should be recorded, and Dr Forsey was agreeable. From that taping, I revived the moribund project and broadened it to include talking to those closely associated with John Diefenbaker and getting them to recall the times and the man.

Among those whom I interviewed were most of the surviving Conservative cabinet ministers, including Howard Green, Donald Fleming, Léon Balcer, George Hees, Davie Fulton, Gordon Churchill, Ellen Fairclough, Alvin Hamilton, Mike Starr, Pierre Sévigny; the movers and shakers in the party such as Allister Grosart, Dick Bell, and Grattan O'Leary; as well as the following executive assistants and aides: Gowan Guest, Merril Menzies, John Fisher, B.T. Richardson, James Nelson, and Roy Faibish. There were the political opponents: Tommy Douglas who was premier of Saskatchewan when Diefenbaker came to power, former Social Credit leader Robert Thompson, and prominent Liberals such as Paul Martin and Jack Pickersgill. I was unable to interview L.B. Pearson because of his untimely death. I also talked with a couple of representative journalists – Victor Mackie, correspondent of the Winnipeg *Free Press*, and Clément Brown who was then with *Le Devoir*, Montreal – and Mr Justice Emmett Hall, who had known John Diefenbaker as a student.

From the above list, it is apparent that those I interviewed were mainly politicians or persons closely involved in the political process as aides or reporters. I did not interview any of the former federal civil servants, although they were an issue at the time, both collectively and individually. This was a deliberate decision on my part. Aside from the question of whether I could persuade them to talk for publication, I felt that if the book were to have any form, it should be confined to the recollections of those who were responsible for (or opposed to, or in a few cases observed) the first and last Conservative government in forty years. James Coyne, for example, had had his 'day in court' before the Senate committee and told his side of his conflict with the government, but this is the first time that Donald Fleming has given publicly his account of what happened.

What follows is not, therefore, the full story of the Diefenbaker era, and this book does not pretend to be that. If anything, it is the recorded table talk of cabinet ministers and other insiders and, as such, is the raw material of history. The definitive work, when it is written, will undoubtedly draw on this book as a source, as well as the full tapes and transcripts of the interviews which are deposited in the Public Archives of Canada and will be available for research after this project is completed.

Each person interviewed was told that the purpose of the interviews was to provide material for this book. The interviews followed a pattern: questions first about the person's initial meeting with Mr Diefenbaker, and then about the events, in chronological order, of the Diefenbaker era, beginning with the Progressive Conservative leadership convention of December 1956. The tapes varied in length from about an hour to more than four hours. Some of those interviewed welcomed the opportunity of recording their memoirs and having them preserved for posterity in the Public Archives of Canada. Several made special trips to Ottawa, and Donald Fleming came all the way from the Bahamas. Others turned me down. There were one or two who asserted that they wanted to write their own reminiscences but gave in to my importuning, for which I thank them.

In the case of George Hees, there was a condition to my interviewing him, and that was that we would not talk about the break-up of the Diefenbaker government (which is not part of this volume). I agreed because I wanted his participation. This may be a weakness of living or oral history, that there is no way of persuading anyone, especially a politician, to say what he does not want to say, although it is probable that the full story would be obtained from the others involved.

As the CBC no longer provided me with an engineer and sound recording equipment to do the interviews, I took to using my portable Sony. I happened to mention what I was doing to Dr Wilfred Smith, the dominion archivist, who put me in touch with Leo La Clare, head of the Historical Sound Recordings Section. Leo dubbed my cassettes onto reels for storage and eventual transcription, and suggested that I make use of the Archives' high fidelity recording equipment, which I did. In fact, most of the interviews used in this book have been done in cooperation with Leo La Clare and using the Archives' recording studio or its portable recording equipment.

In November 1973, Mr Diefenbaker agreed to continue recording his memoirs. We had a couple of sessions in his House of Commons office and, at the time, he suggested that we visit Barbados, where he was going to spend the Christmas holidays, and complete the interviews there. The Archives agreed that this would be worthwhile and sent Leo La Clare and myself to the Caribbean resort, where we were able to finish the job by taping seven hours with Mr Diefenbaker during three morning sessions.

When I began writing and editing this volume, Mr Diefenbaker was actively engaged in preparing his own memoirs and, in November 1974, signed a contract for their publication. He was told that my use of the nineteen hours of interviews that I had with him would be in violation of this contract; although some advisers questioned this, it was decided not to use any part or portion of those transcripts. In any case, the great bulk of my interviews were *about* Diefenbaker and the Diefenbaker period.

Even after this excision, I still had a hundred hours or more of interviews left, which amounted to a million words. I do not expect to use more than a quarter of this verbiage in the two volumes that are planned for the project. Not all of the forty or more persons who were interviewed appear in the first volume which ends with the 1962 election, and the reason is that they did not reach the national stage or make their mark until after this date. As this is an account of the times of Diefenbaker rather than the man, the book has been arranged chronologically; and although there is some overlapping the transcripts have been edited and grouped according to subjects, so that each event, be it the 1956 convention or the tremendous triumph of the 1958 election or the catastrophe of the Coyne affair, can be described by the actual participants. Sometimes what one or another said was clearly irrelevant, and on occasion duplication has been omitted, but as many different versions or viewpoints as existed have been included. Besides editing the excerpts, and deleting my own part in the interview, I have provided a linking narrative.

In the end, living or oral history relies upon the spoken word, recorded on scores of tapes. The accounts, which in the actual interviews depended in part on vocal intonations and person-to-person communication, can be incomprehensible when transcribed because of broken syntax, and missing verbs, and sentences that do not end. The challenge of this book has been to convert the spoken into the written word that is readable, and yet does not lose the emotional quality of spontaneity and direct involvement, and fairly represents the conversation that took place. It must still seem in the mind's eye to be the person talking with all his affectations and idiosyncracies, the actor explaining in his own way the history that he made and lived. I hope I have succeeded.

Ottawa, March 1975

DIEFENBAKER: LEADERSHIP GAINED 1956–62

1
Leadership gained

On a bleak and snowbound day, 14 December 1956, a typical winter's day in Ottawa, John George Diefenbaker was elected national leader of the Progressive Conservative party. At last, after years of labour in the field of politics, he had reached the 'sunlit uplands'; now, there was only one more barrier to overcome before he achieved the ambition he had held since childhood – to be prime minister of Canada. The last barrier, winning the next general election, was formidable, but the delegates made light of it in the euphoria of a leadership convention – no matter that the Liberals had been in power for twenty-two years and had won five successive elections with consummate ease as though they were the only party capable of governing the country.

The convention hall, the rickety Coliseum which was the capital's dingy cow palace, resounded with cheers. Yet the triumph was not entirely auspicious. After the results were announced and while the winner was being hailed, many of the Quebec delegates walked out. Grattan O'Leary, editor of the Ottawa Journal *and an outspoken Tory, came down to the lower barns where the press had its quarters and said that the new leader was a 'phony' and would do the party no good. I remember being slightly shocked by such outspoken comment. While not denying what he had said when I asked him about it years later, Senator O'Leary did soften his criticism somewhat.*

GRATTAN O'LEARY

I remember meeting Howard Green two, three, four, five days after, and he said, 'We've got another John A.' I said, 'Look, Howard, for God's sake, stop that kind of talk. You'll spoil this man.'

Diefenbaker triumphant after winning the leadership over Fleming and Fulton

Howard Green, member of Parliament for Vancouver-Quadra, had sup-ported Donald Fleming at the convention.

The winds of political change – fair winds for Diefenbaker – were blow-ing across the country. Among those testing the winds was George Hees, who had been president of the party from 1954 until shortly before the convention.

GEORGE HEES

For the past two years I had gone across the country, speaking in a great many ridings, organizing, getting them to get candidates nominated. I had run into a tremendous number of Conservatives, people all over the country, and I had learned one thing. If we were ever going to form a government, in my view it was going to be under John Diefenbaker, and therefore we had better get him elected leader.

It was a tremendously interesting experience. I would give a talk on organization – what they should do and how they should pick a certain type of candidate – and then I would answer questions, and at these meetings they were always the same with some variation or other. Somebody would say, 'Well, Mr Hees, you've given us a good plan for organization, but we want to tell you out here that perhaps you can elect new members of Parliament with Mr Drew as your leader back in Ontario, or some other place in Can-ada, but here you can't no matter what, even if you got God himself as a candidate. People don't go for George Drew. Now, if you got John Diefen-baker as leader, we think we can elect a member here.'

I would, of course, naturally stand up strongly for George Drew. But there was no use telling them what they could do in their own area. So I would say, 'Now, I'll tell you what you do – Mr Drew has lost two elections; if he loses the next one, he's through. No leader can lose three elections in a row and stay in. It's automatic; he's out. Get yourselves a good candidate now. Get him in the field. Get him operating. Have him run. If he loses, it's not a loss – he'd have had a lot of good experience, people would have gotten to know him. He'll have had the nomination, and he can get the next one. If Drew loses, he'll be out, and there is no question in my mind that John Diefenbaker will be the next leader. Then your man will be in. He will have had an election under his belt. People will know him. Then, if you say that with John Diefenbaker you can get him elected, let's go and start now.' Well, they went for it and they started nominating.

There was a sense of do-or-die about the Conservatives. Angus MacLean, the member for Malpeque, Prince Edward Island, sensed the Tory mood.

ANGUS MACLEAN

In a strategical sense the party was becoming a bit desperate. It had gone through a lot of lean years. It had tried various types of people as leaders and they were almost uniformly unsuccessful. There was a tendency to believe that time was running out on the party, that it couldn't maintain its strength as a national party if it kept on being so unsuccessful in national elections, and that this was a time when perhaps you had to take desperate chances. There were some people who felt that you needed to give Diefenbaker a chance, but that he was a bit unorthodox and you were taking a bit of a chance in selecting him as leader. I think some people felt like that. But there were a great many people who were devoted followers of Diefenbaker, who were caught up in his personality and the sort of mystic aura that he was able to develop around himself, the sense that he had a mission.

George Drew had led the Conservatives through the epic battle of the Trans-Canada pipeline debate, and some Tories felt that he was finally making a strong impression on the people. But during a holiday late in the summer he fell ill, and on 18 September 1956 he resigned the leadership of the party.

Donald Fleming had been Drew's strong right arm during the pipeline debate; he fought so vigorously that he had been named by the speaker, René Beaudoin, and, as a result, had had to leave his seat for the remainder of the day.

DONALD FLEMING
Whatever thoughts George Drew may have had at any time in 1949 or 1953, or in the interval up to '56, 1956 was not the year that he would have chosen to resign because we all felt that we won a signal victory in Parliament. Our stock was rising by leaps and bounds with the public. We had stirred the public up over a great issue, and public feelings were still running high. George Drew was on the crest of the wave. The public was seeing in him a leader of force and integrity, and it was just at this moment that fate struck George Drew a cruel blow. There can be no doubt about the circumstances that compelled George Drew's resignation at the time: it was illness, a serious question as to whether George Drew would ever be able to resume his duties in public life.

GRATTAN O'LEARY
He was very ill. He was so ill that Ray Farquharson, the famous doctor, told him it was a choice between the quick and the dead; that if he continued as leader he would die within six months. This came to our attention and we had a meeting in Toronto at the home of J.M. Macdonnell. I was there; Jim Macdonnell was there; we brought Léon Balcer, who was the president of the party then, from Three Rivers; Earl Rowe was there; and George Nowlan was there.

We, contrary to what the public thinks, didn't want to get rid of Drew; we wanted to keep him. We were so anxious to keep him, that we said, 'Look here, we are going to bring Ray Farquharson to this home and get the word from him ourselves.'

We brought Farquharson and Farquharson told us, 'He is a sick, sick man. For the sake of his family and for his future, he should give up the leadership of this party. Just because you may not believe me, I am going to bring in another doctor.' He brought in some noted psychiatrist, I have forgotten the name, but it doesn't matter.

So it was decided then that we would go and tell George that he must go. I actually drafted a letter that George was to sign, to resign. Fiorenza [George Drew's wife] and myself and Dr Farquharson, went up to his room where he was sick. We told him what the position was, that it was a question of his family and Fiorenza and his life. He agreed, but very reluctantly, to sign the letter, which he did.

But he was so reluctant about it – I went back to the hotel, I was going home that night, and the phone rang just as I was finishing packing my bag, and it was George, from the hospital. He said, 'Grattan, could you get them to retrieve that letter and take it back.' I said, 'George, you are asking me to do something – Fiorenza knows all about this – that I just can't do, much as I would like to.' So he said okay. There is a public belief that we fired George. Actually we did everything that we possibly could to keep him.

Ellen Fairclough, who was to become the first woman cabinet minister, was a certified public accountant. She was present at the discussion of Drew's resignation.

ELLEN FAIRCLOUGH
I don't think I've told anyone publicly before, but it was I who typed George Drew's resignation. We met in a bedroom in the Royal York Hotel. There was Grattan O'Leary and Jim Macdonnell and Earl Rowe and Bill Rowe and Fiorenza and myself. Fiorenza had come from the hospital. We were perched on beds and chairs. She sat beside me on one of the beds and she told us what the doctor had said about George.

She said, 'I have ruined his life. I have urged him to go on when he shouldn't have gone on.' I never saw a woman weep as she did – the tears didn't roll down her cheeks, they spurted from her eyes. They went straight out. I never saw anything like it, it was just like a shower. She was very much upset.

She said, 'Now I have the hardest job of all, I have to go back and get him to sign his resignation.' Of course we all reassured her, particularly Jim

Macdonnell and Grattan O'Leary, of whom she was very fond. They said, 'Now how are we going to do this so that no one will know?' And I said, 'Well, have you got a typewriter?' Bill said, 'No.' So I said, 'Where can we get one?' Bill said, 'I know, we can go over to the Albany Club and type it there,' I said, 'Well, I can type.'

So we drafted it as well as we could, the bunch of us in the room. Bill and I hopped into a taxi and ran over to the Albany. I typed it and I made three or four copies for my scrapbook, signed by all the people in that room. Not George's signature because he was too sick at that time to realize what had happened. But he signed his resignation.

I know that one of the things that the doctor had said to Fiorenza was, 'Sure he can go back, he can recover and he can go back, but one day you will be sitting in an audience or on the platform and you will see him start to grope for words and he will just disintegrate right before your eyes. Now is that what you want?'

Which is pretty cruel, you know, but I remember Fiorenza saying this. She said, 'Oh no, I want George, I don't want him to be prime minister of Canada, I want George for my husband.'

When Michael Starr, the first person of Ukrainian descent to be elected a member of Parliament, heard about George Drew's resignation, he went to see Allister Grosart. Starr had come to believe that Diefenbaker was the only man who could lead the Conservatives to office.

MICHAEL STARR

I remember vividly when we were at home one night the news came over the radio that George Drew had resigned. I immediately jumped into my car and drove to Pickering to see Allister Grosart. I knew that in 1949 when John Diefenbaker was vying for the leadership opposing George Drew that Allister managed the campaign for George Drew. However, the first thing I said to Allister, as I burst into his house, was 'Do you know that George Drew has resigned?' He said, 'No, I haven't heard.' So I said, 'Well it's true. It just came on the radio. Now I want John Diefenbaker to run as leader. Are you with us or against us?' He sort of stared at me and said, 'Yes. I am with you.' So I said, 'Let's get him on the phone.' We phoned Prince Albert, I got John Diefenbaker on the telephone, and I said, 'Have you heard about George Drew resigning?' He said, 'No, I haven't.' 'Well,' I said, 'he has. Are you interested in the leadership?' There was a pause, and he said, 'Yes.' I said, 'Well, come east fast.'

When he arrived a few days later he stayed at the Royal York. I phoned him and said, 'I want you to meet a person.' He said all right and gave me a date. I said to Allister, 'You prepare, for presentation to him, your plan of campaign for the leadership.' Which he did. I remember coming with him to the Royal York and I waited outside while he was closeted with Diefenbaker.

They both came out after an hour or so, and Diefenbaker said, 'I have just been a babe in the woods.' And that was it. Allister Grosart handled his campaign for him. He won it, and following that we won the election, the minority government election of 1957, and he offered Grosart the national directorship.

ALLISTER GROSART

It happened this way. I was the president of the Conservative association in Ontario riding, Mike Starr's riding. I lived out there and Mike and I were very close friends. One night, Mike burst into my house. He burst in the door and he pointed his finger at me and said, 'If you're not for John Diefenbaker, I'll never speak to you again.' I said, 'What are you talking about?' He said, 'You know George Drew has resigned as leader.' I said, 'I don't know, I never heard it.' He said, 'Oh yes, George Drew has resigned. We have got to have Dief, he's the only man who can win for us.' I said, 'I agree with you.' We talked for a while, and then I said, 'Well, if you're so much in favour of Mr Diefenbaker, have you called him?' So he called him on the long distance phone from my house, and he repeated, 'I'll support you but you have got to have Allister Grosart run your campaign.' I remember he said, 'John, you're a babe in the woods politically; they'll take you again,' referring to the two occasions when he lost the attempt to get the leadership. I asked him, 'What's the matter, calling John Diefenbaker a babe in the woods politically!' He said, 'He is in the in-fighting in the party.' I didn't hear anything for a while and Mike kept calling me and saying, 'Have you heard from him?' I said, 'No, I haven't heard from him.'

At this time I was in business with McKim Advertising and I was busy. I got a call from Mr Diefenbaker. He said he was coming into town and could I meet him. So I met him at the Royal York. He said, 'In talking with friends and supporters, your name has been suggested to handle my campaign for the leadership. How would you feel about it?' 'Well,' I said, 'you remember I handled the campaign of George Drew against you in '48.' He said, 'I know but Bill Brunt and Dave Walker said if you run the same kind of campaign for us as you did against us they are quite satisfied.' Then he asked me, of course, what I thought his chances were. I told him I thought they were good. About two days later I had a phone call from Don Fleming. Don said, 'You know that I'm going for the leadership. We had a meeting in Ottawa yesterday and we decided that you would be my campaign manager.'

I said, 'Wait. Before you go any farther, I have already committed myself to John Diefenbaker.'

'Well,' he said, 'will you come and see me anyway?' So I went to see him at his office on Richmond Street in Toronto. He said, 'You know, Allister, the last thing in the world I want to do is run for the leadership. It couldn't be more inconvenient to me from the point of view of family, business, and other things. But I feel I have to, particularly to make sure John Diefenbaker doesn't get the leadership. I have got great respect and great regard for him. But if he gets the leadership, it's the end of the Conservative party because we will never get a vote in Quebec.' He was sincere, I know that.

I said to him, 'Don, I don't feel that way. My information is perhaps different from yours. I believe we'll get some support eventually with John Diefenbaker in Quebec because the qualities in the man that appeal elsewhere will appeal in Quebec, if we can get them across.'

I was never a supporter of the position with which I identified Don Fleming, rightly or wrongly, but I did identify him with the Tory establishment, and I saw the Diefenbaker campaign – and it was a comment made at the time – as an anti-establishment campaign.

At the time of Drew's resignation, Gordon Churchill, MP for Winnipeg South Centre, was with Duff Roblin, leader of the Conservative Party in Manitoba, at provincial headquarters in Winnipeg. They telephoned Diefenbaker in Prince Albert as soon as they heard the news.

GORDON CHURCHILL.
I think he was not the least bit surprised at Duff Roblin's telephone call, but I have learned in subsequent years that he was rather surprised that I phoned him because he thought that I was not necessarily a supporter and that perhaps I was a supporter of George Drew. But that was quite wrong. I was independent, I was between the two, and with one leader gone, then the search for another leader immediately became important. I had recognized earlier that if a change of leadership did occur that Mr Diefenbaker would, to my mind, be the person that I would support. So we phoned him.

At the same time, Roblin said to me, 'What support will Mr Diefenbaker have in the caucus?' (The caucus consisted then of fifty members.) Within just a few minutes I wrote out on a sheet of paper supporters of Mr Diefenbaker, anti-Diefenbaker people, and in the third column I listed those who were uncertain, and I put down the names of the fifty members. Subsequently I discovered that I had made only two errors in that assessment, and that assessment I put out in front of Roblin and said, 'Mr Diefenbaker will have 80 per cent support in caucus.'

Some time later Mr Diefenbaker was coming through Winnipeg and stopped off and Mr Roblin and I met him. I put this list in front of him and he suggested two corrections, one or two that I had against him were for him and one that I had for him he thought was against him.

Then, we were called down to Ottawa, the members of caucus and the national executive, in order to deal with the resignation of Mr Drew, which obviously had to be accepted, and to appoint a temporary leader. That was done, and Earl Rowe became temporary leader, and discussions were held as to when the leadership convention should take place and where. While I was in Ottawa, Clayt Hodgson, who was a very strong supporter of Mr Diefenbaker, called me to his office, and I met there quite a number of members and we discussed the possibilities of Mr Diefenbaker for leader. I produced my list and the members were quite impressed with it. A day later, another meeting was called, and when I entered the office, Clayt Hodgson, who was chairman and there were about fifteen people present, immediately vacated the chair, seized me, and forced me to take the chair. I found myself then unexpectedly chairman of a meeting of the members to discuss the question of leadership. We went over the list of members again and we decided that 80 per cent of them were in favour of Mr Diefenbaker. We had made another check in the interval.

Well, having determined that, the meeting suggested that a press release should be issued, and I was also commissioned by the meeting to approach Mr Diefenbaker, tell him of the support, and ask him to stand. I did that and saw him and told him. I issued a press release to the effect that 80 per cent of caucus favoured Mr Diefenbaker for leader.

Late in October Mr Diefenbaker was coming down to Ottawa to commence his campaign. He let me know that he was on his way through Winnipeg, so I packed my bag, met him at the station intending to go with him as far as Fort William and then get off the train and come back home. But after talking to Mr Diefenbaker and his wife, Olive, on that journey down to Fort William, I stayed and continued on to Ottawa. Then when I got to Ottawa I thought the best thing to do was to hang around for a while. Mr Diefenbaker didn't ask me to do anything, but I volunteered to assist in any way that I could. I got into my room at the House of Commons and commenced to get in touch with the members.

Somewhere along in that period Al Grosart appeared on the scene as a supporter of Mr Diefenbaker. I met him and I found that with no formal arrangements being made that I was supposed to be chairman of the committee of the Conservative members sponsoring the Diefenbaker campaign. That's the way it turned out. So I stayed on in Ottawa, and worked with Mr

Diefenbaker and with Al Grosart, phoned and wrote to the various members to see what they were doing and see how active they were.

From time to time, some of them would come to Ottawa and give me a report. Then, I journeyed with Mr Diefenbaker and Mr Grosart to one or two places and George Hees joined our forces so that we had Mr Diefenbaker, Al Grosart, George Hees, and myself, who formed the nucleus of the organization for Mr Diefenbaker's campaign.

That's how I stumbled into it. There is nothing formal about it. I hadn't yet been appointed chairman of the committee to organize for Mr Diefenbaker for leadership. It just happened. I was active and I plunged in, and that's the way Mr Diefenbaker operates, you know. If somebody volunteers, well, he will make use of him. And he appreciated assistance.

ALLISTER GROSART

I remember when they called the first meeting of the backbenchers who were supporting Dief in George Tustin's office. George Tustin was party whip then. The atmosphere was really charged. There was real animosity because this fellow was going with Fleming, this fellow wouldn't come with us. Already you were hearing things, 'What he said,' and 'This fellow is spreading this rumour.'

I was a PR man, and by this time I had quite a bit of experience, and I listened to this, and I said, 'Oh my God, this is '48 all over again.' Because in '48 Mr Diefenbaker's supporters, not him but his supporters, ran this same kind of campaign; everybody who wasn't with us was a SOB and this and that and another thing. In fact they put up a big sign in the Château, 'Vote for the man from Main Street not Bay Street.'

After all, you don't wash your dirty linen in public, at least you didn't use to. It has become popular now, but in those days it was unusual for anybody to wash the party's dirty linen in public. So I said, sitting in George Tustin's room, 'Here it is again.' I think the anti-establishment people tend to have more chips on their shoulders, they have all kinds of grievances against the establishment and against headquarters and so on.

I remember Dief wasn't saying much, just listening, stretched out on the couch. I got up and I said, 'Listen fellows,' and I didn't know them all very well, I said, 'Look fellows, I don't think I'm going to run this campaign.'

Dief had introduced me; the Ontario ones of course knew that I had been active. I had a bit of a reputation since I had been on the right side for three elections. It is unusual for any Tory to be on the winning side for three elections.

So Dief got up and said, 'What did you say?' I said, 'Just a minute. If

I'm going to run this campaign I have got to insist we have one motto.' Dief said, 'What's that?' I said, 'We love everybody.' Then I explained to them. I said, 'This will kill you; you will kill John with this kind of campaign. We have to go out and love everybody. No more of this. John's got enough qualities to talk about.' Then we started to talk about the things that really mattered.

> It was evident to the most anti-Diefenbaker Tory that the tide was running strongly in favour of the man from Prince Albert. Even so, and despite the politician's propensity to climb on a bandwagon, a desperate effort was made to stop him from getting the nomination. Dick Bell, who was Diefenbaker's greatest friend when he was first elected a member of Parliament, and whose roots in the Conservative party go back to the days of R.B. Bennett, was part of a group that tried to find an alternative. The ink was hardly dry on Drew's resignation before Grattan O'Leary was looking around for successors.

GRATTAN O'LEARY
Somebody suggested the premier of Ontario, but Frost wouldn't touch it.

R. A. BELL
When the party leadership became vacant, I concluded, along with a number of others, that it seemed almost inevitable that Mr Diefenbaker would be elected leader, that he was not of the temperament and of the staying capacity, we believed, to do a successful job, and I was one of a group who met on the night the convention was called in the Château Laurier. Amongst the group were J.M. Macdonnell, Earl Rowe, Léon Balcer, Grattan O'Leary, George Nowlan; Donald Fleming came late. We discussed whether Fleming had the capacity to do the job or the capacity to stop Diefenbaker and concluded that he had neither. Fleming took this exceedingly well.

We reached a conclusion of which I was fully a party, that approaches ought to be made at once to Sidney Smith, then president of the University of Toronto. My recollection is that the following day Nowlan and Balcer, as the delegates of this group, went to Toronto and saw Smith. They had some initial encouragement. It certainly was argued that Smith was the only individual we could see across the country who might be successful against Diefenbaker.

I have notes of a subsequent telephone conversation I had with Smith. I was on rather intimate personal terms with Smith. I was an admirer of his and liked him in all respects, and found a tragedy his subsequent career when he entered politics. In any event, I have my notes of the conversation in which he told me ultimately, ten days or so afterwards, that he would not do it. He had consulted his doctor; his doctor had told him that while he was in no immediate danger, he did have a heart tremor which made it undesirable. He said that if it were back on the 1942 basis he would jump at it. But the years had rolled on and he thought he was too old to start a new game. Incidentally, just to go back to 1942, of course, as you know, he was the most disappointed man when [John] Bracken stepped in.

Meanwhile, the Diefenbaker bandwagon was rolling. There was a formidable triumvirate in charge: George Hees who, as he himself said, did the political spade work; Gordon Churchill, the contact man with members of Parliament; and Allister Grosart, the supreme image-maker. David Walker, who was one of Diefenbaker's closest friends and who nominated him the first time he ran for the leadership in 1942, was the official agent, the liaison with the two other candidates, Donald Fleming and Davie Fulton.

The campaign of Donald Fleming who, by default more than anything else, had become the only other serious contender seemed hardly to have started.

ALLISTER GROSART

In a campaign, you look at your pluses and you look at your minuses, and you try to exploit your pluses and do what you can to try to minimize the effect of your minuses. So we looked at these, and the people said, 'Oh yes, a lot of people still call him Diefenbacker.' I said, 'Well, now, how do we get around this?' I thought, maybe a little song.

Then I couldn't find an English rhythm. As you probably know I have spent a good deal of the time in my life being interested in English poetry and I couldn't find a rhythm that would fit Diefenbaker. Then it first came to me – a Scotch rhythm, 'Comin' thro' the Rye' or 'Lochinbar.' So taking the 'Comin' thro' the Rye' tune, I made up this little song:

Diefenbaker, Diefenbaker, Diefenbaker, Yea!

He will lead us on to victory on election day.

John's a man who's ringing, swinging, swinging back our way.

It's Diefenbaker, Diefenbaker, Diefenbaker, Yea.

My two daughters, who were about seven or eight at the time, sang it. I will never forget that we sat down with Dief and the two girls sang it to him. In the campaign we had a very strong young people's support for Diefenbaker. It was the first indication to me that he was a pretty sure winner. We got those kids singing the Diefenbaker song.

GRATTAN O'LEARY

I supported Fleming. Allan Lawrence was the chairman of Fleming's committee. I was in Europe, as a matter of fact, and I got a cablegram from Fleming, asking me if I could nominate him. When I got to New York, I called him up and said, 'Look, I am the kiss of death for you. I can't nominate you, it will murder you.' I came home and saw Allan Lawrence and said, 'Bring me up to date on what has happened.' Lawrence said 'Actually there is nothing to bring you up to date on because nothing has been done.' This surprised me because I always felt that poor old Donald Fleming had a good well-organized meticulous mind. But he didn't, not in a case like that.

Davie Fulton knew that he could not win the leadership, and his candidature had a harmful effect on his relations with John Diefenbaker, as he ruefully recalled. There were never any personal recriminations, but he felt that Diefenbaker had hoped for his support at the convention and was disappointed that he did not get it. What, then, were Fulton's reasons for running?

DAVIE FULTON

I suppose the actual occasion was the urging of my friends who were mostly younger members of the party. They urged me to run on the basis that although I could hardly be expected to win I could probably make a respectable run, and that, in their view, to preserve their allegiance to the party and the long-run interests of the party, it was desirable that a younger member of the party strike out a position now with a view to the future.

And the other reasons are that, I suppose, in fact I know, that increasingly the thought was entering my mind that one day I might be qualified for and possibly be elected as leader of the party. You know, as you succeed in any endeavour, as you move up the ladder on the basis of preference and success, it is only human nature that there comes into your mind the thought that maybe one day you will be at the top of the tree. I had been in Parliament then for eleven years, and I think had made a useful contribution as a member of Parliament. So the thought was not very far from my mind that one day I should make a move to establish a claim for leadership, and so in 1956, when my friends came to me with this urging, I decided to accept.

As the leadership campaign proceeded, Fleming found that he was losing the support of those whom he expected to be strongly for him.

DONALD FLEMING

More and more of the figures in the party who didn't want to see John Diefenbaker elected leader, who thought that he was too temperamental or that his health wasn't equal to the task, and who for that reason might have been expected to throw strong support behind me, began to show themselves as less and less willing to expose their opposition to Mr Diefenbaker's candidature because it was more and more likely that he was going to be elected leader. This is precisely what happened.

I toured the country. Diefenbaker had great advantage here because he had been touring the country a great deal. I had been much more tied to the House of Commons than he and I had to keep an eye on my professional responsibilities in Toronto at weekends. There was no doubt that throughout the country he was better known, although I was undoubtedly known widely, particularly after the events of that 1956 session. I didn't attempt to capitalize personally on those in a personal sense but I was perfectly well aware that, in going into that convention, I was the underdog.

At the convention, there was great pressure exerted, there was undoubtedly a strong organization that had built up and supported Mr Diefenbaker. Some of my friends, some who had wanted to support me, came to me and said that they had been put under strong pressure by either their local people or, in some cases, by newspaper policy to give their support to Mr Diefenbaker. So I went into that convention as an underdog. To my knowledge, I put up the best fight that I could.

Dick Bell was joint chairman of the convention with Léon Balcer, president of the party. Balcer's voice gave out during the convention, so Bell presided during most of the sessions, in French as well as English. He was asked to be convention chairman some time after his meeting with the anti-Diefenbaker group in the Château Laurier, and he maintained that he had had no idea at the time of the meeting that he would be appointed to this job.

R.A. BELL

I resolved that there was nothing that I could do but preserve a judicial and impartial position, and I did so throughout. Mr Diefenbaker does not agree with that. He has told me he doesn't, and he told me at the time of the convention and the foolish little incident on the afternoon before the convention. I was on the platform looking over the final arrangements, and the first thing I noticed because of my height was that the podium had been built much too low. I immediately called the carpenters together with instructions that this had to be raised. I was in the process of these discussions when Mr Diefenbaker arrived to look over the scene, and I said to him, 'John, these crazy people have put the platform podium away down there. It is no good for you or for me.'

'Ho,' he said, 'You are building it for Fleming, eh? – up to your old tricks.'

Well, what can you do in relation to a situation like that? As I say, Mr Diefenbaker will not give me credit for having preserved a total impartiality and judicial approach as chairman, and there is nothing I could do to convince him of it.

Among the delegates to the convention were Douglas Harkness, MP for Calgary North, Alvin Hamilton, president of the Conservative party in Saskatchewan, and Gerald Baldwin, an Alberta lawyer who had just been named the PC candidate in Peace River.

DOUGLAS HARKNESS

There is no question that the great majority of people at that time thought that John Diefenbaker was the only logical man to succeed George Drew. I thought so myself and supported him on that basis.

ALVIN HAMILTON

The Saskatchewan delegation was absolutely 100 per cent for Diefenbaker in '56, as I recall, and really there wasn't much work to do. You did your best here and there. I was the party leader at this time in Saskatchewan, but I don't recall doing too much. I worked along calling delegates. Mr Churchill seemed to be the general commander and chief of the campaign and I would report in to him every day on the people I would see, and he would give me a new list, and that was about all I would do. I would act like a canvasser but I wasn't in charge of anything as I remember.

It was soon apparent that the real struggle at the Conservative leadership convention was not between the candidates – it was a foregone conclusion that Diefenbaker would win – but over the formal nomination of the man from Prince Albert and whether it should be seconded by a French-speaking Canadian. The captains were divided: Gordon Churchill supported the candidate's desire to be nominated by an easterner and a westerner; George Hees wondered whether it was wise.

The battle was joined in the Diefenbaker suite at the Château Laurier. One of the fighters was Pierre Sévigny, a newcomer to the federal political scene, who had become an ardent supporter of Mr Diefenbaker and hoped to nominate him. Most of the Quebec delegates were up in arms, and the issue led to the ugly scene of Léon Balcer and a number of French-speaking delegates walking out of the convention. However, one of them, Jacques Flynn, understood Diefenbaker's motives. Senator Flynn, the grandson of the last Conservative premier of Quebec, was supporting Donald Fleming.

JACQUES FLYNN

It was so obvious that a very large majority of the French delegates were favouring either Fleming or Davie Fulton that, maybe, Mr Diefenbaker considered that it was useless to try to woo the Quebec delegates and was trying to balance his support by having Hugh John Flemming from New Brunswick and General Pearkes from BC. It was, I would say, a practical decision

– tactical decision, if you want – based on these facts. I don't think it was intended as a rebuff of the French language, but it was rather, I would say, based on the fact that he had not enough support in Quebec and would not get any support by having a French-speaking seconder.

At that time it was supposed that Pierre Sévigny, who was one of the delegates supporting Mr Diefenbaker, would nominate him. Pierre was so furious about the decision that it created quite a turmoil. He took it as practically a personal insult, and told Balcer that he should denounce Diefenbaker.

GORDON CHURCHILL

He had selected George Pearkes from British Columbia and Hugh John Flemming from New Brunswick to move and second his nomination. George Pearkes was one of the distinguished members of the House of Commons and one of Canada's most distinguished military men, and he came from British Columbia. Hugh John Flemming had very recently been elected premier of New Brunswick, so his standing was extremely high within the party. It was the first provincial breakthrough that we had had, and Mr Diefenbaker, and I concurred, thought that having somebody from the west coast and somebody from the Atlantic provinces would be satisfactory for nomination.

Well, all sorts of trouble then arose because this was considered to be an affront to Quebec. Mr Diefenbaker passed through an extremely difficult time because of the pressure that was exerted upon him to alter this plan. Both George Pearkes and Hugh John Flemming volunteered to withdraw. I argued that if they withdrew, and somebody from Quebec was to nominate Mr Diefenbaker, then he would pretty obviously have to select somebody from Ontario. And, I said, once again, once again, western Canada and the Atlantic provinces will be left out on the fringes.

However the decision was not mine to make; it was Mr Diefenbaker's. But I did indicate this to him, that having a nominating person from Quebec would not give him one extra vote at the convention. We had found out, going down to Quebec on more than one occasion, that antagonism against Mr Diefenbaker was so pronounced that the only support he would get from Quebec would be a handful of delegates. The delegates were not selected by constituency organizations, which were non-effective and virtually non-existent. They were picked by Léon Balcer and his advisers and Léon Balcer was very much opposed to Mr Diefenbaker becoming leader of the party. Outstanding men like Paul Lafontaine and Ivan Sabourin, who were supporters of Mr Diefenbaker, were not given the privilege of becoming voting delegates. My estimate was that there wouldn't be more than four or five voting delegates from Quebec favourable to Mr Diefenbaker, so having someone nominate him from Quebec would do nothing to his contest for the voting delegates at the convention.

He was under tremendous pressure. In the last twenty-four hours prior to the convention people kept coming in and out of his room, pressuring him to change his plan. On one occasion he called me down and, in an adjoining room, I met for one whole hour with Pierre Sévigny and his wife, who were disturbed about the situation and were hoping that Mr Diefenbaker would change his mind. It was a great test of courage and determination. As far as I was personally concerned, it would have been decisive in so far as my support of Mr Diefenbaker was involved. I would have continued to support him, but I wouldn't have had confidence in him had he changed his mind. He didn't change his mind, he went ahead with General Pearkes and Premier Hugh John Flemming nominating him.

GEORGE HEES

I felt, and I think Grosart felt also, that he should have been nominated by an English-speaking Canadian and seconded by a French-speaking Canadian – which was the way those things were usually done because, after all, the French-speaking segment of the country is about a third. I thought, as I remember, at that time that that was a mistake. But, after all, Diefenbaker was the candidate and he had asked George Pearkes and Hugh John Flemming to do the job and that was it. There wasn't any great fight about it. He had made up his mind and that was it.

GEORGE PEARKES

I took the position that I would be very happy to second his nomination, or, if it was in the interests of Diefenbaker, why I wouldn't feel the least bit hurt if he asked a French Canadian.

LÉON BALCER

The tradition that there would be a French seconder or a French mover for each candidacy dated back from the previous convention. An argument developed that from a distance might not appear too important. A lot of people from Quebec felt that 'This man is going to be the leader of our party and right off the bat he is going to show to all of Canada that the Conservative party is not much interested in any support from Quebec because they are going to break with this very recent tradition.'

A lot of people were talking about it, and a lot of sincere Conservatives thought, 'Well, we should be going in Quebec and really start a good campaign.'

All kinds of caucuses and meetings of the Quebec delegations were held, and this thing was building up into a pretty strong affair. The press was following it very closely. I talked with many people in Mr Diefenbaker's organization. They sort of stopped this idea and said, 'Well, you people just get in line and that's all.'

I resented that very strongly, and the same day I told the press that it was a real mistake and that the Quebec delegation would resent it very much. That was the start of a misunderstanding between Diefenbaker and myself that lasted for quite a long while.

ALLISTER GROSART

This decision was not deliberately anti-French. I know that because I remember when the storm blew up I had to help put out the fire. Mr Diefenbaker was from the West, not, in political terms, a national figure yet. People regarded him as a national Lone Ranger. Their thinking, as they told me, was that if we had somebody from the Atlantic and the Pacific, that made sense. It is what I think [R.B.] Bennett had done. There wasn't a tradition in the Conservative party of an English and French nominator and seconder.

It wasn't a deliberate insult as it was taken by a good many Quebeckers. Léon Balcer inadvertently said it was an insult to French Canada, not knowing he was being quoted. This was when he was sharing a taxi with Ross Munro (of the Vancouver *Province*) and the editor of the Winnipeg *Tribune*, Carlyle Allison, who later became a vice-president of the BBG – everybody was doubling up in taxis going from the Château to the Coliseum, and he didn't know who Ross and Carlyle were. There was a degree of polarization on the French- and English-speaking issue between the candidates.

It was bitter for a while but, as you know, Dief's feeling was the opposite. He was always a One Canada man. If you stop to think of all those years Parliament went along without simultaneous translation, and one of the first things that he did was to bring it in. I remember how excited he was when he came up with the name of Georges Vanier as governor general. One of the anomalies of politics is the frequency with which a man gets somehow in the public mind an image which is exactly the opposite of his feelings.

PIERRE SÉVIGNY

It was contrary to tradition, and it was of the nature of offending the sensitive minds of Quebeckers. So, I for one strongly objected and said, 'This doesn't make sense, and just through this little thing we could possibly lose a great deal of the support that we have in Quebec. What is much worse is that when campaigning time comes along, when the election finally is called, this could be used with great ill effect in Quebec so that Mr Diefenbaker would be represented as being anti-French Canada and all that sort of thing.'

Naturally there were some heated arguments over this, with Churchill for one, with Grosart for another. George Pearkes was very reasonable. Pearkes more or less approved what I said and was quite willing to withdraw, though really in the back of his mind he did wish to second Diefenbaker because he was his friend and he was very loyal and fanatically devoted to Diefenbaker. But we had these discussions in the Château Laurier, I remember, in that suite that Diefenbaker occupied. Eventually, in due course, I was accused of being the one who wanted to make the speech, which wasn't true. It would have flattered me to make the speech but I was looking ahead, thinking that this was a faux pas, and it proved to be a very serious faux pas because the moment it was learned among the delegates that there would be no one from Quebec to second Diefenbaker, we lost immediately at least fifty or sixty votes which definitely would have been for Diefenbaker.

I took it up with Mr Diefenbaker, and that's when I saw for the first time, maybe, one of the worst traits of the Diefenbaker character, that terrible indecision which has characterized so many of his actions as the years went by. Diefenbaker at that time should have come out and been either for my idea of a French-speaking seconder, or looked at me and said, 'Well look, I want it to be this way: Flemming and Pearkes,' and that would have settled the issue. But he didn't do it and the decision was not taken by Diefenbaker but by others. And eventually some clumsy effort was made at representing that the East was proposing and the West was seconding, national unity and harmony and so on, but it was really a major mistake, one which cost Diefenbaker at least sixty votes at the convention.

HUGH JOHN FLEMMING

After it became quite an issue, we gathered in Mr Diefenbaker's room [in the Château Laurier], and one of his lieutenants mentioned to him that there was a feeling that there should be one of each group, of French and English background, you know [to nominate him]. He had, I suppose, already spoken to General Pearkes from British Columbia about seconding his nomination. At any rate, he gave it considerable thought. I said, 'Mr Diefenbaker, the fact that you've requested that I move your nomination shouldn't be a contributing factor to your decision, because, as far as I am concerned, you should do what's best in your interest and in the interest of the party, and it will be all right with me.' I gave him a free rein to make a decision whichever way he wished.

He said, 'No. The die is cast. I've made the decision. I've asked you, and I'm not going to change. You go ahead. Get out there and prepare your speech.'

As everyone expected, Diefenbaker won on the first ballot. The result was: Diefenbaker, 774; Fleming, 393; Fulton, 117. This was Diefenbaker's moment of triumph, made all the richer by the years of struggle. He stood in the floodlight's bright glow, for this was the first television convention, before a tossing sea of Diefenbaker placards, and the rickety Coliseum reverberated to the roar of the delegates. He was sixty-one years old; with his shock of grey hair and piercing blue eyes, he looked the part of a political leader, and in the euphoria of the convention the delegates caught a flash of his confident, charismatic appeal. Donald Fleming and Davie Fulton raised his arms in the victory salute.

DONALD FLEMING
I moved that his selection as leader be made unanimous. I meant it, and I conducted myself in that relationship from that point on. Unfortunately, just at that moment a large portion of the Quebec delegation, to demonstrate their disapproval of the party's selection of Mr Diefenbaker as leader, got up from their places on the convention floor and walked out. I deplored this and certainly made my own feelings of this point known widely.

From that time on I dedicated whatever lay in my power to try to build support for Mr Diefenbaker's leadership within the party wherever I had opportunity. I took the simple view that once the convention is over there are no more contestants for leadership, there are no persons who stand number two or number three or number four, there is a leader, the other members of the party are followers, and it's their duty to conduct themselves accordingly.

LÉON BALCER
I think this walkout has been exaggerated. The convention ended at four o'clock in the afternoon and the train was at five o'clock. There were no planes at the time, and everybody was taking the train, so everybody moved out. But there is no doubt about it, that a few of the Quebec delegates said, 'Well we came, we saw, and we are walking out. Never mind the Conservative party. We have seen enough of it.' But that was not general; there were a few of them, maybe about ten of them.

GORDON CHURCHILL
No harm resulted from this walkout. It was a great tempest in a teapot at the time, terribly oppressive, awfully hard on Mr Diefenbaker.

2
The road to the Coliseum

John George Diefenbaker had been born in Neustadt, a village in Grey County, Ontario, on 18 September 1895. He was the son of William Thomas Diefenbaker, a descendant of German and Dutch settlers who had come to Waterloo County, Ontario, around 1820, and of Mary Florence Bannerman, a descendant of one of the Selkirk settlers, whose family had moved from Winnipeg to southern Ontario.

William Diefenbaker was a studious man who was quite content with his life as a school teacher. But as a young man attending normal school in Ottawa, he had spent much of his spare time in the public gallery of the House of Commons, and his tales of the great parliamentary debates of 1890 and 1891 and of the last days of Sir John A. Macdonald enthralled his son John. Teaching was an ill-paid profession in those days; the Diefenbakers knew hardship and sacrifice, but they never lacked books, and John learned to love Shakespeare at an early age.

At the turn of the century, the West was being settled and thousands were on the move. The Diefenbakers joined the great trek in 1903. John remembered that railway trip, the colonist car in which they travelled, the stations on the prairies crowded with Ukrainians, Poles, Hungarians, Germans, and French – where every language but English seemed to be spoken.

Some time later, William managed to get a homestead when a virgin area on the north side of the North Saskatchewan River was opened for settlement. John and his younger brother, Elmer, helped their father measure off the quarter section and build the family's first home, a two-room shack.

Often members of the North West Mounted Police stayed at the home-

Diefenbaker addresses the 1948 leadership convention

stead, which was on the Battleford Trail near Batoche and the site of the Battle of Duck Lake. Young John heard stories of the Riel Rebellion from Sergeant Pooke and other Mounties. As a small boy he saw Gabriel Dumont, the great buffalo hunter and Indian warrior who had been Riel's chief of staff. He became immersed in western history and folklore and he learned what it was to be poor and exploited.

In 1910, William sold the homestead and the family moved to Saskatoon. The new provincial university was being built there and in time John became a student. In 1915, he joined the armed forces along with the rest of his graduating year. He went overseas but was injured and sent home in 1917. One of his companions at university was Emmett Hall, whom he was to appoint some fifty years later to the Supreme Court of Canada.

Diefenbaker's first jury trial was in Humboldt. A Ukrainian farmer had been charged with attempted murder in connection with the shooting and wounding of his neighbour. There was a story that the jury brought in a verdict of not guilty because it was the young defence counsel's first case and coincided with his twenty-fourth birthday; but Hall dismisses this tale.

EMMETT HALL

There has been a great deal said about that first trial that he had before Chief Justice J.T. Brown. I had been in Humboldt a while and got to know the local people a bit, so I sat in with him when we were selecting the jury. It used to be that jurors were known for their propensity either to acquit or to convict, and the convictors soon became widely known. Anyway, I was watching the trial for him, as a friend.

The essential element of the defence, if it was to succeed or not, lay in the extent of visibility. It had to be such that a man might reasonably mistake a coyote for a man, or a man for a coyote. John was spending quite a lot of time stressing the element of darkness.

Chief Justice Brown, whom I succeeded as chief justice of the Queen's Bench almost forty years later, was really a fine judge and a fine man. I think he appreciated that he had a lawyer with his first case, and it was an important one, and an important one for the accused as well. I was living in the Arlington Hotel and having lunch with the chief justice in the dining room, and he allowed to me that he thought John was stressing this darkness a little too much. The first thing you knew, you wouldn't even be able to see the coyote. Whether the judge had some idea that I might pass the message along I don't know, but he certainly didn't put it that anything that we were talking about was confidential. So immediately following this I drafted a note to Mr Diefenbaker, telling him about this conversation, and sent it to him. Then of course for the rest of the trial there was a little more light and it resulted in the acquittal, but this is part of the story. Now, his birthday may well have coincided but I didn't hear of it as being an important factor. He won because it was a meritorious defence.

But here is something. As you know, Mr Diefenbaker never parted with any papers of anything, and two or three years ago I got a note from him sending me a photocopy of my note to him of that day, with this notation: 'Your handwriting has hardly changed in x number of years.' So he still has the original document, the memo that I sent him about this question of darkness.

Although the reciprocity agreement of 1911 made Diefenbaker and his father suspicious of the Liberals and the way they were flirting with the Yankees, it was really the war that turned John into a Conservative. He could not understand why the Liberals had opposed service overseas; as he was to say later, he chose the Conservative party because it believed in maintaining the Empire and the Commonwealth and would not permit itself to be led into an American orientation.

Still, it was a strange choice for an ambitious young man to make. There were few Conservatives on the prairies, and the provincial Liberal party under Jimmy Gardiner dominated Saskatchewan. The Liberals, always on the lookout for a bright young man, went so far as to appoint him secretary of the local party organization without his knowledge, when he opened his office in Wakaw. They even sent around the books. He returned them unopened.

Altogether, Diefenbaker ran for office five times before being elected. Shortly after he moved his law office to Prince Albert, the Conservative Association persuaded him to stand for Parliament. He was defeated in the 1925 general election. The following year, he lost again in a byelection called to find a seat for Liberal leader and former prime minister, William Lyon Mackenzie King. In 1936, he ran for mayor of Prince Albert and was defeated by the narrow margin of twenty votes. Also that year, he was chosen as leader of the provincial Conservative party. He contested Arm River in the provincial election of 1938 and was defeated as were all the Conservative candidates. Finally, in the 1940 federal election he won in Lake Centre, a constituency in the heart of Saskatchewan.

During that 1940 campaign, T.C. Douglas met John Diefenbaker at a radio studio where they were both making political broadcasts. Douglas was then a CCF *member of Parliament.*

T.C. DOUGLAS

I was rather pleased to meet him because at that time he was having a difficult time. My sympathies were all with him for two reasons. The first was that he was running against a Liberal, Fred Johnston, who had been elected originally as a Progressive and was waging a rather vicious campaign. Most of the constituencies in Saskatchewan were multiracial constituencies, but Lake Centre, while it had multiracial characteristics, had a fairly large percentage of Anglo Saxons who, of course, were very strong in their support of the war. Fred Johnston, more than by innuendo, very deliberately tried to portray Diefenbaker as a German. Every time he referred to him he referred to him as my opponent, 'Mr Diefenbacker,' and made it as guttural as possible at a time when, of course, anti-German feeling was very high. This was an unfair thing and it made my gorge rise and my sympathies were all with John Diefenbaker. The second thing was that, as Diefenbaker himself has said, the only protection Conservatives had in the days of the Jimmy Gardiner machine were the game laws, and the Conservatives were pretty scarce. The New Democrats, or CCF supporters as they were known in those days, weren't very plentiful either. So we had a sort of mutual feeling of being underdogs.

Davie Fulton was elected to Parliament in 1945 as a khaki candidate. He found Diefenbaker to be a happy, friendly fellow member who enjoyed enormously his role as an opposition critic and who took an almost fatherly interest in Fulton as a new member.

DAVIE FULTON

He was a brilliant performer in the House of Commons, a terrific debater, a man who attracted a following not only because of his personal personality but because of his public personality. The way he shone just made him a very attractive man. A man of generous instincts, a man who befriended me, guided me, whose door was always open to somebody seeking advice. Whether it be a detailed matter such as: 'How do I address the prime minister? I want to write him about a problem that affects my constituency.' Or a question of tactics or strategy: 'How will I go about tackling this problem?' As well as advice with respect to speeches in the House: 'What activities of what departments should I specially interest myself in?' He was very good to me – I can't put it in more simple terms than that.

When we were in the opposition, I have seen him in the House of Commons bait hooks for various ministers: Jimmy Gardiner, who was a particular antagonist of his, or C.D. Howe. He would make a comment in the course of a speech, one minister would get to his feet to refute it, and Diefenbaker would club him – he had the answer all ready. A few minutes later, precisely the same treatment for another minister. On one occasion I remember seeing three of them swallow the bait, get up – and the fish was landed.

Diefenbaker won the 1940 election by the narrow margin of 280 votes; in 1945 he increased his plurality to 1009.

EMMETT HALL

Then they started to gerrymander the constituency; they were going to gerry-mander him out of business. First, they cut off the city of Moose Jaw. Jimmy Gardiner was handling this thing. In exchange for that they added to the constituency a whole area to the east down near Melville, Punnichy, Quin-ton, Elfros, and so forth, where there was a very heavy foreign vote – Ukrain-ian, Hungarian. That posed a very difficult problem because no Conservative votes had come out of that area for twenty-five years. It looked as though they had really cooked his goose in that sense, by adding these thousands of votes from the east and taking away his support in the Moose Jaw area.

Elmer and I were detailed to organize that part of the constituency, and we did, with our headquarters at Punnichy. Elmer was probably the best polit-ical canvasser for a rural area that I ever saw. Actually he did most of the work, but we put in two to three weeks at this. Believe it or not, we came out of that area with a majority.

That hadn't worked. In 1949, Diefenbaker increased his plurality to 3432. So they obliterated Lake Centre altogether.

Here he was now [in 1953], a man without a country, and at this stage we ran into a little of what we could call perverseness with him. Saskatoon was wide open; basically there was always a strong Conservative element in Saskatoon. With Diefenbaker's reputation at this time we felt we could win Saskatoon in a walk, and we put the pressure on him: 'Forget everything else. You have got to stay in the House. It's the only way that you are going to get to the top, and you have got to be there. Saskatoon is yours for the asking, literally.'

'No I won't do it. I am going to run in Prince Albert.'

Well, my God, there hadn't been any Conservative votes in Prince Al-bert for fifty years, not since Knox had been elected in 1917. We attributed this in a sense to a letdown after [his first wife] Edna's death. He was almost going to make what we looked upon as being a sacrificial effort in Prince Albert.

It's true that many years before, in '26, he ran against Mackenzie King there. He had a respectable following in Prince Albert, because the man had been practising there and had been the most successful lawyer in Prince Albert over the years. But Prince Albert was just an element in a very large constituency that extended halfway across the province, way east to Nipawin and west to halfway between Prince Albert and Battleford; it took in a great area of French-speaking votes at the Big River line and in that area, from

Shellbrook west. It was the country part with which we were very much concerned.

Anyway, he decided he was going to run in Prince Albert, so that was it. Fortunately for him at that time, some former Liberals in Prince Albert decided, 'This is our opportunity to get a real member.' There would have been half a dozen of them and they formed the nucleus of a very powerful group in the city. This was a shock for the Liberal party in Prince Albert.

The problem then was the French Catholic vote in the northwest corner of the constituency. There was going to be a Social Credit candidate, a very nice fellow, a French merchant at Debden. Now I had taught school just out of Debden in the Shell River district back in 1916, which was a long way back, but it was an opportunity for me to go back and say, 'I know these people.' Besides anybody who could speak French in the Conservative party at that time in western Canada was very welcome. Davie [Fulton] and I worked the church picnics and that kind of thing, and again came out with a majority. [Diefenbaker won Prince Albert in 1953 with a plurality of 3001.]

Not much more than two years after becoming a member of Parliament, John Diefenbaker put his name forward for the party leadership. He was, as a friend said, persistent and supremely confident of his own destiny. He had run five times before being elected and he was to run three times to win the leadership. He was an unsuccessful candidate at the 1942 convention in Winnipeg which chose John Bracken, who had been the Progressive premier of Manitoba for twenty years. In 1948 he lost to George Drew, premier of Ontario. He finally succeeded eight years later.

At the first of those leadership conventions, in 1942, Diefenbaker was the candidate of the Young Turks in the party, and was nominated by one of them, an aggressive young Toronto lawyer, David Walker. He was then in his forty-seventh year, but to Ellen Fairclough, he was 'more like a young man in his early thirties,' although given to 'rather elaborate histrionics' which, in her view, did not suit his youthful appearance. The Winnipeg convention was held in the midst of the war, and Diefenbaker's German-sounding name became an issue.

R.A. BELL

One of the joint chairmen was H.R. Milner, QC, of Edmonton. He introduced Mr Diefenbaker as 'Mr. Diefenbacker' and he barked it out, when you can imagine what the sentiments during wartime were. I don't think any incident that has ever happened to me politically made me as angry as that. I was sitting next to Milner and I told him what a bastard I thought he was for doing it. Milner, I suppose, has paid well for it. Since that time he has undoubtedly been the leading Conservative in Alberta, and deserved more than anybody else within the province, and he did not become lieutenant governor, he did not become a senator, he just did not, period.

> *When Diefenbaker was first elected to Parliament, his greatest friend was Dick Bell, the young private secretary of the leader of the opposition. They were in each other's offices every day; they talked over events for an hour every evening; Bell saved press clippings for the new MP, and did research for him. However, this close and happy relationship turned to bitter opposition and charges by Diefenbaker that his erstwhile friend was conspiring against him.*

R.A. BELL

This goes back really to the 1942 convention where he bitterly resented the fact that I, as his friend, did not take a part and did not support him on that occasion. Such misunderstandings as we have had, and we have had many of them over the years, stem from my failure to support him in 1942. During the period of time that I was national director I supported only one person, and that was the leader, and throughout I have been a leader's man. Subsequently he took a further scunner, and I can only describe it as that, in which he attributed to me, quite falsely, that he was not successful in being chosen as the leader of the opposition, and that he was defeated by Gordon Graydon. I was the leader's secretary and took no part whatever in the caucus which chose Gordon Graydon, but Mr Diefenbaker has from time to time made mention that I was a conspirator against him.

DONALD FLEMING

Mr Bracken, after accepting the leadership, did not enter the House for the two and a half years that remained in the life of that Parliament. It became necessary, therefore, to select a House leader and it was up to the national leader to make this selection. Undoubtedly Mr Diefenbaker hoped to be the House leader. And why not? He was recognized as a front-rank debater, he had gathered more votes at that national convention than any other Conservative member sitting in the Commons, and undoubtedly he had every right to expect to be seriously considered for the appointment. However, Mr Bracken chose Gordon Graydon. Graydon was a very personable member, greatly liked by everyone, highly respected, and evidently Mr Bracken concluded that, while Mr Graydon was not as effective a debater in the House as was John Diefenbaker, nevertheless he might be an easier person to work through in conducting the affairs of the House and he might possibly be an easier leader for the other members of the House to follow. This situation may have contributed to some of the rumours that Mr Diefenbaker was a lone wolf. I think he was keenly disappointed at not being appointed House leader.

R.A. BELL

As I recollect, since I was not a member of the caucus, the candidates for the leadership of the opposition were: Gordon Graydon, MP for Peel; John Diefenbaker, MP for Lake Centre; J.H. Harris, MP for Toronto-Danforth; Howard Green, MP for Vancouver South, and the Honourable Grote Stirling, then member for Yale. Ultimately the contest came down to being between Mr Graydon and Mr Diefenbaker. Mr Graydon was successful, my understanding was, by quite a narrow margin.

Mr Diefenbaker has always bitterly resented his defeat in caucus for the leadership of the opposition at that time. Certainly he was sharper in debate than Graydon, but I query whether he was able to get along with people, and he had put, even then, a number of backs up amongst his colleagues, particularly amongst his senior colleagues in the House. I think there was no doubt that the senior men, including the retiring leader of the opposition, Mr Hanson, were in favour of Graydon rather than Diefenbaker. I suppose one of Mr Diefenbaker's reasons in feeling that I was involved was that I was Hanson's private secretary and therefore what my chief's attitude was, was mine; which of course, doesn't follow at all. As a person who never was permitted to set his foot inside the caucus door, I had no part of any kind in the decision.

Although John Bracken did not win the 1945 election, he did well enough to elect sixty-seven members under the new 'Progressive Conservative' banner; this was almost double the Tory membership of the two previous Parliaments. He had won forty-eight seats in Ontario, which was a remarkable achievement for a former Manitoba premier. Yet within three years Bracken resigned, and another leadership convention was held. It was this convention, in Ottawa in 1948, that had such a serious effect on Diefenbaker.

R.A. BELL

He felt that the formal structure of the party was against him. I think there is no doubt that the president, J.M. Macdonnell, who presided at that convention, was against him. Macdonnell always looked upon Diefenbaker as temperamentally and emotionally unstable – and it wasn't new then, it went back years. So no doubt Macdonnell, as chairman, was against him. I think [Léon] Méthot, the joint chairman, was against him.

So far as the instructions which were given to the organizers went, it was total neutrality.

I think if I had been taking any part, and I was not because I believed I had to be neutral as a national director, it probably would have been on behalf of the man who was my closest friend, Don Fleming. He was a candidate then and I didn't think he was ready. Fleming didn't forgive me, particularly because, when he asked me whether he should run, I said to him that I thought he had to get a little more warmth into his personality. I thought, before he became a candidate for party leadership, he should go out and get drunk and sleep with somebody else's wife. He didn't think that that foolish illustration was an apt one. But it did illustrate the weaknesses that Fleming had, brilliant orator and administrator and so on, but unable to communicate the warmth, the personality which was underneath him.

However, back to the situation, so far as any formal organization of the 1948 convention is concerned, I deny absolutely that there was any stacking in favour of Drew as opposed to Diefenbaker, or Drew as opposed to Fleming. The actual organizers of the convention went right down the line to give everybody a fair chance.

DONALD FLEMING

I was the third contestant for the party leadership at that time. I had been in the House then little over three years. I suppose it is fair to say that I had been very active in debate, and many people in the party had convinced me that I should stand for election. There was always the possibility that with two strong contestants both senior to myself, the convention might have ended in a deadlock, and it might have been necessary to turn to someone else as a means of resolving the deadlock – this was a possibility. On the other hand my candidature rested on very strong support from Quebec and from the younger element in the party. These were the two principal sources of strength. I was the young man of the three at that time. John Diefenbaker was ten years older than I, George Drew was a year older than John Diefenbaker. I was forty-three years of age and there was always the possibility that the party might decide to invest its future in a younger man. This is the way things shaped up before the convention. At the convention the weight of support for George Drew became increasingly apparent; from the day the convention opened one could feel a gathering of strength in his support.

Mr [William] Brunt, who later became Senator Brunt, was a very close friend of Mr Diefenbaker and directed his campaign for the leadership. He told me afterwards that he had made a serious mistake at the convention. Mr Diefenbaker had no support in Quebec, and I had. It was a question of whether Mr Drew might claim support in Quebec as well as enormous support in Ontario and in other provinces. The fact is that Brunt, whether he is right or wrong, said that, in the events of the program, he should have seen that Diefenbaker supporters gave me strong applause to build up in the minds of the Quebec delegation the impression of strength of my candidature. They didn't, and a good deal of my Quebec support drifted over to Mr Drew. The Quebec delegation did not want Mr Diefenbaker to be elected, and many of them decided to support Mr Drew as the man more likely than myself to defeat Mr Diefenbaker when the poll came. In the end, Mr Drew won an overwhelming victory.

LÉON BALCER

One of the people from Three Rivers who was supporting very strongly this western lawyer, John Diefenbaker, was Bill Whitehead, who was president of Wabasso Cotton and whom I knew slightly. He heard that I was at this convention and he called me and insisted that I should meet Mr Diefenbaker and have a chat with him. So I met John Diefenbaker at the Château Laurier. I remember he was alone in his room and I was accompanied by a newspaperman from Three Rivers. I must admit that he was a fascinating man. He is a great conversationalist and full of stories and at the same time very aggressive. I knew that right off the bat. After the second sentence, he started trying to impress on me that he was not anti-French, anti-Quebec. He was getting the papers to show me that he had defended the school people in Saskatchewan at the time of the Catholic schools question. This defensive attitude of his surprised me, coming so soon. But on the other hand I found it a very interesting meeting. After that I met George Drew, and I must admit at the time I got along very well with George Drew and I decided to support George Drew.

ALVIN HAMILTON

I was in charge of the Saskatchewan delegation and out of ninety-three potential votes, we delivered ninety-one for Mr Diefenbaker. In the first days of that convention in '48, when the delegates first came in, I thought that there was a very even chance that Diefenbaker would take it. But in the three days of the convention we couldn't match the power of the people who came up from the cities, particularly Toronto, and all their persuasive arguments. I saw whole delegations that were trying to vote for Diefenbaker swung over to the Drew side at that time. It was a very powerful campaign in many ways on Mr Drew's behalf.

Only one ballot was needed to decide the leadership of the 1948 convention; Drew's 827 votes were almost twice those cast for his two opponents. The results were a bad blow for Diefenbaker. He concluded that there was little or no hope of there being any change in the leadership in the years ahead. It seemed to be the end, and he became more and more depressed about his own and the party's future prospects.

In February 1951, his first wife, Edna, a gay and loving companion, died. He was bereft. Davie Fulton, who had come to regard Diefenbaker as his mentor, went to Saskatoon at the time of the funeral and got the impression that 'for two pins he would give it all up and not come back to Ottawa.' There was a report that he had been offered the position of counsel to a large law firm in Vancouver.

However, he carried on. The passion for politics from his boyhood days overcame his frustrations and disappointments and made him continue. Victor Mackie, who covered the 1948 convention for the Winnipeg Free Press, *had known Diefenbaker in triumph and in trouble since the thirties.*

VICTOR MACKIE

The thing that haunted him, and it really hurt him, was his name. He used to often talk to me about it and say, 'Isn't it a crime that a man with a name like Diefenbaker can't win the national leadership of a political party – because of his name!'

I think he was right. In those days, the name Diefenbaker was high around his neck and he couldn't get rid of it. I remember the campaign leading up to the national leadership convention in which he ran against Drew. He gave Drew a very good run, but he lost. He was broken hearted about that. And he blamed it on his name. He said if his name had been Anderson or Mackie, or something like that, he would have won. But because Drew was Drew – and, of course, the Bay Street boys! – he blamed the Bay Street boys and the James Street boys for having discarded him because of his name and because he was from the West.

To Allister Gre—

with affectionate

good wishes for [illegible]

inspiration and a

matter of [illegible]

[illegible] devotion

Diefenbaker

[illegible] 10" 1957

3
The turning point

Less than seven months after being elected leader, Diefenbaker was to win the 1957 election and become the thirteenth prime minister of Canada and the first Conservative prime minister in almost a quarter of a century. After that historic victory, there would be no doubt about his supremacy in the party. But at the leadership convention he had been the outsider, the prairie radical and populist, challenging the party establishment; and when he had won the leadership, he found that the establishment had packed its bags and quietly gone.

The leader of the opposition's ornate corner office in the Parliament Buildings was empty; it had been vacated by Earl Rowe, who had occupied the office since George Drew's resignation. The Progressive Conservative party headquarters in an old Ottawa residence near the Lord Elgin Hotel was nearly deserted. The party's national director, Bill Rowe, Earl's son, had departed without leaving a resignation or forwarding address. The bureaucracy had collapsed. One of the new leader's first tasks was to get the party organization functioning, and Diefenbaker turned to Allister Grosart, the man who had fashioned his successful leadership campaign. Grosart had returned to his job as executive vice president of McKim Advertising.

ALLISTER GROSART
In January [1957] I got a call from Dief, and he said, 'Who have you got at headquarters?' I said, 'I haven't got anybody at headquarters.'

Kate Kearns was at headquarters and had been there from time immemorial. Actually she had been Sir Robert Borden's secretary before moving to headquarters. Unfortunately, she was identified with what Mr Diefenbaker regarded as the anti-Diefenbaker establishment and he felt she had been part

The photograph that dominated Tory advertising in the 1957 campaign, inscribed by Diefenbaker to Grosart of his opposition and resented it because after all this was the civil service of the party.

'Well,' I said, 'Look it's none of my business, I'm not a politician. I'm not getting into it.' I didn't think of myself as an *eminence grise* or anything like that, which I wasn't.

So he said, 'We have got to get a national director and the boys think you should do it.'

I said, 'No, I don't want any part of that. I hate Ottawa and I'm not going down there.' I was, let's see, just around fifty, and I had good earning years. I had worked my way up into a position where I had a piece of McKim, and I had set my pattern for life.

'Well,' he said, 'Will you come down and we'll talk about it.'

So I came down. As a result, George Hees, Gordon Churchill, and I were appointed a committee of three to find a national director. The logical man was Mel Jack, who had, more than anybody, been responsible for the fine image, if you like, that Diefenbaker had in Ottawa in the Press Gallery. He had been the PR man at headquarters. George Drew had fired him peremptorily on the grounds that he was doing PR for Diefenbaker and not for George Drew. Now, I'm not judging that, but that was the reason given. Mel had a bad time but finally got a job. The Liberals gave him a government job. Mel was itching; he loved politics. One day he would say 'yes' and then next day he would go home and his wife would say that if he got back in politics again, thinking of the peremptory end of his career and the hard times they had for a while before he got another job, she would leave him. She meant it. Eventually, we thought, Mel would come around. Then that year Mr St Laurent announced the date of the writ; it was unusual, but for some reason he announced that the writ would be issued for the election on June 10th. Dief called the three of us in and said, 'Have you got a national director?'

We said, 'No.'

Well, he hit the ceiling. He said, 'We can't even take over the party, what's the sense of us pretending we can take over the country?' When he finished telling us what he thought of our efficiency in getting a national director, he said, 'Allister, what do you say?'

I said, 'John, I've seen Barrymore do the second act of *Hamlet* and I was pretty well satisfied until now, but I won't be satisfied until I see you do it. That was the greatest second act of *Hamlet* I have ever seen.' He started to laugh. To make a long story short, I said, 'Look, I'll come down two or three days a week and take over headquarters until we get somebody.' Famous last words!

I was working morning, noon, and night, and midnight to start the organization. It was a shambles, naturally, because it had been built, right across the country, around the establishment, who, understandably, had been supporters of Don Fleming. There had been no contact, no new direction, and nobody knew where they were.

A condition that I made with Dief was that there would be no announcement. I said, 'I'm not taking any title because I'm staying with my business. I've got clients and if it's suddenly announced that I'm national director of the campaign, McKim may censure me because maybe their sympathies are Liberal or something.' So that was agreed.

I remember there was a constituency map on the wall of the office there. I looked at it and I said, 'I couldn't get 20 per cent just on naming the constituencies. I can't run this thing; I don't know anything about it.' There was no question I was an amateur. I said, 'What am I going to do? There's only one thing, and that's to call the boys in.' I said to Kate Kearns, 'Give me the names of the five or six people with whom you correspond most in each province, who are our people.'

After a few days, Dief went out on a tour of Canada. My wife called me one night and said, 'It would be nice if you would keep your wife informed about what is going on, but congratulations anyway.' I said, 'On what?' She said, 'It has just been announced that you're the campaign manager and national director of the Conservative party. Mr Diefenbaker announced it in Fredericton.' I said, 'Oh my God.'

When he came back I asked him. He said, 'I'm sorry, but everywhere I went, people were saying, what kind of a campaign have you got? who do we talk to in headquarters? who is running the show?' because they had always been used to Dick Bell, Cappy Kidd, and so on. He said, 'The organization is Allister Grosart.' Of course, these fellows knew I had run the leadership campaign so I wasn't a stranger, and they said 'Oh, that's fine.'

Dief didn't say in so many words that he hadn't broken his promise but he said enough. Strangely enough I was never appointed anything. There was never any appointment saying, you are national director, you're campaign manager. It just fell in my lap that way.

The first thing I discovered was that Kate Kearns had a loyalty to that chair. She was a real blue Tory. It didn't matter who it was, the minute I sat in that chair, I had her complete loyalty. Dief could never quite understand this but I kept her there.

Although the pipeline debate was almost a year old, John Diefenbaker insisted on making it an issue in the 1957 election campaign. Allister Grosart argued that the public's memory was short and the issue would not have much impact. Some Tories even suggested that it could backfire; the pipeline was by this time being built, and the Liberals could say that the great unifying project had been undertaken despite the obstruction of the opposition. Also, Diefenbaker had not played as prominent a part in the debate as had his rivals for the party leadership, Donald Fleming and Davie Fulton. However, Diefenbaker saw the use of closure in the pipeline debate as a supreme example of Liberal arrogance, a trampling underfoot of the rights of Parliament and of the people, and Diefenbaker was a House of Commons man.

ALLISTER GROSART

I remember when we got our campaign committee together and Dief came in and talked about how he saw the issues. He stressed Parliament. One fellow got up and said, 'Well, John, that's a year ago, that pipeline thing. People have forgotten about it.' A lot of them said, 'People don't care that much about what goes in Parliament.'

He said, 'That's the issue and I'm making it.'

I had my doubts as to whether this could be made the big issue. In his first speech at the opening of the campaign, he stood there and put his hand on his heart and said, 'I am a House of Commons man.' He made it stick as only Dief could, relating the House of Commons to the interest of the average man.

WILLIAM HAMILTON

Diefenbaker sensed and understood better than most of us that there was a moral issue in the '57 election. The arrogance of the Liberals in two or three debates in the House – the pipeline was the final one, but there were others like the one on the Emergency Powers Act – was pretty frightening to people who have a great trust in having a free Parliament and letting the Parliament be the spokesman for the people.

ANGUS MACLEAN

I think the pipeline debate was one of the main factors in exposing them as an overbearing government. The Liberals believed that there was almost a divine right for them to be in power. They had been in power for so long, it was automatic that they should be elected indefinitely. People resented this attitude, and this attitude became glaringly apparent during the pipeline debate.

The new Conservative chief seemed to understand better than anyone else the traumatic effect the pipeline debate had had on so many opinion-makers. Eugene Forsey, then research director of the Canadian Labour Congress,

and other concerned democrats were incensed by the Liberals' invocation
of closure to end the debate. Forsey described a party he attended given by
Walter Gordon whose report on Canada's economic prospects had just come
out.

EUGENE FORSEY

As far as I can recall, every last one of them [at the party] was a very
strong, well-known member of the Liberal party, with the exception of Dana
Porter and myself. I said to Porter, 'Well, you and I seem to be the only
heathens here,' and he looked at me rather sourly and said, 'Some of us
sometimes think that you are too conservative for us.'

Anyway we sat around and chatted, and after a while in came Pickersgill, whom I had known ever since we were at Oxford together. He was
taken around and introduced to people. When he got to me, he looked at
me for a minute, and I looked at him for a minute, and there was rather
a strained silence, and then he put out his hand and said, 'Hello Eugene,
how are you?' and I said, 'Hello Jack,' and we shook hands.

Somewhat later, I said, 'I'm afraid that I must ask to be excused because
I have to get up early and be hard at work.' A very very high and very
eminent civil servant, one of the best that we have ever had in this country,
I think – I am following a great Canadian tradition of not naming names but
if I did name him, everybody would agree that he was a man with most outstanding capacity and quality – said, 'Well, I have got a hard day tomorrow
too, I think I had better go,' and we went out together.

This was not very long after the pipeline debate. When we got out in
the hall, I said, 'When I get home tonight I am going to get a whaling from
my wife.' He said, 'Oh. Why?' I said, 'For shaking hands with a member of
the Liberal cabinet.' He said, 'Why would she be so annoyed about that?'
'Well,' I said, 'both she and I, after the pipeline debate, felt, with old General
Pearkes, that it was going to be very difficult to associate with these people
on any level of friendship.' 'I quite agree of course; the conduct of the opposition in the pipeline debate was simply scandalous.'

I looked him in the eye and I said, 'All I can say about that is that if
I had been leading the opposition the only difference would have been that
the row would have gone on longer and more bitterly. I shouldn't have
stopped when they did.'

He said, 'Oh!' as if I had told him the Pope had joined the Orange
Order. He couldn't have been more surprised. He said, 'What makes you say
that?' It was perfectly clear that to him it was a foregone conclusion, simply
axiomatic, that the Liberal government was right.

By this time we had got on a bus together and were getting to his stop and I said, 'It would take me a long time to tell you why I feel that way, but I have written something on it and I will send it to you,' and he said, 'Thanks very much.' So I did. But the significant thing there was that this man, who was of quite exceptional quality and I am sure not consciously a partisan, a man of extraordinary intellectual attainments and what we call in French, *formation supérieure*, educated up to the sky and with vast experience internationally, had become so accustomed to one party being in power and had become so completely associated with them, without any intention of being partisan, that it just never crossed his mind that they could be wrong. It was the dyer's hands subdued to what it works in. He had undergone what you might call an immersion course, total immersion, in Liberal policies and legislation and it just meant that he couldn't see the thing from any other point of view. This was what frightened me terribly. This was really frightening to anybody who looks upon the non-partisan, independent civil service as one of the bulwarks of British parliamentary government.

Gordon Churchill was credited with the strategy that brought about the turning point of the 1957 election. In 1954, as a rather junior backbencher, he had set out to discover why the Conservatives had been so unsuccessful at the polls. He had studied electoral campaigns and concluded that it would be possible for the Conservatives to win a federal election without increasing their meagre representation in Quebec. His findings were largely ignored until John Diefenbaker became leader.

Gordon Churchill was no Tory maverick. Although he became Diefenbaker's most loyal lieutenant, he had been a true blue supporter of George Drew when the latter was leader. As he said, he was 'accustomed to serve in any capacity in the army and serve whoever happened to be in command.' The army had been the first of his four careers, and Churchill described himself as basically a soldier.

Churchill was born at Coldwater, Ontario, on 8 November 1898. His father, a United Church minister, had moved to Winnipeg by the time the First World War began, and young Gordon was barely out of school before enlisting and serving as a machine-gunner at Vimy Ridge. After being demobilized, he joined the militia and received a commission. In the Second World War he organized and commanded the First Canadian Armoured Personnel Carrier Regiment, 'The Kangaroos,' which served with the British and Canadian forces in northwest Europe. His regiment carried into action fifty-four battalions of infantry, before the Rhine and across the Rhine, ending in Germany at Oldenburg.

Between the wars, Churchill was a teacher, the principal of the Collegiate Institute at Dauphin, Manitoba, for ten years, and of St John's Technical High School, in Winnipeg, for a year. After the Second World War he studied law and was called to the bar in Manitoba in 1950.

Politics was his fourth career. In 1946, while still in uniform, he was elected the army representative in the Manitoba Legislature. His first attempt to win a seat as a federal Conservative candidate was in Winnipeg South Centre in 1949. He was defeated, but won the seat in a by-election two years later and was returned to Ottawa in the 1953 general election. It was after that campaign that he made the famous study on which future Conservative strategy was based.

GORDON CHURCHILL

We had gone into the election of 1953 rather strongly, and the results were disappointing and shattering. We left the House of Commons with fifty members and we returned with fifty members. There had been some changes, naturally; some people dropped out, some were defeated, and some new men came in, but our numerical strength had not increased. Although the St Laurent government lost twenty seats, the beneficiaries were the CCF and Social Credit.

I then commenced to study the elections from 1867 on, just to see what had happened; and to get the thing clearly in my own mind I drew a graph, federally and by provinces, showing the distribution of seats in each of the elections from 1867 to 1953. I also got the figures for the total vote for the various parties during all that period. I made a very intensive study of it. Then, constituency by constituency, I examined the situation in the provinces, and I was shocked by the vast majorities in the province of Quebec for the Liberal party and the Conservatives just barely making a showing.

Having examined all the elections from 1867 to 1953, I reached the conclusion that the Conservative party, if it continued to put its time and its energy into the province of Quebec, would never have any success whatsoever. It came to my attention that in 1953, 45 per cent of the funds available for the Conservative party federally had been ploughed into the province of Quebec and only four seats emerged, and out our way we were starved for assistance. What struck me as so odd was that Walter Dinsdale and I, who had captured two strong Liberal seats in the by-elections of 1951, received no financial support in the general election of 1953. So far as I know, nobody out West received any support whatsoever. It struck me as rather odd that the Conservative party would fail to support people in western Canada, particularly in view of the fact that two of us had made some slight inroad in the province of Manitoba. I was shocked to think that so much money went into the province of Quebec.

All these things combined led me to the conclusion that if the Conservative party would spread its energy more equitably across the country, and reinforce success and not failure – a military maxim – that we might have some chance of achieving victory. I estimated that if we could gain sixty seats in the nine provinces exclusive of Quebec, and hold our own in Quebec, that we might form a minority government.

It was on that basis that I wrote that paper and urged that the policy of the Conservative party be altered and that not so much time and attention should be devoted to Quebec. Not to ignore Quebec – in fact, in the paper I said if Quebec produced twenty seats we would form a majority over-all. But I didn't think we were wise to place our confidence in Quebec.

The strategy as I understand it of the hierarchy of the Conservative party at that time was to gain seats in central Canada, Ontario and Quebec, where the majority of the seats are, and then take their chance on the Atlantic provinces and western Canada. In addition, the Conservatives who were then in charge of events were unhappy about western Canada, which was split four different ways politically – Liberals, CCF, Social Credit, with the Conservatives trailing a bad fourth. One of the Conservative senators, the late Senator Hackett, at one meeting that we had prior to the election of 1953, had expressed grave doubts as to whether there was any hope at all in western Canada. Even as early as that, I had raised the objection that it was quite wrong for the party not to give more attention to western Canada. But at that time I didn't have all the facts and didn't know very much about the federal scene.

Actually I wrote two articles in 1954, one on Ontario and one on Quebec, based on the statistical study that I had made. Being naive and unfamiliar with the activities of the press, I showed these articles to the late Judith Robinson and I left them with her over the summer, expecting that in the fall of 1954, when the House reassembled, Judith, who was a good friend, would talk to me about them because I was not confident that I had the right idea or anything of that nature. But Judith was a first-class newspaper woman, and she saw that there was a story here. So she wrote four articles based on my preliminary studies – never told me a thing about it. I didn't even see the articles until I got phone calls from headquarters at Ottawa, pointing out the error of my ways. My difficulties with Quebec stemmed from those articles.

Well, when I returned to Ottawa in September 1954, the session being resumed, I sensed that I wasn't a popular figure within the party and the only person who spoke to me about those articles happened to be John

Diefenbaker in the lobby. He was just going into the House, I was standing there, and he said to me, 'Those were good articles. You were dead right.' That's the only comment he made. Nobody else said a word about it, and I could feel that it was better for me to be seen and not heard for some considerable time.

Dick Bell was one of the former campaign chairmen whom Churchill was implicitly criticizing.

R.A. BELL

The question of reinforcing success is a matter of judgment in the individual circumstances. It may be that it is preventing collapse, and such money as was poured into Quebec, which was not anything like what is alleged, was just for the purpose of preventing a total collapse. If the Conservative party had become a completely Anglo-Saxon party in 1953 and in the years prior to that, it would have done it more national harm than anything else that could have happened.

There always are in campaigns certain earmarked funds. I remember that one of the largest companies earmarked a substantial amount of its contribution for a particular candidate who, I knew, had not a ghost of a chance. The amount of the money was $30,000 and I called the president of this Canadian company, with international ramifications, and said, 'This is ridiculous. You are pouring money away.' He insisted – the candidate was a solicitor in the area for the company – and $30,000 was spent and the man got fewer than 3000 votes. Now there are in Quebec some earmarked situations of that sort which a campaign chairman, a national director, simply is totally unable to control.

One of the problems in Manitoba was that the organization, from a financial point of view, was so weak that they could not raise the amount of money that they ought to have raised within the province. Again it becomes a matter of judgment by the man who has central control of the party funds. How much does he hold back from a province in order to compel them to do their own digging for funds?

When I took over in 1945, the general attitude in the West and in the Maritimes was that there was an unlimited pot in Montreal and Toronto. They did not have their own finance committees; they could sit back and let Toronto and Montreal finance the rest of the country. I resolved that Vancouver was a city of no mean wealth and that Winnipeg was a city of no mean wealth and that they had to put their own financial structures, their own houses, in order, and in every election that I had control of I gave them basic guarantees but insisted that they must put their own financial house in order and that they couldn't rely on Toronto and Montreal.

PIERRE SÉVIGNY

Gordon Churchill said something which was rational and plain common sense. It was obvious that the Conservative party, because it was identified in those days as being an imperialist-minded party, a colonialist-minded party, and also militarist party, was unpopular in Quebec. The best proof was that in 1953 we had won four seats out of seventy-five, in 1949 two out of seventy-five, in 1945 one out of seventy-five, in 1940 none out of seventy-five.

Gordon Churchill said that it was wishful thinking and plain folly when election time came along to pour money which was scarce in those days into ridings where there was no chance of success. He said something which was very close to the truth. He said, actually, 'In Canada we have got 265 seats. Let's say if we win no seats in Quebec, but we win let's say 150 seats elsewhere, well then we still win the power without Quebec.' He did not advocate starving out Quebec and giving it nothing. But he advocated a common-sense policy which was to use the little money that the PCs had in a better way, in a more rational way than had been done. And I must say that I had to agree with him.

In fact, in those days, we discussed it, and I said, 'Look, if I am going to organize in Quebec, the little funds we have we should put where it will serve our cause best. When we get to the seats where we haven't got a snow-ball's chance in hell to win a victory, let's put a minimum, maybe a token sum, for our candidate and hope for the best.'

As I say, Gordon Churchill was misinterpreted and he was viciously accused in many circles because of this statement. Eventually, history proved that he was right, because in 1958 Mr Diefenbaker and his Conservative party came to power with 208 seats out of 265 seats; 50 of these seats were won in Quebec. It is plain common sense and simple arithmetic to realize that if we had not won these 50 seats in Quebec, Mr Diefenbaker still would have had 158 seats, a majority government in the Commons. Of course, politics being the nice polite game that it is, Mr Churchill's and Mr Diefenbaker's and all of the Conservatives' enemies took advantage of this declaration to represent Churchill as the enemy of Quebec and French Canada and that kind of nonsense.

GORDON CHURCHILL

I developed the strategy paper of January 1956 [from the election studies] but, having developed it and written it carefully, I didn't know what to do with it, because I was afraid I would get into more trouble. I showed it to Angus MacLean and to no one else. I thought it should be made public, and yet I had no controlling influence in the party and I didn't particularly want to cause trouble, so I just sat on the thing. It was after Drew's resignation, when I was on the train going down to Fort William with Mr Diefenbaker, that I produced that strategy paper as well as the earlier ones and showed them to him. He was very much interested in them and his wife read them as well. We didn't discuss them at any length but he was appalled at the statistical figures with regard to the city of Montreal, where the majorities for the Liberals ran up to 25,000 and 30,000, you know. At any rate, I had enough gall or courage to show this strategy paper to Mr Diefenbaker, and at least he had the information. And I think he did follow the strategy in the 1957 election.

Dick Bell agreed that Churchill's plan of reinforcing success had been adopted.

R.A. BELL

I think they ran a perhaps more limited campaign in Quebec than previous campaigns, yes. They were prepared to risk a possible collapse and the risks turned out in their favour. It is a case of nothing succeeds like success. Everything was starting to go for them at that time.

When the election was called, Allister Grosart got together Conservative workers from across the country, three or four from each province, for a three-day meeting at headquarters in Ottawa. He set up a national campaign committee – something the party had never had before. In his opinion it proved the organizational key to success in 1957.

ALLISTER GROSART

By this time I had come up with a concept for the campaign. I knew what money I'd have and it was a shoestring campaign, believe me, because it was half the money the party had in '53. I can remember it very well. It was $1,000,000.

Now this was appalling because that headquarters fund has to provide campaign funds in the constituencies. There are always complaints from the constituencies and from the provinces that the distribution of money is unfair. Up to my time it had been done from headquarters, because someone like Dick Bell, for whom it has been his whole life, knew every constituency; he was as good a judge as anybody as to where to put the money. Well, I couldn't do this. I said, 'I'm not going to decide. I couldn't tell you what constituency.'

There had been a feeling, and it was true, that the tendency in those days was to say, 'Where can we win? We will put most money in Ontario.' There was always a feeling – I thought it wasn't altogether true – that Quebec was getting more than any, that the Conservative party had been putting a high proportion into Quebec and never coming out with a result. There was always dissatisfaction. It doesn't matter how you do it. The fellow who doesn't think he gets enough will always have stories that somebody else got more. I would have to say that some candidates get a little proud and talk around that they got more money out of headquarters than they did. All of these things contribute.

Anyway, I explained to them: 'I don't know the business. You fellows have to run the campaign. I'm no politician. You fellows are. You know how. You have run campaigns before. What do you want from me?'

They said, 'This money business?'

I said, 'All right. I've got $1,000,000. I'll give you three-quarters of it. That will be $3000 a constituency.'

GORDON CHURCHILL

I had some influence on the apportionment of the funds. When we had the meeting of that committee in Ottawa, I propounded my thesis that there should be an equitable distribution of funds for the election of 1957, contrary to what had happened in 1953. When I found out from the finance people that there was a very limited amount of money available, I said, 'Well, in those provinces where money can't be collected to finance the campaign, a basic figure of $3000 should be allocated for each constituency.'

This was accepted and it made a tremendous difference to us in Manitoba. In 1953 we had virtually no money at all. In 1957 we got a grant from the general fund of $42,000, and we collected other money ourselves in Manitoba, but what that meant was that each candidate would at least make a start. He could rent a committee room, get out some advertising, and hire stenographic help without having to run down to the bank and borrow money or mortgage his home or something of that nature.

Naturally Quebec was upset because they wanted $10,000 per constituency and to get only $3000 – well, they didn't like that at all. I think that turned quite a few Quebec people against me. But fair play is fair play and it paid off as far as we were concerned.

There was little money for the Conservative campaign in 1957, and the little there was came in slowly – a clear sign that the business community thought the party's chances were poor. Indeed, the campaign in the key province of Ontario might have collapsed before it began had not George Hees ridden (in a taxi) to the rescue. The opening meeting in Massey Hall, attended by the province's eighty-five candidates, proved such a success that Diefenbaker described it as the turning point of the campaign.

GEORGE HEES

It is so extraordinary how things happen. I was having lunch with somebody, I don't remember who, downtown on that day. I had been out in my riding, and was driving downtown. I had a few minutes to spare so I dropped in at the office of Harry Willis, the Ontario organizer, just to say, 'Hello, Harry. How are you doing? How are things going?' not thinking that things weren't going well at all. He was sitting in his office and he looked like a condemned man.

I said, 'Harry, what the hell is the matter with you?' He said, 'We are never going to get going, never going to get going.' I said, 'Why not?'

'Well,' he said, 'these people are coming in from around the province tonight to be on the platform. I have to give each one of them $1000 to get the campaign going.' This was only five weeks before the votes went into ballot boxes, and they hadn't gotten any money yet. He said, 'Bev Matthews,' who was our chief collector, 'tells me,' think of this, 'that he can only give me about half the amount, about $45,000. At least half of these candidates have told me that if they don't get $1000 tonight, they won't run. They're not going to bankrupt themselves if we are in such bad shape that I can't give them $1000 to start their campaigns five weeks before election day. We are in terrible shape and they are not going to bankrupt themselves by going head over heels into debt. What am I going to do? There is nowhere I can get it. Bev Matthews says that we may get it sometime later but not now. He hasn't got it.' Business didn't have any confidence in us at all.

So I said to Harry, 'I can get some money for you.' Of course, he looked at me with complete disbelief.

I went down to the Royal Bank. I bank at the Royal Bank, and our firm has always banked with the Royal Bank, which was the main thing, and therefore my credit was pretty good because the firm's credit was pretty good. My uncle had been a vice president of the bank. I went to the bank manager and said, 'I will come back here in an hour and I want eighty-five packets, and in each packet, done up with an elastic, ten $100 bills. I want eight-five such packets, and I will be back in about an hour. Can you get it?' Well, he just about gagged, you know. This was the damndest thing he had ever heard. I said I would sign a note for it.

He said, 'What do you want this for?'

I said, 'Never you mind what I want it for, I want it, and I will be back in an hour. Will you get it?' Luckily it was the main branch. I came back in an hour, and he handed me this brown paper parcel of eight-five $1000 packages, all in negotiable money, and I called a taxi. If that taxi driver had ever known what he was driving uptown, I think he would have fainted.

I got to Harry Willis' office. I will never forget it. He was still, unbelieving, sitting behind his desk, like a man who had been condemned to the electric chair. I said, 'Harry, here is your dough.' He was just like a child on Christmas morning. He nearly wept he was so happy.

That is how close we came to not even starting the 1957 election. If we had had half our candidates, or even a large group, saying they were not going to run, this would have been disastrous nationally. We never could have made it. It was a cinch for me because I said that I would do this on the understanding that the first $85,000 that came into the kitty I got. I knew it was coming. I wasn't taking any chances. It was lucky that I was able to get it.

I will tell you exactly when the turning point was. It was three weeks before election day and, up to this point, we were just going along, ho hum. Dief was a new leader and a new type and people thought this was okay, and we were going to get some more new seats and so on. That's it, we had not taken off until this point, and we went to Vancouver, and they organized there for him the first big meeting that he had.

There were only 2700 at Massey Hall, and we had brought them in from all the ridings around Ontario. Only 2700 in that hall was shocking, for a meeting like that. The Liberals, for instance, in Toronto at that time got 15,000 at the Maple Leaf Gardens: we only got 2700.

In Vancouver, a fellow called John Taylor was quite an organizer, a nice guy, Cyclone Taylor's son. He became our member there, John Taylor from Burrard riding. He was the prime organizer in staging a meeting of over 5000 people in Vancouver, which for Tories out there was big, big, big. They had it well organized, the cheering sections were well orchestrated, and so on. He [Diefenbaker] got a terrific round of applause when he got in. It got him excited and that was it and he made a hell of a speech. They had it on radio, and I don't know if they had it on television, but anyway, it got all across the country. Diefenbaker, I think for the first time, really branched into the things that he was going to do for the country, and he started talking like a man who was prime minister. But it was the crowd that did it. The word came back across the country that Diefenbaker had had a tremendous meeting in Vancouver, and the crowd went wild, and people were excited and so on. Everybody said suddenly, 'Maybe this guy could do it.'

ALLISTER GROSART

In the '57 campaign the turning point was the big rally the Liberals had in Maple Leaf Gardens.

The pipeline thing, the arrogance bit, was getting across pretty well. But you keep on and on, because our election campaigns are that long, and your big theme tends to die. People say, 'Will you shut up? I'm getting fed up with that.' The Liberals decided to go for the Maple Leaf Gardens because Dief was drawing crowds. This worried them because no Conservative leader had drawn crowds like that for a long time, and these crowds were getting bigger. It was getting around that it was exciting to get out and hear Dief really going and handling the hecklers and so on.

To fill Maple Leaf Gardens they put on quite an extravaganza and they made a terrible tactical mistake. They hired the Bell singers – you know, 'Annie Laurie' and 'Roamin' in the gloamin'' and so on, these things they sang so well under Les Bell, and this of course filled Maple Leaf Gardens. But their appeal was to the dear old Tories; more than half the audience were old Tories, men and women out to hear the Bell singers.

At some point – Mr St Laurent was of course there – some Conservative kid got excited, lost his head, and dashed up on the platform to hand some paper or something, a wacky kid. A Liberal alderman sitting there, who was on the platform I think, decided to make himself a hero, dashed out, pushed this kid and the kid fell off the thing, and cracked his head. You could hear it all over the Gardens. That, of course, went across and the question was, 'Was the kid conscious?' He was taken to hospital. 'That's it, they'd push a young kid off.'

Pick [Pickersgill] used to always claim that I put this kid up to it; this was part of the Machiavellian scheme. I had nothing to do with it. It was a sheer accident.

G.W. BALDWIN

I think it was the beginning of May, the spring anyway, 1957, and the Diefenbaker campaign was beginning to catch fire, and he was a man walking on air. We had a farm outside of Peace River and he came out there with a lot of the fellows in the press who were then starting to attach themselves to him in large numbers. I had known of him before and I had met him in the leadership campaign, but it was obvious watching him how he was so detached from the mundane things of life, because he seemed to feel that he was going to win that election and the press fellows began to feel the same way.

This was the first time that a national leader had ever come to our country. We arranged for the two biggest halls we could find, one in Peace River and the other in Grande Prairie, and filled them both. Some people came hundreds of miles. Some northern Saskatchewan people wanted to say hello to Diefenbaker, others to see him.

He came into Peace River an hour and a half late. I don't think it was his fault – it was the Edmonton people that kept him. Of course, my wife and I and our few supporters were on tenterhooks. As soon as he and his party arrived, I said, 'I think we should go down there to the meeting.'

'Oh no,' Mrs Diefenbaker said, 'he hasn't had anything to eat.'

So I got one of my friends who was there and we drove him down to the farm. They said, 'He doesn't want anything substantial, just a little light snack, milk, crackers, and cheese.' He wasn't a very heavy eater. I tried my damndest to get him moving but he walked around and started to admire the pictures on the wall. He was perfectly oblivious of the meeting. I think that he was so keyed up after the exciting time he had had in Edmonton that his wife felt, probably quite rightly, that he needed a few minutes to relax before coming to a meeting in Peace River and then another flight to Grande Prairie and a meeting in Grande Prairie.

At last we got him going, and on the way he said to me, 'Now look, Baldwin, this is one of the days that I have to make some national news. You know I have got these press people with me. This is your local campaign, of course, but then there is a national campaign going, so part of the speech I make will be directed in your interests and the interests of the party here, but part of it will have to be on issues which have a national connotation because I have to make some news.' That was understandable, and he asked me what were the local interests. He knew something about the railroad, not too much. I sketched it in, and he caught the ramifications right away. I said this is the issue of people versus corporations, the Edmonton people don't want the railroad this way but the Peace River people do and here are the reasons. So he went onto the national issue first, I forget what it was, and then he started on this railroad. And it was Dief saying, 'Send Baldwin down to Ottawa and you will get your railroad.' I had only given a very short speech, and I had given the most wonderful of Lincoln's quotations, about the house divided, and the west had to get together with the east, etc. He picked it up and referred to it and just went right into his speech with no notes on the local issues and spoke for about three-quarters of an hour altogether. He got great applause.

Then he had to go to Grande Prairie, but he stayed and talked, especially to anyone from northern Saskatchewan. When we got to Grande Prairie we were two hours late and there was a big crowd to meet him at the airport.

ALLISTER GROSART

Let me just say this in answer to your question, 'Did you structure that whole campaign on the personality of John Diefenbaker?' The answer is 'Yes.' The great criticism that developed after that was that Grosart was an image-maker, that I just took Diefenbaker and threw away the Conservative party. I did and I said so.

We had this one big ad, three-quarters of a page. It was a very sympathetic picture of Mr Diefenbaker and then some quotations going back over the years from different papers, particularly some that were opposed to us, but that time they were praising Diefenbaker. That was our ad, 'It's time for a Diefenbaker government.'

The Liberals had their big Ottawa rally, and Mr St Laurent was there. They wrote a script for him and he had this ad. He said, 'Here it is. This isn't the Conservative party. Look at it. The smallest type you can get on bottom: "Published by the Conservative Party." It's time for a Diefenbaker government.' He had about ten minutes of this. I've got the picture in which he holds this up, he looks at it, tries to read it, and he scowls. This wasn't Uncle Louis – oh, ugly. I got the tape, had it typed out, and put it in an envelope and sent it to every Liberal candidate. My thinking was, if these fellows would start this, it is exactly what I am trying to get across: 'It's Diefenbaker. It's Diefenbaker.' Because I felt by this time that there were people who would vote for Diefenbaker. I just sent it out to them all, and, happily, they assumed this was the party line, which it was. I didn't make any comment; this was just Mr St Laurent's text.

That was in the last analysis, I would say, responsible for our last four or five seats. It was good enough for that: 'It's Diefenbaker.' Because you have to go back and remember how low the Conservative party was in the election before it. I think we got 28 per cent of the vote. Now we went up by 10 to 38 per cent.

Merril Menzies, the economist whose proposal for northern development became 'the Vision,' worked as a speech writer during the 1957 election. He replied to charges that Diefenbaker had been overly lavish in campaign promises.

MERRIL MENZIES

In point of fact I only remember one specific promise that he made during that whole campaign – a promise that was designed to help one constituency, and it happened to be Paul Martin's constituency.

For a long time there had been a surcharge tax on automobiles. I forget the origin and I forget the end. In any case, going down from Toronto – there was Eddie Goodman, myself, and Harry Willis – and somehow or other the argument got around to whether in the speech that night he should promise to eliminate that tax. I always avoided any specific commitments like that. He asked my view, and I said that really I was opposed. Subsequently, should he form the government, it should be studied, there might be an overwhelming case to remove the tax, but without such a study it seemed to me just a little too obvious. He asked Eddie Goodman, and he said exactly the same thing. He asked Harry Willis, and Willis was all for anything that would sound good politically. So it was in fairly even balance. He still didn't know what to do. We had a very delightful head porter or waiter. His name was Blue. He'd been in the CNR for years. In fact, he'd been in charge of the King and Queen's coach in the 1939 royal visit. As Diefenbaker often did, he went to the grass roots. He asked Blue what his view was. 'Well,' he said, 'it couldn't matter less to me. I don't drive a car.'

In the end, what he did do was really the worst thing he could have done. He promised to reduce the thing somehow or other. It was neither quite one thing nor the other. And that really got him into trouble. It kept coming up time after time after time. But it was the only promise. These great claims of billions of dollars of specific promises – they weren't made. I know it.

However, there was another campaign promise, and it was to cost the Conservative government $25,000,000 a year, in adjustment grants split among the four Atlantic provinces. The promise was made in line with the campaign strategy of appealing to Canadians outside the central provinces of Ontario and Quebec.

HUGH JOHN FLEMING

We felt down here that we should press for what we called special treatment. The reason for the special treatment was really the Confederation agreement and the fact that the two provinces down here went into Confederation along with Ontario and Quebec with the general idea that they were going to try to develop a country on an east-west basis rather than a north-south basis.

Up to that time, the Maritime provinces had been fairly prosperous due to their trade with the New England states. That was our natural market. No question about that. We have been fighting geography for over a hundred years.

Now I don't say that we would have been better not to have gone into Confederation, but, having gone in, I felt that we should get a special adjustment grant due to those reasons plus the general economic situation. We could easily prove that our per-capita income was several dollars lower than the national average and about half as much as in the central provinces. Mr St Laurent never accepted this as being a reason for preferential treatment. We felt that we should press Mr Diefenbaker to accept that. So, when he came I went to see him along with Mr [Donald David] Patterson, who was then minister of finance down here, and we enunciated our ideas along that line. He said, 'Look, you've made a good case. I can't give you a decision about what I'll do or what the party will do when we make up our platform. But I'm glad to hear of this and certainly it will receive very careful consideration.'

Finally, he did come out in support of a special adjustment grant. You remember that was established and five years later it was increased some. I've always felt that these provinces – it was after I left [as premier] – were very unwise when they allowed themselves to be talked into giving it up.

The 1957 campaign was the first in Canada in which television played a major role. The Conservatives concentrated on their leader, giving John Diefenbaker all the free political broadcasts. The CCF did the same with M.J. Coldwell, and the Social Credit with Solon Low. The Liberals, however, divided their time up among the senior cabinet ministers. This was largely because Prime Minister St Laurent did not feel at ease in front of the cameras and would make only a couple of appearances. A survey of homes with television sets in populous southwestern Ontario showed that Diefenbaker made the strongest impression.

J.W. PICKERSGILL

I have never been able to understand or appreciate the appeal that Mr Diefenbaker has on television. I am forced to believe that he has an appeal. He has none for me. I don't go quite the length many of my friends do, of turning him off, because I wonder what new horrors there are going to be and I am a little curious. But he has no appeal to me at all. I like people to be consecutive and orderly and finish their sentences and know what they are talking about. I just never could understand why he gets all the publicity he does, because he never says anything. People say he is a great performer, but you know, I have always preferred opera to rock!

PAUL MARTIN

St Laurent didn't like TV. He could have been very good at it if he had had a chance to acclimatize himself to its implications and to its advantages, because he was a good-looking man, he was a man of serenity and quiet composure. These are useful qualities, I should think, on television. But it was a new instrument. He was preoccupied with many problems. He wasn't well at the time. He lacked his normal self-assurance, and for that reason he didn't take well to television.

Actually, I wasn't very impressed with Mr St Laurent's performance generally. None of us were. It certainly wasn't the St Laurent of the election before. He had aged considerably, spoke at great length, repeated himself, and quite obviously we were not the masters of the election ship as we had been.

Nevertheless, I wasn't sure that we were going to be defeated. Perhaps I was looking at that election in the light of my own situation. I actually got the biggest majority I ever had received up to that time in that election. I suppose I misjudged the national picture, which was catastrophic.

Pierre Sévigny, who was organizing the Conservatives' campaign in Quebec, was worried about the party's chances in the province. He consulted an old friend of his, Maurice Duplessis, premier of Quebec.

PIERRE SÉVIGNY

Duplessis, who always liked a good political talk, received me, put everything aside, asked how it went, and laughed at me. In due course he became intrigued and interested. But he was still refusing his support and he used to laugh at me and say that we would win nothing, that we were just idiots, that the future in politics was with him, the great Maurice Duplessis, and not in Ottawa.

I persisted and I would meet him either at his office in Quebec city or at the Ritz Carlton in Montreal where he came weekly. And, in time, I realized that he was becoming interested. Anyway, one day I became annoyed at this reluctance of Mr Duplessis to give us his support and I looked at him and said, 'Well, Mr Duplessis, the election will be in June most probably and if you don't support us we're going to win nothing. I mean we have four seats now, we will have none then. Maybe we will keep Léon Balcer through your influence, but that's all. Maybe Bill Hamilton because he has got a personal level of support, but that's all. And then the people will be justified to say that the strong man of Quebec is not Maurice Duplessis, but Louis St Laurent.'

He was sitting in a chair and he jumped about this high. 'What's this you say? What's this you say' I repeated it. I said, 'That's common sense.' So he started twisting around and he ordered an orange juice. That man was drinking orange juice by the gallon. Then he said, 'Well, let me think of this and come see me tomorrow. See what we can do.'

The next day I went to see him and he said, 'You know, what you said yesterday has merit.' And he went on, 'Maybe we must make an effort, I mean to support this man, Diefenbaker.' He said, 'From what you tell me he appears to be in favour of the theory of provincial autonomy; he seems to be very strong for Confederation.' That's one of the fallacies about

Duplessis; he has been represented as the arch-enemy of Canada, yet he was the greatest man for Confederation that there was and his complete provincial autonomy theme was the preservation of Confederation and the respect of its terms.

'Look,' he said, 'I will support your man but your man has got to come forth with something which will give me a reason to tell my supporters to support him and a reason for me to do that.' And then he scribbled a few notes on a piece of paper. It was simply that he would respect the terms of Confederation and see to it that the fiscal powers of the provinces were returned to the provinces as per the terms of the Confederation pact. I mean it was really a very indifferent statement and I figured, after my talk with Mr Diefenbaker, that it would be very simple to get him to say these things.

Now, Duplessis, who was a great strategist and also a great tactician, said, 'This has got to be started at some meeting. You have got to give some sort of a function, and Diefenbaker will come, and that will be his keynote speech in Quebec.' So we arranged a dinner. Then we had to sell tickets. It was not easy. Nobody wanted to come. In due course, it cost me a fortune because I had to buy most of the tickets and give them to people.

But it was one thing to give a dinner. It was another thing though to get Mr Diefenbaker to say what Duplessis wanted him to say. I had thought it would be simple. I saw Mr Diefenbaker in Ottawa and told him, 'Look, we have the support of Mr Duplessis, providing you say this.' I picked up that paper and I said, 'Here's what he wants you to say.'

He said, 'Never, never, no, no. I will never say that. Never, never, preposterous. I can't say that.'

I said, 'Look, the fact is you told me you stood for – '

'Yes, but not that thing.'

Then the fight started. Either I got Mr Diefenbaker to say what old Duplessis wanted him to say and Duplessis backed us, or Mr Diefenbaker did not say what Duplessis wanted him to say and everything went wrong.

Eventually, as I was much younger in those days and maybe a little more adventurous, I conceived a plan. I told Mr Diefenbaker, 'You will have to speak French at that meeting.' He reluctantly agreed that this was a necessity. Diefenbaker's French has never been of the best and was worse in those days than it eventually became.

'Well,' he said, 'I can't speak at length in French.'

I said, 'No, no, no.' I said. 'Half a page is enough, two minutes, maybe one, but you have got to say something in French.'

'Well,' he said, 'prepare something.'

I prepared a speech for old Dief in French which he changed at least a dozen times, and which eventually he practised. I would sit in one chair and Marc Drouin in another and we would coach him how to pronounce 'Québec' in French and 'Canada' in French and say the right words, and it was a battle. I could see that he was getting nervous when we got him to do that. In any event, he had what he said in French, which was about ten lines, no more.

On the great day, we met him at the airport, took him to the Windsor Hotel, and there I said, 'Mr Diefenbaker, we have got to brief you one last time for your French remarks.' He said, 'Yes.' I had typed on a sheet of paper exactly what Duplessis wanted him to say and I arranged it so that it was exactly the same length as the speech that he had so studiously prepared himself. When the rehearsal was over I took my little sheet of paper, placed it where, in the part of the speech, he would speak in French and took the other one out and put it in my pocket.

We got to the Mont St Louis arena where the dinner was being held and I was nervous as hell. 'My God,' I said, 'This is the nearest thing to a fraud that I have ever committed in my life. Now what's going to happen?' By then I knew about his temper.

Old Dief was in great form that night and he cracked a few jokes and he did not read his speech. He turned the pages you know, but would speak off the cuff. Eventually he came to that part where he had to speak French and I remember what he said. He said, 'Just to prove to you that in this party Mr Sévigny is not the only one who can speak French, I have got a few remarks of my own.'

So he picks up the paper and starts reading the ten lines. By the time he had finished the ten lines he realized that it was not exactly what he had said, and his head started shaking – but it was said on the air, and Duplessis was listening. Then he carried on in English and when the speech was over he shook hands with a few people, and I remember I was introducing him and he was looking at everybody but me.

Eventually, the time came to come back to the hotel and he said, 'I want to see you.' If you think I had received hell before and I received hell after, you should have seen the blast that I got that time. Finally, I told him, 'Look, you certainly didn't say anything wrong.' I denied being the one who had substituted the thing. I remember my wife got mad, and said to him, 'This is your one chance to win and there you go screaming and yelling at this.' Olive was there telling him to quiet down and my wife was giving him hell. Oh, it was terrible, really.

Anyway, the next day the reports were fabulous and Duplessis called me up and said, 'I want you to tell your man that he made a fine speech.' I said,

'Why don't you tell him yourself?' Which Duplessis did. He sent a wire of congratulations. Then Diefenbaker started realizing that really this speech had been extremely well received. There were no criticisms for what he had said. One day he called me up and said, 'I have got to see you.' I knew I had been forgiven for my terrible sin, which I have never admitted to him.

From then on Duplessis was sold on Mr Diefenbaker. One day, about a week after that speech, he asked me to come to Quebec city, and when I got there he called in some of his ministers: Antoine Rivard, the solicitor general, and Onésime Gagnon, who was minister of finance, [Antonio] Talbot who was minister of roads, [Antonio] Barrette, who was minister of labour, and another one, Paul Sauvé. These were his key men and he said, 'We are going to go all out for the Conservatives, but we are going to do it according to plan.' He glanced at me and went on, 'Look, here is the province. In at least fifty seats you have no chance at all. So we will put token candidates there, but in twenty-five seats you have a good chance, and that's where we will put strength, power, and good candidates.' He ordered these ministers to go all out and put the strong machine that the National Union had to work behind the Conservatives.

After that, Duplessis asked to meet certain of the organizers from Ottawa and I arranged a meeting at the Ritz Carlton. I forget who came from Ottawa. If I remember, there was a chap called Art Burns who was present and who was a publicist for the party. Senator [Louis-Philippe] Beaubien, I think, was there. In his own inimitable way Duplessis said, 'We are out to win this thing. It is impossible for you to win as Conservatives in Quebec. The reason I changed the Conservatives to National Union in 1935 is because I realized that as Conservatives it was impossible to win votes in Quebec because the memory of the 1917 days was too vivid in the minds of too many. The Liberals were too strong, were too much identified with being the right party for Quebec. But you have something that you can sell. You've got this man Diefenbaker.'

'In his own way,' he went on, 'Diefenbaker is a pretty boy, he looks good – nice hair, nice eyes – he speaks well, he is good orator, presents himself well. He almost looks like a man, which is saying something for a Conservative. I like him. He's got something. What you should do is sell him as a man. Forget about the Conservatives, forget about the party, but build that man up. Now, what he said about Confederation is what needs to be said. Build him up!' I remember his words. 'You have got to make him a combination of Churchill, de Gaulle, Moses, God, and maybe the Devil, because he has got a bit of that in him. This combination usually wins votes. Do that.'

These guys were a bit shocked but they listened and, anyway, this is certainly what we did in Quebec. We forgot about the PC party in our publicity and started talking about Mr Diefenbaker. When the election was decided, we benefited from the stupidity of the St Laurent organization. The St Laurent people were so sure of winning that they didn't bother to really organize as they should have done or to campaign as they should have done. They tried to perpetuate the Uncle Louis image, and they were very lackadaisical. On the other hand, we were working like mad, following the theory of Duplessis to promote Mr Diefenbaker as the man. Gordon Churchill was very pleased because we didn't ask Ottawa to supply us with much money, because we had Duplessis supplying the money. He supplied in fact in twenty-five ridings the sum of $752,000 and he ran the campaign himself. Daily I had to report to him, and he was following everything and very curious about it. On the eve of the election Duplessis called me and said, 'I have made my last calculation. Here's the way it is going to be.' So on the night of the election the miracle happened.

As for the Liberals, most of them were supremely confident to the very end. Jack Pickersgill said to me while the campaign was in progress that they deserved to lose, but would win because there was no alternative. Lionel Chevrier, the former transport minister who was in charge of building the St Lawrence Seaway, had been persuaded to return to politics in time for the 1957 election. While he was still head of the Seaway authority, he had reported monthly to Prime Minister St Laurent and they had in passing discussed political prospects.

LIONEL CHEVRIER
I would ask him how were things going and so forth, and what do you think our chances are. When George Drew was leader of the opposition, he said to me there was no doubt about the result, that we would win – and I too was sure that we could win. Then, when Mr Diefenbaker was chosen, in my monthly visit I said, 'What do you think of the position at this time?' [Mr St Laurent] said, 'You know what I told you earlier concerning Mr Drew; it will be ten times worse, so far as I'm concerned, in favour of the Liberal Party. Of that, there's no doubt at all.' And I think everybody felt the same way because here was Dief from way out west. What influence had he in central Canada, even the Maritime provinces? He was relatively unknown.

J.W. PICKERSGILL
I won't pretend that I had any thought that we would lose until the night of the election. I was in the Château Frontenac before the polls closed in Que-

bec and I telephoned Charlie Granger, who was my executive assistant. He was in the Newfoundland Hotel and Charlie had his radio on. I heard over the telephone the radio report of the first few returns from Halifax. I said to Charlie, 'Did I hear those right?' and of course, the Tories were way ahead in Halifax. He said, 'Yes.' Then he started to say we had done well in Newfoundland but had lost the St John's seat, which I knew we would anyway. But Halifax was another kettle of fish.

This was in the bedroom, and I came out into the sitting room and my wife said, 'You look as though your best friend had died.' I said, 'The government has been defeated.'

I was at the St Laurents' on election night. It was really dismal! When you are prepared for a great victory – and then that. I remember when the results began to come in from Manitoba – until Manitoba the Liberals had been in the lead – and the two parties were getting closer and closer, I remember Mr St Laurent saying to me, 'I hope they get at least one more seat than we do so we can get out of this appalling situation.' I said, 'So do I.'

ALLISTER GROSART

You remember the famous remark that Dief made in the plane going down to Regina on election night – he had to go down there to get on the national network. When the announcement was coming over the radio that another cabinet minister had gone, in an exuberant mood he shouted down the plane, 'Allister, how does the architect feel?' Well, you remember the press picked that up. It was only his generosity. But the Liberals used it – they were not prepared to admit that Diefenbaker had defeated them – so they claimed it was due to Machiavellian Grosart and Madison Avenue tactics, which was a lot of nonsense.

The official results of the 1957 election were: Progressive Conservatives, 112; Liberals, 105; CCF, 25; Social Credit, 19; others, 4. Nine Liberal cabinet ministers were defeated, including C.D. Howe, who was virtually deputy prime minister, Walter Harris, the finance minister and heir apparent, Robert Winters, Hugues Lapointe, and the newest minister, Paul Hellyer, who was sworn in when the election was called.

Most of the Tories I interviewed, but not all, agreed with Allister Grosart that Diefenbaker was responsible for ending twenty-two years of Liberal rule.

4
Leadership exercised

The day after his extraordinary victory, Diefenbaker went to Lac La Ronge in northern Saskatchewan to fish. There was no telephone or any other communication with the outside world. Everything seemed to be going his way, and for a couple of days he had the most successful fishing he had ever had. He was out on the water when an urgent message was delivered: the prime minister wanted to communicate with him. He went ashore and drove to the nearest telephone and rang St Laurent, who asked when he was coming to Ottawa.

Diefenbaker flew down the next day. He called on the prime minister, who said that he would not make his final decision until the armed forces vote was counted the following Monday. This could not, however, change more than two seats. St Laurent made it clear that he was not going to stay in office, despite pressure on him to do so by the former agriculture minister, J.G. Gardiner.

When Diefenbaker was asked to form a government in the week after the election, there was no one with cabinet experience whom he could consult. Earl Rowe had had a passing acquaintance with the privy council, as he had been made minister without portfolio by R.B. Bennett during the election campaign of 1935, but Earl Rowe was part of the dead Tory past. Among those whose counsel the prime minister designate sought were his old friends, General George Pearkes and W.R. Brunt. Diefenbaker's long reading in Canadian history and constitutional law also helped.

GEORGE PEARKES

I think that it is an exaggeration to say he consulted me. He did tell me what his decisions were and asked for my comments. I think that I was the

Diefenbaker, with reporters, on his way to see St Laurent to begin the transfer of office (the author is at right)

first member to be nominated by him to the cabinet. He told me what his plans were in many cases and asked me what I thought of this and that person or what we might do with somebody else. It was Diefenbaker who made all the decisions and thought them all out really. I think that when he told me, it was mainly my concurrence with his suggestions that he was seeking.

Bill Brunt was in his office quite a lot during this period and I think that very likely he discussed his cabinet proposals with him. I think there were others too whom he consulted separately.

Among those Prime Minister Diefenbaker named to his cabinet was Michael Starr, member for Ontario riding, and the first Canadian of Ukrainian parentage to be made a minister of the Crown. He was appointed minister of labour and held the portfolio for the whole period of Conservative government.

Michael Starr was born in Copper Cliff, Ontario, on 14 November 1910. He was mayor of Oshawa from 1949 to 1952 and, as the first mayor of Ukrainian descent, he opened the door for other Ukrainian Canadians to become mayors, such as William Hawrelak in Edmonton and Steven Juba in Winnipeg. Starr was an aggressive mayor who got city hall moving so impressively that Premier Leslie Frost wanted him in his cabinet. When Starr ran provincially in 1951, however, he lacked an organization and lost. Then George Drew asked him to run federally in 1952; despite his wife's objection, he did run, and won.

Starr recalled how he had been appointed to the cabinet.

MICHAEL STARR

I was sitting at home, after the election, reading the papers, and I saw that Doug Harkness was in Ottawa, and he saw the prime minister and so did Howard Green and Davie Fulton. My wife said, 'Don't you think you should go to Ottawa?' I said, 'What for? I don't understand what they are doing there really – it is all strange to me.' 'They are probably there,' she said, 'to try to get in the cabinet.' I said, 'Mr Diefenbaker has a telephone and he knows where I live; he has got my telephone number; if he needs me, he will call me.'

Anyway, all of a sudden Dr Blair died in Perth. [William Gourlay Blair was a prominent Conservative MP who would probably have been minister of health and welfare had he lived.] John Pallett and I drove to Perth together for the funeral. When we came out of the church after the service, somebody came up to me and said, 'The prime minister wants to see you.' I walked over to the car and Diefenbaker said, 'I have been looking all over for you. I wanted to see you.'

'What did you want to see me about?'

'Oh, I've got to see you in Ottawa.'

I said, 'Mr Prime Minister, I wasn't prepared to go to Ottawa. I just came for the funeral and I was going right back. I have only a handkerchief in my pocket.'

'Oh, I've got to see you.

I went back over to Pallett and said, 'If he wants me tomorrow, I could go back home and come back properly equipped for any stay at all. But he said, 'He is the prime minister and you have got to go.'

So I went to the cemetery; Peter Dempson was there and I rode to Ottawa with him. I arrived at about five o'clock and went to the prime minister's office in the Centre Block. I saw people walking in and out until seven o'clock and I was getting exasperated. All of a sudden, Dief walked out and said, 'Oh, I've got a lot of decisions to make.'

I said, 'Look, Mr Prime Minister, you said you wanted to see me. But if you're tired, I guess I better go.' He said, 'No, come and have dinner with me. Come on, we will go down to the Château.'

We had dinner in the main dining room there, and he was telling stories, shaking hands with people, bowing at everyone. After we came out, I said, 'Mr Prime Minister, don't you want to see me about something?'

He said, 'Michael, you try and be in my office for eight o'clock tomorrow morning.'

By that time, I was getting put out. My wife must have been wondering where I was. All she knew was that I had gone to the funeral, and I wondered what to do. Then I remembered Allister Grosart was down at the Beacon Arms Hotel. I found him and told him the story.

He said, 'You have got to stay overnight. You can stay here. I have got two beds, Mike, and I am alone.' I phoned Anne and I told her and she said, 'If he wants you, you better stay over.' I said, 'I haven't got a clean shirt for tomorrow,' Allister said, 'What size?' I told him and he said, 'Just my size.'

Next morning, I was up bright and early. I was in the Centre Block at eight o'clock and waited for about two or three minutes before the prime minister walked in. He said, 'Come on in, Michael,' and he told me about the responsibilities, et cetera, that he had. Finally I said, 'Well, you wanted to see me.' He said, 'Mike, I just can't see you now. Do you mind waiting outside? I have to see a few other people first and then I will.'

I sat outside and I sat until noon and no answer. I could see delegations walking in and out and I dared not go for lunch in case he wanted me, so I sat until five o'clock and I got up and, exasperated, I said, 'The hell with it,' and I went out. I went back and I was pretty disgusted and I said, 'I am going home.' Allister Grosart said, 'Okay, Mike, but let's go out and eat.' So we had a few drinks and had something to eat.

We came back and there was a note on the floor underneath his door and he picked it up and it was for me. 'The prime minister wants to see you in his suite at the Château Laurier tomorrow morning at eight o'clock.' That was the morning when they were going to be sworn in. I phoned my wife and she said, 'You better stay,' and I said, 'Okay.'

I borrowed another shirt the next morning. At about five minutes before eight I appeared in the lobby of the Château Laurier and there was Bill Hamilton standing there. We looked at each other and he said, 'I guess we are going to the same place together.'

We got on the elevator and went up. The door opened and Mr Diefenbaker was there, the prime minister. I hadn't had any breakfast but he was chomping away at his breakfast, and he told us to sit down on the chesterfield back of him. Then, he turned around to Bill and said, 'Well, have you made up your mind?' Bill said, 'Yes.' And he said, 'Well, okay.'

He turned around to me and said, 'You are minister of labour,' and I said, 'Thanks very much.'

I started to go out and he said, 'Just wait a minute, Michael. I want you to walk up to the House with me.' So he finished his breakfast and we came downstairs and he is shaking hands and Bill Hamilton says to me, 'I don't know what I am.' I said, 'What are you talking about?' 'Well,' he said, 'he gave me a choice of two and all he asked me is if I made up my mind and I said, yes, and he said, okay, and I don't know which one.' I said, 'Bill, don't worry, at eleven o'clock when you get sworn in they will tell you what you are.'

Anyway I walked with Mr Diefenbaker up to the Parliament Buildings. I wanted to get out to get some breakfast because at eleven o'clock we were supposed to jump into taxi cabs, the barefoot boys in the taxi cabs.

I will never forget that. I was pretty nervous. In the taxi cab there were about four of us. Ellen Fairclough was one. I had just lit a cigarette when we arrived at Rideau Hall. The cigarette was half-burned so I snuffed it out and put it in my pocket. We went in and got sworn in. After we came out for pictures, I pulled out this damned butt and automatically put it in my mouth. I said to the press, 'Hey, has anybody got a match?' and one guy rushed over to light it up. It was all in the papers, and my wife gave me hell for that.

WILLIAM HAMILTON

When I heard that Diefenbaker was forming a government, I hustled up to Ottawa by train and I was there by ten o'clock, and immediately phoned his office. Diefenbaker was occupied, but George Pearkes was there. And George allowed as how he was very happy that I was in town. No, to his knowledge they hadn't been trying to get me, but he would certainly let Mr Diefenbaker know I was in town. My wife and I had a little apartment in Ottawa and I went there, and waited patiently. I don't know how long it took, but the call came, again from Pearkes. Mr Diefenbaker would like to see me. I went up and had a rather vague conversation with Diefenbaker about whether or not I would like to be in the cabinet, and what kind of a portfolio I might be interested in. I remember him mentioning Citizenship and Immigration, Northern Affairs. Then he went into the Post Office Department, and said that I had been a critic and had been quite vocal about that – this might be a very good portfolio for me, but, on the other hand, perhaps my criticism had been such that it would have antagonized the staff of the postal organization. If that were the case another portfolio would be better.

He also said that he was only going to appoint a portion of his cabinet at that time, and there would be others later on, so I might have another crack at it, if I decided against it on this occasion. Well, anyone, it seems to me, who has any kind of an opportunity to get into the cabinet and doesn't grab it quickly is being stupid, to say the least. I wanted to be in the cabinet and I wanted it very badly, and I think this was obvious, and I didn't care which portfolio I got. In any event he said to me, 'Go away and think about it overnight, and come back and see me tomorrow morning at eight o'clock, and we can have another talk.' The next day had been announced as the day on which the cabinet was going to be chosen.

So I went away, and I wondered about this antagonism within the postal department. They did the estimates on the floor of the House in those days, and a couple of departmental officials sat in front of the minister. One of them, a chap named Bill Griffiths – he's now dead – who was controller of the department, was there along with the deputy, and Bill used to, I'm sure of it, when I was on a good point, look across the House at me, smile rather happily and wink. I felt that here was a sort of sympathetic soul, and one that might understand my position. I found him somewhere in the hinterland of Ottawa that evening, and I put the question to him: 'If I became minister of your department, what would be the reaction of the people in the department?' He gave me an answer which I thought was pretty indicative of the attitude with which the civil service as a whole greeted the Diefenbaker government. He said, 'If you come into our department with the same kind of an antagonistic attitude that you displayed as a member of the opposition, and a critical attitude, an almost unreasoning attitude that you displayed as a member of the opposition, you're not going to get very much cooperation, and people won't be very happy. But on the other hand, if you are someone who is happy to be in the department, then I think you'll get wonderful support and you'll get along very well.'

The next morning I went back to the Château Laurier, and I was there a few minutes early. I was sitting in the lobby. Mike Starr came along. I looked at Mike and Mike looked at me, and I said, 'I suppose you're going upstairs?'

He said, 'Yes. Are you?' I said, 'Yes.'

We went up together. Diefenbaker was in his suite. He and Olive were having breakfast. He greeted us warmly, and had us sit in a little loveseat against the wall. Olive was facing us at the other side of the table, and Diefenbaker was there with his back to us. Once in a while he'd turn around and look over his shoulder, but most of the time he just went on attacking his bacon and eggs, and with his back towards us, but talking to us.

I remember not being particularly offended, but nonetheless thinking that it might have been done in a somewhat more considerate way. He might even have swung the table around.

Be that as it may, the conversation was almost completely with Mike Starr initially. Then he moved over to me, and he just asked me – very short, very abrupt, very directly – 'Well, have you thought about what we talked about yesterday, and what your reception might be?'

I said, 'Yes, and I'd like to try it.'

He said 'Humph.' Sort of a snort. Then he swung around in his chair, and he looked directly at Mike Starr, and he said, 'You're minister of labour.' That was really the end of the conversation. I didn't feel as if I wanted to ask the man who in two hours was going to be prime minister of Canada whether 'humph' meant yes or no. I positively learned that I was going to be a minister and postmaster general from George Nowlan, driving out to Government House to be sworn in. He had the list, and he confirmed it.

GORDON CHURCHILL

I was appointed minister of transport when the government was formed, and was it for forty-eight hours, and then before we were sworn in I was switched to trade and commerce, and George Hees, who had expected to be minister of trade and commerce, took over transport. I was caught in a trap; I didn't want to be minister of trade and commerce but some trouble had arisen and some major change appeared to be advisable. The late Senator Brunt and Allister Grosart were sent by Mr Diefenbaker to apprise George Hees that he would be taking over transport and not trade and commerce.

They then came to see me and dragged me down to see the Chief, who informed me that I was being shifted from transport to trade and commerce. I pointed out all the difficulties that would arise from that but I had earlier said to Mr Diefenbaker that I would undertake any job that he gave me. I wasn't even looking for a position in the cabinet to begin with, and I had no special field that was open. My interests in the House of Commons had been in defence, veterans affairs, and external affairs, largely. Obviously, I wasn't fitted for external affairs. George Pearkes was the natural choice for defence, and Alf Brooks was the natural choice for veterans affairs because they had been head of our caucus committees for years on those subjects. When it came to this crisis, it was difficult for me to say, 'Well you know, I can't take it on.'

I had to take over the 'empire' of C.D. Howe. I suffered from shock for two full hours after I returned to my own office and sat down to think about it because nobody in his right mind would want to succeed C.D. Howe. You know, you can't succeed God. I suffered for a miserable two hours, and then I went back to see the chief and I said, 'This is all wrong, it shouldn't be done.'

He said, 'You're an organizer, aren't you?'

I said, 'Yes, it's one of my chief interests.'

'Well,' he said, 'it's organization.' I said 'All right.' So I was saddled with trade and commerce and enjoyed it immensely, but it would not have been my choice.

GEORGE HEES

I was called down to Ottawa like so many others and saw Mr Diefenbaker and he asked me what I would like. I said I would like Trade and Commerce. This is what I had been engaged in all my life. I had been a business man. I had taken a great interest in those things while in the opposition and that was the portfolio that I would have liked at that time. Mr Diefenbaker said he would consider it. The next day, I was told that he couldn't give me Trade and Commerce, that he was going to give that to Gordon Churchill, that I could have Transport. I didn't know that much about transport, because a central Ontarian is not very much interested in Transport. As it turned out it was the best thing that ever happened to me because it turned out to be a fascinating portfolio.

LÉON BALCER

I was made solicitor general. At that time, I was the only minister from Quebec, and also with a very minor post, because solicitor general was even much less important than it is now. I mean it was the bottom of the totem pole. On the other hand, Quebec, at that general election of '57, had elected only nine members. Some of them were unknown and inexperienced. Then, the [walkout at the] convention was very strong in the mind of Diefenbaker and the people around him. Diefenbaker had this argument, 'Give me the men and we will give Quebec the representation it deserves.'

DONALD FLEMING
I told [Mr Diefenbaker at a meeting in Ottawa] that my first choice would have been external affairs. I eliminated finance from consideration, as I told him, because I assumed and hoped that my dear friend, Jim Macdonnell, would be appointed minister of finance. I think it is true to say that in all the budget debates and debates on fiscal questions in the years leading up to 1957, I had taken a very active role, second only to that of Jim Macdonnell. Mr Diefenbaker made it quite clear immediately to me that Mr Macdonnell would not be appointed minister of finance. I think the reasons were probably personal and also he felt that Mr Macdonnell was a little old and his health might not be adequate to the rigours of what is by far the heaviest of all the portfolios.

There was some possibility of my being appointed, I thought, minister of trade and commerce, because I had been critic on trade and commerce and defence production, the two departments headed by Mr Howe in the six years leading up to 1957. There was also the possibility of the Department of Justice, but my personal choice was external affairs.

I went back to Toronto after this meeting. He was in touch with me, as a matter of fact he consulted me about a number of the appointments to the cabinet. I was back once again about two days before the swearing-in and at this time he made it quite clear to me that finance was to be my portfolio.

DAVIE FULTON
When he offered me post A, he asked me if I would be prepared to accept the nomination as speaker of the House of Commons, and I know he had very good reasons for it. The speaker, you remember, in the pipeline debate had come under very severe attack, and we had ourselves taken the position there should be some permanency attached to the post of speaker and he should be neutral – you know, somebody who would really be neutral. To the extent that I would have been generally acceptable to the other members on both sides of the House, and to the extent that I had a knowledge of the rules of Parliament, and that Mr Diefenbaker may have wished to move towards the establishment of a permanent speakership, these were valid reasons.

I never resented it, or felt that it was beneath my dignity, or that it wasn't a proper offer. I never felt that a bit. But I did have this feeling, and indicated it to him, that my role for some time to come would be in the political battle, and I both wanted and felt I would perform a greater service in the ranks of the cabinet, rather than as speaker, and he accepted this.

Again he may have been rather annoyed with me, but he never reproached me. He never said, 'You are a beggar because you wouldn't take what I offered you.' Later he said, 'Go and think it over and come back.' We set a time, and I went back, and he said, 'Well, what do you think?' I said, 'I am afraid I have to say my position is still the same, I am sorry about it.' So he said, 'Okay, how about justice?' and that was the end of it. I was very happy. My justice committeeship was my major function as a member of the opposition, and it was a logical, and to me very acceptable, appointment.

Diefenbaker appointed the first woman cabinet minister in Canadian history. Ellen Louks Fairclough came of United Empire Loyalist stock. She was secretary of the United Empire Loyalist Association and an executive officer of the Imperial Order of the Daughters of the Empire. She was also a certified public accountant. She could be counted among the members of the Tory establishment and among his enemies in the Conservative caucus.

Born and raised in Hamilton – she represented Hamilton West in Parliament – she had become involved in politics at an early age. She was vice president of the Young Conservatives of Ontario in the early thirties. Just after the war she ran for alderman, but lost by three votes. Subsequently, when an alderman retired, the Hamilton City Council appointed her to complete his term, and she served from 1946 to 1949. Then she ran for Board of Control and headed the poll, becoming deputy mayor in 1950. After being defeated in the federal general election of 1949, she ran in the by-election of 1950 and won by a narrow margin.

The first time Ellen Fairclough came to Ottawa after the 1957 election was when she was on her way to Dr. Blair's funeral in Perth. She found 'things were in a great old uproar' with several people who wanted to be ministers or who wanted special concessions hanging around.

ELLEN FAIRCLOUGH
When I met George Drew, he asked me if I'd like a ride out to the funeral with him and Fiorenza. The three of us drove out in the front seat of his car, and he said, 'Has Dief called on you yet?' I said, 'No.'

Fiorenza laughed and she said, 'Well, if he hasn't called on you yet, it won't help to ride out to the funeral with us,' which I thought was highly amusing.

I was standing with the Drews and with somebody else twenty-five or thirty-five feet away from the prime minister. He looked at me and he jerked

with his head for me to come over; so I went over to see him, and we exchanged pleasantries, and he said. 'Are you free to come and see me later on
today?'

I said, 'Yes, what time?'

'Well,' he said, 'say about six o'clock.'

So I went to his office and I could see for myself the mob that was hanging around. I sat down and he let me cool my heels for some considerable
length of time. Although he had asked me to be there at six, I guess I sat there
for half an hour, three-quarters of an hour. Finally I went in and sat down
and said, 'How are you?' He said, 'Fine, and how are you?' I said, 'Fine.' I
said, 'I guess you are having your problems trying to organize things, and
get them in some reasonable order.' He said, 'Yes, I am. Looks to me as if I
have to compose a cabinet of my enemies!' Imagine, that is exactly what he
said. I didn't answer. I would not feed that fire of his.

Then he went on and he was determined to bait me: this is when he made
the comment that I had supported Fleming. I said, 'I don't care whether you
believe it or not but I did not support Don Fleming. If you doubt that you
can ask Don Fleming because I told him in my own living room that I would
not support him.' I told him that I had not supported Fulton publicly but I
voted for him. I said that Margaret Aitken and I were the only two women
there and we had discussed the matter. We had agreed between ourselves
that we would not support any one candidate publicly – not even Diefenbaker
even though it was obvious that he was going to win. Anybody could have
jumped on the band-wagon; that was easy. We decided that it was unfair for
us, in the spotlight in which we stood, to come out and actively support any
one candidate, so we stayed neutral.

I don't think he believed me, but some time later, two years later, I had
occasion to call on him for something or another, and he said, 'Ellen, I want
to thank you, you have been extremely loyal.' I had told him on the first
occasion, 'George Drew and I were bitter enemies, but once he was my
leader, he was my leader and I have never been anything but loyal to him!'

I didn't get the cabinet post I expected. I expected to get labour, and I
thought that with my accounting background if I didn't get labour I would
probably get national revenue. I readily admit that I felt terribly let down.
I almost refused to go into the cabinet. I went back and I discussed it with
George Drew. I said, 'He has offered me secretary of state.'

George said, 'Oh dear, oh no.'

I said, 'Yes, that is what he offered me and I don't think that I am going
to take it.'

George said, 'Don't be a fool. Even as secretary of state you will be the first woman cabinet minister in Canada. Take it, and you will be changed before long.'

What happened was that right after the next election he gave me the post of immigration, which was a dirty post. There is not a bit of doubt in my mind that it is the worst post in the government. Then, after the '62 election, he asked me to take postmaster general. By that time, I had been in immigration longer than almost anyone else and I was glad to move out.

PAUL MARTIN

I'm sure that I never thought the day would come when John would ever be a member of a government, let alone head of it. When that happened, the world had come to an end as far as I was concerned. So, when John did become prime minister, I sent him a message, a wire to Prince Albert, congratulating him, but I found it very difficult to believe that he was actually the head of the government.

I was certain that he was going to have a tough job. I was certain that he was going to have to learn that government was quite different from what it looks like from the ranks of the opposition. He had never been in government, he had never administered anything in his life. I don't think he'd ever been on the town council or the village council in Saskatchewan. If you have had no experience in administration, anyone who has had it is bound to conclude that the poor chap who comes in untutored is going to have a tough time. That was my feeling about John and his crowd.

I met him one day about a week after the election. I was coming down from the main block, going down to the Château Laurier to have a swim, and there was John, shouting at me, 'Paul!' I walked over, and he had his hands in his pockets, and he said, 'Are you not going to congratulate me?' 'Well,' I said, 'I have congratulated you, but if you had an efficient prime ministerial office, you'd know this and you would have by this time acknowledged my wire.' 'I'm so sorry,' and I'm sure he meant that.

But there he was, he was proud of himself, and he had every reason to be. It was quite an achievement. Many in his party didn't want him, and he'd circumvented that. Here he was, actually *gloriamente regnante*, actually in office, prime minister of the country!

Somehow or another, he seemed to be very happy to convey that fact to me, that he was the prime minister. He took me up to his office. We walked along to the privy council office, and he said, 'Would you like to come in and see my office, and see what I've done to it?' And I said, 'Well, I'd be very happy to visit the office of the prime minister.' I had a feeling of envy, you know, to think that he had succeeded. We went into his office and sat down. And you could just see the exhilaration. All of this is very understandable.

The office had changed. There was a picture of Sir John A. Macdonald; I remember that.

The first Conservative government in twenty-two years, since 1935, was sworn in on 21 June 1957, just eleven days after the party's triumph at the polls. John Diefenbaker had to move quickly because the Commonwealth Prime Ministers' Conference was due to be held in London shortly and he was determined to go, despite the fact that there was much to do at home. He did not have time to complete the selection of his ministry and there were only fifteen members of his first cabinet, with the result that some had to double up. For instance, Douglas Harkness was minister of northern affairs and national resources as well as agriculture, and Alf Brooks had to keep an eye on health and welfare in addition to veterans affairs.

It was a joyous occasion, Diefenbaker's first official visit to London. The prime minister had a private audience with the Queen, and Mr and Mrs Diefenbaker were invited to lunch by Winston Churchill. The new Canadian leader caught the fancy of the British public as soon as he stepped off the plane and announced that he would propose a Commonwealth trade conference to be held in Canada. There had been reports that the British government was considering entry into the European free trade area, a course of action which the British public viewed with hostility and suspicion. Diefenbaker, by his support for the Commonwealth, became an instant hero in the popular press and was described by the Daily Mail *as the New Strong Man of Commonwealth.*

When he got back, Diefenbaker made more appointments to his cabinet. Alvin Hamilton was named minister of northern affairs and national resources.

ALVIN HAMILTON

Of course, the resource portfolio was just tailored for me. I couldn't have asked for a blanker sheet of paper to start writing on. It was a new portfolio set up in 1953. It was not called natural resources, it was distinctly labelled national resources because they wanted to include human resources in it. This is where I got started in my study of city problems, as a human resource, because I took this very seriously. If you go back to St Laurent's speeches when he set up the department in 1953, he made quite a thing about that. I seized on this to give me the right to monkey around with the cities, much to the concern of some of my cabinet colleagues.

There was one portfolio that Prime Minister Diefenbaker retained after completing his cabinet: external affairs. Mackenzie King had been minister of external affairs for most of the time he had been in office. Despite this precedent, Mr Diefenbaker did not keep the portfolio long. In September he appointed Sidney Smith, president of the University of Toronto, to the post.

Once the new ministers were sworn in, they had to take over their departments. This proved a trying experience in some cases. Even more difficult, some found, was answering for their departments in Parliament.

MICHAEL STARR

After the swearing in, I went home for the weekend, and when I arrived back in Ottawa on Monday I felt I should be down at the department. I decided to ask, 'Where is the Labour Department?' They told me, 'In the Confederation Building.' I said, 'Where is that?' I lived in the Parliament Buildings and in the Lord Elgin; that was the extent of my Ottawa situation.

I drove there. I couldn't find any parking space around the building and I drove around a couple of times. Then I spotted an empty space with a sign that said, 'Minister of Labour.' I stopped the car and I said, 'Well, that is me.' So, I pulled in there and parked and went in.

I came out in the evening and there was a ticket on the car. This went on for about three days – the RCMP tagged me every day.

GORDON CHURCHILL

One of the strange things about my appointment as minister of trade and commerce was that Mitchell Sharp phoned me and said that the department offices in the temporary buildings would not be available for ten days because they were redecorating. Actually, they were getting rid of the files. But that was all right. I sat up in the House of Commons. Then I moved down with a small staff of four or five to the coldest reception that I have ever received in my life. It affected the staff as well. C.D. Howe was gone and here was an unknown, insignificant person coming down to take his place. The Conservatives were in power and the department was completely upset.

Later on, when Sharp left in 1958 and I got John English appointed as deputy minister, he told me quite frankly, 'When you first came down here you were hated by everybody in the department, right down to the most junior office boy.' But John English fixed it up. He was a very diplomatic chap, and I liked him very much.

That was my introduction to trade and commerce. What an experience!

George Pearkes was named defence minister.

GEORGE PEARKES

I was going home. Quite a few of the officers had been in my division; others had been cadets at the Royal Military College when I was an instructor there; and I felt I was among friends. Charles Foulkes, who was then chief of staff, had been a brigade major at the beginning of the war and had been a brigadier in my division. I had known him for years and it was the same with many of the others. After I was sworn in at Government House, I phoned the deputy minister, [Air Marshall] Frank Miller at that time, and asked him to have lunch with me. We had lunch in the Château, and I went for a walk with Frank and we discussed things generally, and I said, 'I will be over tomorrow morning after the announcement has been made.' He then showed me where the office was and introduced the senior officers of the department, most of whom I knew.

When I was in the Defence Department in 1935, Ian Mackenzie became minister and he met the senior officers, much the same way I did, but he laid down the law. He said, 'I expect loyalty from you. Most of you have been appointed under the Conservative government, and things will be different now. I am minister and I expect you to be loyal to the Liberal party.' I didn't do anything like that. Why, I knew the officers of the permanent force and I knew that they would be loyal to any minister. That's traditional. They had no politics.

GEORGE HEES

None of us had experience in these portfolios and I particularly had no experience in transport. I had sitting opposite me in the House two former ministers, Mr [Lionel] Chevrier and Mr Marler. So they were stacked against me with a lot of knowledge that I didn't have. It was a rather terrifying experience.

The very first question that was asked of me was asked by Mr Chevrier, about a matter of which I knew nothing and really couldn't be expected to know. It had to do with a canal employee who had been removed from his job, as a result of a Conservative member, Mr [Arza Clair] Casselman, who had notified my department, and theoretically me, that this man had worked against him in the election. The way Ottawa works is this: if you are a member of the civil service, you cannot be removed because of political activity unless you are removed by the Civil Service Commission. It is a very lengthy trial period, and so on, and quite rightly so. But if you are a casual employee, and canal employees were classed then as casual employees, you came under a different ruling. If a casual employee had worked against a member of Parliament during the election, and that member wrote a letter to the minister, simply stating over his signature that this man or woman had done thus and so contrary to the practices of the civil service, and had worked against that member, and recommending somebody to take that person's place, automatically the change took place. There was no question about it. Theoretically it was done by the minister, but a minister of transport had so many things to look after that he had no time for those details.

It was a routine matter, and the letter didn't even come to my atention. It was automatically done and the man was replaced and that was that, but I didn't know anything about this. Mr Chevrier got up and made a terrific case about this, asked what I knew about this person being summarily dismissed, inferring, of course, that it was very unfairly done, that this was the action of a cruel and a new government.

Having never heard about this kind of thing before, it was rather shocking. I didn't know really what I had done, but I said I would take note and give an answer the next day. Fortunately, one of my top civil servants, the secretary of the department, said to me afterwards, 'I think I can dig out some things that can be useful to you, Mr Hees.' I said, 'I certainly hope you can because this looks as though I am in a rather tough spot. I have to answer to what sounds like a very heartless action by me personally against this poor man and I would like to know how I stand.'

The next day he dug out a letter from Mr C.D. Howe, written in the fall of 1935 just after he had taken over as minister of transport, in reply to a Prince Edward Island Liberal who stated in his letter that this man in Prince Edward Island, a casual civil servant, had worked against him. He wanted him dismissed and recommended Mr So-and-So to take his place. Mr Howe's letter said, 'I have got your letter. The man has been dismissed and we are appointing your nominee Mr So-and-So in his place.' Which was exactly what had been done in the case that I was involved in, and it happened to be the same department.

Then he dug out a speech that Mr Jimmy Gardiner, who was still in the House at that time as former minister of agriculture, had made in the House in early 1936, when he was accused of doing terrible things to all of the casual civil servants who were members of the PFRA [Prairie Farm Rehabilitation Administration], the farm inspectors who were casual employees. When Jimmy Gardiner got in as minister of agriculture in '35 he fired every Tory appointment over the past five years and replaced them all with Grits. He was greatly criticized in the House for this. He got up in the House and made this great speech saying that he had researched the whole thing back to Sir John Macdonald's time and found out that this is the way that these cases had always been handled. People who were casual employees had been let out and others put in who suited the government. That was the way it was, and this was 100 per cent okay.

There was also a speech by Mr Coldwell who criticized the Liberals in 1935 and '36 for this kind of treatment and said it was a dreadful thing and railed on that this was heart-rending and unfair and cruel and dastardly, and this should never be, and so on – a very definite speech by Mr Coldwell.

I had this information that was very useful to me, but I wanted to make sure that I knew how to use it well. So I went to see Mr Diefenbaker, and I said, 'John, here is the information that I have got in answer to that question Chev asked me yesterday. How do you think I ought to use it?' Here is the advice he gave me and it was just great: 'Now you have really got him. This is the information you need to just fix him for good. Here is the way to play it. Get up in the House on a question of privilege and say: "Mr Speaker, I was asked yesterday about this case." Then act rather awkward and a little stupid and bumble a little and act as though you didn't know much about it and you are kind of sorry it happened – as if you didn't know much. Look stupid and look awkward. Then sit down and look very embarrassed. Then Chev will jump and he will roar into the attack and he will tear you limb from limb and he will really lay you all over the place. Then when he is through get up and say, 'Mr Speaker, in view of what the honourable gentleman said, here are some facts that I think might be interesting to the House.' Then read these letters and speeches and so on and outline what they were. You will murder Chev. It will be great!

I said fine, and I did exactly as he said. He knew what would happen, being an old campaigner and old criminal lawyer; he knew how to draw in the opposition. Chev leaped up and he castigated me and the Tory government for being cruel and thoughtless. Here I was laying off this man who had five children and a wife and here I was laying off these people who were obviously starving. I had no thought and no mind and no kindness in me and so on. It was a great, great speech and he was raging and he was tearing his hair. The Liberals were all pounding their desks and they thought they were just going to murder this new Tory government right off the bat and show that we never should have been allowed in. We had no hearts, we were cruel, we were to be despised. So he roared and thundered for about ten minutes.

Then, Coldwell got up and said, 'Mr Speaker, I have never heard of anything like this before in my whole experience here in Parliament. I have been here for many years and I have never heard of anything like this before, in this House or outside of it.' He gave about a ten minute diatribe and what a dastardly, terrible thing this was, and how rotten I was, and the Tories even more so, and this is what you expect if you elected Conservatives.

He sat down, and I got up and said, 'Mr Speaker, I just happen to have a few things that might be of interest to the House.' I read C.D. Howe's letter that showed that he as a Liberal minister did exactly what I did. I read Jimmy Gardiner's speech. He was sitting right in front of me and of course he was a good enough sport to nearly die laughing, because he recognized the old speech of twenty-two years ago. There were the words he had said, justifying what I had done, 100 per cent.

Then, of course, the killer was M.J. Coldwell, the holy man from the West, who had said he had never heard of anything like this before, and here were his words of twenty-two years ago, describing exactly what I had done in the same terms that he had that day, describing what Jimmy Gardiner had done in even more vociferous terms.

It was a great day, and it was the kind of thing that a new minister needed very much indeed. It set me up and got me going. It meant a great deal to my political life because I was on the offensive from then on and I had confidence instead of being put in the gutter, as I might have been if I had been wrong and didn't have this information.

The last half of 1957 was a testing time for the Progressive Conservatives and their new leader. They had to show the country that they could govern, even though they had no experience. Most, but not all, Tories agreed with Donald Fleming that John Diefenbaker came through brilliantly in his new role of prime minister.

R.A. BELL

I believe that the government between June of 1957 and the election in 1958 was one of the best governments this country has ever had. As a minority government, it went immediately at a number of things and tidied them up.

PIERRE SÉVIGNY

More was done in a few months by the Diefenbaker team of 1957 than had been done, possibly in ten years, by the St Laurent team. Then this [Duplessis] image of Diefenbaker as a combination of God, Moses, de Gaulle, Churchill, Napoleon, and a few others, really bore fruit. The people were surprised by the extraordinary results. Diefenbaker in no time flat had become a changed man, and this is one of the phenomena of that particular year of phenomena.

All of a sudden he tasted power. The first time was when he went to the Commonwealth Conference, which was held soon after his election in 1957. Then he changed. He became much more the leader. He gained a certain assurance. He spoke with strength. He could feel from the press and what was said about him that he had the wind in his sails. He demanded that even his closest friends stop calling him John and call him Mr Prime Minister. I remember one day I dared to tell him that he needed a good tailor, and he called me up, much to my surprise, and said, 'Take me to a good one.' And I took him to a man who made him many suits. From a shabby dresser, Diefenbaker became a tailor's dummy straight from Savile Row, and the image of the man changed completely for the better.

I must say that he showed the spirit of decision in these first few months after June 1957, which he unfortunately did not maintain during subsequent years. He settled the question of old age pensions. The social security program was vastly improved. He poured money into the construction industry. He opened up new markets. He settled questions which demanded to be settled in double quick time. And he promptly gave a new image to a nation, which had been run more or less as a corporation before. That, of course, galvanized the people and made them ready for the stunning victory that resulted from the March 31, 1958 vote.

GRATTAN O'LEARY
Quite frankly, as I remember it now, it was not a good government. It was not what you would call a strong government. Diefenbaker dominated the whole thing. Now, you take his western people. I doubt if many of them could have gotten into a Laurier cabinet or a Borden cabinet.

ALVIN HAMILTON
I think, objectively, if you put a measuring scale of brand-new legislation brought in and took all the governments of Canada since 1867, there is only one period that would challenge the 1957 government and that would be the period from 1932 to 1935 under Bennett. There was a tremendous rush of brand-new legislation then.

DONALD FLEMING
I would begin by saying that there was a new spirit in Parliament. After all, those who had fought for the supremacy of Parliament had won. I think we can look back on that as a major contribution. There were individual measures also that won us support and approval on the part of the Canadian people. Many of these were fiscal, tax reductions. Some of them were related to pensions: we increased the old age pension, we increased the provision for veterans. Some were legislative measures related to agriculture because these had played a large part in our appeal to the public for its support. The question of cash advances on farm-stored grain became something of a

clarion call. The Liberal government said that this couldn't be done. We did it, and I can remember Mr Diefenbaker using this as an example time and again in speeches both in Parliament and elsewhere. He would ring the changes on that theme, 'They said it couldn't be done; we did it.'

ANGUS MACLEAN

The Atlantic Provinces Grants, which were made without any strings attached, had a tremendously potent effect. For the first time in many years, it was felt that there was a government in Ottawa that appreciated and understood the problems of the Maritimes and was prepared to try to do something about them. We believed all Canadians should be entitled to a basic level of public services, and the fact that some areas were so economically depressed that they couldn't provide this shouldn't continue – the federal government should make a contribution to improve the situation. And that was what was done. It had a tremendous effect in the Maritime provinces.

Prior to that, when the St Laurent government was still in power, the government of New Brunswick was building the Beechwood Power Development on the Saint John River in an attempt to provide cheaper electric power which was one of the keys to economic progress and industrial development, and they had requested the federal government to guarantee their bonds. If this were done, they would have been able to borrow money at 1 per cent or 2 per cent less and, of course, the cost of money was a very big factor in this project. They were turned down flatly by the federal government. Yet, at the same time, the federal government was building a dam in Pakistan, a power development there, for free. There was a growing feeling in the Maritimes, in those days, that if we were some underdeveloped country somewhere else, they would have greater concern for us than they did because we were part of the country.

GORDON CHURCHILL

Everything in that 1957 session pointed to an advancement of Canada, and the public responded.

5

The Liberals commit suicide

The Diefenbaker era began with a flourish of trumpets and the splendour and pageantry of a royal visit. On 14 October 1957, Queen Elizabeth II opened Parliament. Her Majesty rode past cheering crowds to Parliament Hill in an open landau, accompanied by the Royal Canadian Mounted Police, with the guidons of their lances flashing in the sunlight. It was the first time since her coronation that she had visited Canada, and the royal presence seemed such an appropriate tribute to the resurgence of the Conservatives that it was assumed to be the work of John Diefenbaker. The visit had, however, been arranged by Louis St Laurent before the election. Even before Parliament met, St Laurent had told his confidantes that he wanted to resign as leader of the Liberal party. In the late summer of 1957, L.B. 'Mike' Pearson, who was already regarded as the heir apparent, received a telephone call asking him to see the former prime minister at the family summer home in St Patrick, Quebec. He knew this meant that Mr St Laurent wanted to retire but he did not want to be the only former minister to advise him on this matter. So he asked Lionel Chevrier as the senior French-speaking privy councillor to accompany him. Chevrier recalled the weekend visit.

LIONEL CHEVRIER

It was rather pitiful, in more ways than one. We were asked to go by his son-in-law, Dr [Mathieu] Samson and by his son, Reynaud. He [Mr St Laurent] told us that he felt he should resign because he didn't think that he was equal to the task physically. The doctor confirmed that. Mike was very worried about this because he didn't want to leave the impression or create the impression that he was seeking the leadership. But he was prepared, I'm sure, to take it on if it was offered to him.

Ellen Fairclough and Donald Fleming after being sworn in as ministers

We met the whole family at dinner, but we didn't discuss these matters with them. We discussed them exclusively with Mr St Laurent, the son-in-law, and Reynaud. It was finally decided that he should resign – I shouldn't say that, he decided that he should resign. He was fearful that it might create some difficulties for the party.

We withdrew and went to the boarding house where we were staying and Mike proceeded to draft his [St Laurent's] letter of resignation. Mike's hand at drafting these things is far superior to mine. I only had a few comments to make. It was signed by him the next day. He felt that this is what he should do. He felt that he had let the party down, which was certainly not the case. He was so sure that he would win the '57 election as he had won the others that, I think, it took a great deal out of him.

PAUL MARTIN

I remember being at a weekend place with Pearson in September when we talked about the leadership. Walter Harris was there and a few other people. I remember Mike and I having lunch together somewhere near the Bay of Quinte, and he told me then that he was going to go after the leadership of the Liberal party. It was a foregone conclusion that he would, just as it was a foregone conclusion that he would succeed. I myself had no intentions of running at that time.

J.W. PICKERSGILL

As everybody knows, Walter Harris considered very seriously being a candidate. At that time, Walter was one of my closest friends. Stuart Garson and I realized what a tremendous service he had done for the government and the party. I thought he would have been a very good prime minister; however, I didn't think that he could ever get the leadership if Mr Pearson was a candidate, and I didn't think he would have anything like the appeal to the public that Mr Pearson would have. I have no apologies for that judgment. It is still my judgment. I remember the day I gritted my teeth and went to Walter and said, 'I want to tell you that I do not think you should be a candidate because you are not going to get the leadership. In any event, I have got to tell you that I think it's our duty to try to salvage the party and try to get the maximum unity and the best possible candidate who is most likely to have the maximum appeal. I think that's Mr Pearson, and I propose to tell him that I will give him whatever support I can.'

I went to see Pearson the next day, and I told him that I had come to offer my support. He said, 'I am very surprised, I thought you would be supporting Walter Harris.' If he hadn't said that I wouldn't have said anything, but then I told him. I said, 'Walter is a much better friend of mine than you are, but I think that you have a much better prospect of salvaging the Liberal party and I certainly think you would be a competent leader.' I didn't really, honestly, think at that time he would be as good as he turned out to be. I thought he was far and away the best bet we had and I supported him loyally throughout.

I don't say that my attitude was decisive as far as Walter Harris was concerned, but I think it was pretty compelling. The one thing that has always pleased me very much about this is that it never made any difference to our relationship.

LIONEL CHEVRIER

I made sure that the delegates from the province of Quebec would support Mike [at the leadership convention]. Unfortunately, this meant that I ran counter to the wishes of Paul Martin – he had expected, perhaps, that I, being of French Canadian extraction, would support him. But my view all along was that it was the turn of an Anglo-Saxon as had been the tradition of the Liberal party over the years. I supported Mike and I am sure that the vast majority if not all of the delegates from Quebec supported him.

> Paul Martin was born in Ottawa on 23 June 1903. He studied at the University of Toronto, Osgoode Hall, Harvard Law School, and later at Cambridge University and the Geneva School of International Studies. But politics had a much greater attraction for him than law, and in 1928 he ran unsuccessfully for the Ontario legislature. In 1935, he was elected to the House of Commons as the member for Essex East (Windsor), and was never defeated again.
>
> Martin had unusual experience in foreign affairs. As an alumnus of the Geneva school, he was the only academically trained diplomat Canada had before the Second World War. Later, when he led the Canadian delegation to the United Nations, he was one of the very few delegates who had also been a delegate to the League of Nations. But he was not by any means Canada's best-known diplomat. He always seemed to be walking in Lester Pearson's shadow.
>
> At the 1948 convention which had picked Louis St Laurent as leader, Martin had been nominated. He himself said he had no intention of running then, but some of the young Liberals put on a campaign for him which annoyed the Liberal establishment before his name was finally withdrawn. For the 1958 convention, Martin received encouragement from a strange quarter.

PAUL MARTIN

I don't know whether Diefenbaker came to me or called me, but we met and he said, 'Now, it's none of my business what you do, but you've been in Parliament a long time now, and you must have political ambitions. It's a worthy thing to want to be leader of your party. Why don't you go after this?' I was rather amused by his interest in me and in the leadership of the party. I never knew whether he thought this was a way of perpetuating his own political tenure or whether he was genuinely interested. I suppose he really was generally interested as a friend.

Towards Christmas time, I began to get pressure from people in my own section of the province particularly and, very reluctantly, I did become a candidate for the leadership at that time. I didn't think I'd have a chance, the principle of alternating [francophone and anglophone leaders] was so strong and so widely accepted. Then, Pearson had increased his stature by winning the Nobel Peace Prize. However, Mike and I had a talk, and he said, 'Whatever you do is your own business. We're friends.' I had known him longer than anyone else in Ottawa. My first visit to the Parliament buildings was with him in 1925. 'Well,' I said, 'I'll have to think this over.'

When I did make my decision, I made it at a meeting in Windsor. I returned to Ottawa not very happy with myself. Not that I didn't think I had the right, not that I didn't think I could do the job, but I just felt that I couldn't win, and if I did win, would I not be faced with a very difficult political situation?

What would that situation be? It would be this: here was a man, a French Canadian himself – because after all, I am three-quarters French – succeeding a French Canadian from Quebec, having stood in the way of an English-speaking Canadian, an eminent Canadian. If I'd lost the election, as I likely would have, just as Pearson did, it would be said that the reason we lost the election was primarily because I became the beneficiary of a change in the system of alternating. I felt that very keenly. I'm sure people would have said, 'Here's a second French Catholic now leader of the Liberal party. The principle of having a French Canadian now and then is all right, but to have two succeeding one another is too much for non-Quebec Canada.' My instincts, my judgment, suggested to me that that would be the judgment, and it was for that reason I did not want, really, to run. But I had been in politics; I had a lot of friends; I had people who believed in me; and those who haven't been in situations like this will find it difficult to understand how you can be forced into a situation like that against your will. But that is what happened in my case. I'm sure it was the kind of situation that faced Adlai Stevenson, for instance, in the second nomination that confronted him as a candidate for the presidency. In any event, Mr Pearson won, as I knew he would.

I really was very relieved, because I knew that I couldn't possibly win the next election against John Diefenbaker, just as I was certain Mike Pearson couldn't. Diefenbaker had just been elected a short time before, and people were going to give him a chance. We, the Liberals, hadn't justified ourselves yet in the public mind.

Our convention of 1958 helped. I think it was a good convention, a surprisingly good convention. It created a lot of enthusiasm. If I hadn't run, Pearson would have got it by acclamation. That would have made the whole affair a pretty dull one.

Four days after he was elected leader of the Liberal party, Pearson introduced an ingenious non-confidence motion which, in effect, asked the Conservatives to turn the government over to the Liberals without an election. The man popularly regarded as the father of the motion was Jack Pickersgill.

John Whitney Pickersgill was born in Wyecombe, Ontario, in 1905 and grew up in rural Manitoba. He studied at the University of Manitoba and Oxford and like another civil servant who became a politician, Lester Pearson, he lectured in history before joining the Department of External Affairs. He was teaching at Wesley College, later to become the University of Winnipeg, when he took the civil service examination. He came first and a year later, in October 1937, started work as a third secretary probationer.

After a couple of months in the attic of the East Block, Pickersgill was seconded to the prime minister's office. Eleven years later, when Mackenzie King retired, Pickersgill stayed on to serve under St Laurent, whom he grew to 'almost worship.' In 1952, he became secretary to the cabinet and clerk of the Privy Council. A year later he resigned from the civil service and was appointed to the cabinet. In the 1953 general election he won the seat of Bonavista-Twillingate.

As for the extraordinary amendment of 1958, Pickersgill described the events that led to its conception.

J . W . PICKERSGILL
My view, which was expressed at length in Mr St Laurent's speech as leader of the opposition in October when Parliament met, was that the Liberals should not move an amendment to the address in reply, and they didn't. They should say that the Conservatives had a program, the program they put before the electorate, and should be allowed to carry it out, and should be allowed to do any other thing that the Liberals didn't feel was really contrary to the public interest, even though it hadn't been on their program. I think that policy should have been followed.

But I was not consulted about the speeches Mr Pearson made at the convention, especially his acceptance speech where he breathed fire and slaughter and was going to move a motion which, if it had been carried, would have forced an election. He committed himself to such a motion. I thought the last thing we wanted was an election, and I was naive in one respect.

Perhaps, in retrospect, I see things that I couldn't have seen then, but I thought if we moved a straight vote of want of confidence in the government that the CCF and the Social Credit people would have to support it. That would defeat Diefenbaker and give him the election he wanted. Therefore, I said, having got ourselves into this mess by breathing fire and slaughter and saying we were going to try to bring the government down, we had to find some weaseling motion that we would be sure the small parties would not vote for so that Diefenbaker would not be defeated. He would get what he would claim was a vote of confidence and would have no excuse to precipitate an election. Now, that is the real reasoning behind it, and I have never said it publicly before.

Perhaps in my whole career my most serious weakness as a politician – no doubt I have lots that nobody has told me about or I don't agree with, but I agree with this one – is that I tend, unless I am very careful, to say that people can generally understand very complicated things if they are explained carefully. I tend also to think that when I see something clearly it's because it is clear and other people will see it too. I learned slowly and painfully as a politician, and I have never learned completely, that you should always try things out, if you can possibly do it, before you try them out on the public to see what the effect is, but that was impossible in this particular case.

I also made another mistake that I regret. Maybe that motion was worse than some alternative course would have been. Maybe the best thing for Pearson to have done would have been to move a straight vote of want of confidence. Probably there would have been enough absentees from the two small parties, and even perhaps a few from ours, to make sure it wasn't carried. But it was a terrible dilemma. We should never have got into it, and I had nothing to do with getting into it. I told him I would support him but I had never been one of his advisers. I was concerned at the convention with making sure that Mr St Laurent was looked after properly. I helped him write his speech, and I had a great deal to do with the general organization of the convention because it was Mr St Laurent's ultimate responsibility and he relied on me. After we were defeated, I lapsed into the old position of being the person he leaned on – I had a room right next to his office as leader of the opposition.

I wasn't the least bit concerned with how Pearson ran his campaign, and I don't know who was responsible. All I know is that I was shocked by it. I thought it was imprudent and unwise. I thought the line that we had laid down in our caucus was the right one: that we should let the people challenge them for not doing the things that they said they would do and keep them in office long enough that the public would see what they were really like. I had a very strong feeling that if we could just keep the Diefenbaker government in office for two or three years, in this precarious position, we could defeat them. I still think probaby that judgment was right.

I realized after the convention, and this was where I made another mistake – what my motives were God alone knows, but I had been so used, from 1939 until Mr St Laurent ceased to be the leader, to dealing with the prime minister as the leader of the party, making sure that something was ready, that there wasn't a vacuum – at any rate, after the convention I realized that nobody, Mr Pearson and nobody, nobody was prepared. Nobody seemed to know that there was going to be a supply motion to which we had to make some kind of response except me. I went to Mr Pearson and I talked to him about it. I said, 'You are going to be faced with this very great problem. How are you going to deal with it?' That's how I sucked myself into doing it. It wasn't that I regarded it as a very pleasant task, but it just came to me that here was something nobody else was doing anything about. It was perhaps a silly kind of boy scoutism, but it certainly wasn't wise.

The purpose of the motion, although it was a non-confidence motion, was to make sure the CCF and Social Credit wouldn't vote for it, and thus keep the Diefenbaker government in office. I don't know how clearly Mr Pearson appreciated that. I think he did, but I know that was my motive because I was sure that if we had defeated the government we would have been slaughtered in an election.

I wasn't totally the author of the motion. It was checked with several people and it was changed a bit. But I suppose substantially I was. I think I would call it a Simple Simon motion rather than a Machiavellian motion. It was incredibly naïve.

I gave Mr Pearson tremendous marks for never blaming people and for no recriminations. Mind you, he was a little chary of my advice for the next six months or so, and I wasn't anxious to give it either.

LIONEL CHEVRIER
There was nothing the matter with the decision [to move an amendment to the Speech from the Throne]. It's a normal thing to do – criticize, castigate,

raise the roof with the government – but to have worded it in the way in which it was immediately after the election, asking them to resign and we take over, that was, I think, going a bit far.

Whose responsibility it was, I don't know. Let it not be forgotten that it was discussed with the so-called shadow cabinet before it was submitted to the House. We all knew that it was coming. We all had an opportunity to say, no, there is no sense to this, or all right, let it go; and we did express our opinions. But it was quite clear that we were going ahead with it.

I wouldn't say that I opposed it. I think I would have to say in all fairness that I went along with those who felt that this should be done. Again, I repeat, not as an excuse or a defence of myself, I had been away from politics for three years, so I didn't pay the attention that I should have, otherwise I would have opposed it and objected to it in stronger terms. At any rate, a decision was taken and it was a wrong decision.

Prime Minister Diefenbaker seized on this non-confidence motion and delivered a slashing attack on the new leader of the opposition. At the same time, he produced a confidential report, prepared by civil servants, which had warned the previous government of an imminent economic downturn accompanied by rising unemployment. He said the Liberals, on leaving office, had hidden that report. It was a devastating performance.

PAUL MARTIN

This was Diefenbaker's great hour. I remember that speech. It was one of his best speeches, and he just tore us to pieces. Now, the use of that report cannot be justified. I've talked to him about this. He knew that that was a secret report. Someone, with or without his knowledge, had taken off the word 'restricted' or 'confidential' – in any event, he knew it was a confidential report. I always felt that a man who was prime minister should have known that there could be no justification for the use of such a report. He could have achieved the same result by using some other reports that were not confidential. This was a report prepared by officials for the use of the minister of trade and commerce. There could be no justification for anyone in government using it publicly. But there's no doubt that using it, together with our *gaucherie* in the amendment that we put forward, gave him an opportunity of making one of the greatest devastating speeches, certainly within my memory.

The non-confidence motion had the desired effect, as Pickersgill had planned, of allying the CCF and Social Credit members with government. It was easily voted down. However, this did not prevent the election that the Liberals so

much feared. The following week, Prime Minister Diefenbaker flew to Que-
bec city and called on the governor general. He returned to Ottawa to tell
the House of Commons that although St Laurent had promised cooperation
the new Liberal leader had made it clear that this would not be the case. So,
Diefenbaker said, there was no course left but dissolution and an election.

J.W. PICKERSGILL

There is another thing that nobody has paid much attention to: Mr Diefenbaker had no right whatever to a dissolution of that Parliament. If the constitutional precedents which Davie Fulton, when he was in opposition, had written about had been followed, the governor general would have said: 'I see no excuse whatsoever for an election. You got everything through you have asked for. You haven't suffered a single defeat in Parliament. We had an election last June. There is no reason on earth why you should ask for an election.' Diefenbaker himself was a little hard put to think up any excuse for it. In fact, what he did was to say that the situation was so unstable and so on. It wasn't anything like as unstable as he was claiming.

I think he based his position on the 1926 precedent, which was not really applicable He thought he would get away with it and, of course, he did. The governor general was right to give it to him because if he hadn't that would have given him another issue which might have been even better. But it was a shocking abuse of office, in my view, and I think that it brought its own retribution. He would have been far better never to have had 208 members. If he had gone along and got himself defeated after about a year and put on a good record, he would have got a decent majority and he might have been prime minister a lot longer.

6
Too great a triumph

Timing is crucial in politics, especially in that climactic act of the British parliamentary system, the calling of an election. Allister Grosart was keenly aware of this. As the country entered the winter of 1957–8, unemployment was over 6 per cent and was increasing. What effect would this slowdown have on the vote? Grosart thought that the Conservatives would not be blamed for the recession until they had been in office for a year: there was something magical and terminal about a year. And Grosart, as national director of the Progressive Conservative party, was at the controls of the federal machine, such as it was. More important, he felt he had the confidence of the prime minister.

ALLISTER GROSART

There were those also in a position to advise the prime minister who were saying, 'Oh no, we mustn't go while there's this high unemployment.' Now this became the point of decision. I can't say what was in the prime minister's mind, but I know what I wanted. I wanted an election before June of the next year, before we had been in power for a year. I think the majority in the cabinet took the other view, understandably. I remember saying, 'Well, I simply have to get the prime minister's ear.'

It is never easy: there are all sorts of people advising the prime minister, and he has to look around and get the views of many people and put them together and arrive at his own decisions. I didn't feel I was having very much luck, because of course he was meeting cabinet every day, and I never sat in the cabinet. I thought that if I could get him away from this atmosphere, I might be able to convince him of my viewpoint. So I suggested to him that he

Grosart confers with Diefenbaker at a Government House garden party needed a holiday away, since he had been under tremendous strain. 'Why don't I arrange for you to go down to Nassau, to the Bahamas, and take a rest?' He agreed to that at New Year's, and we set it up.

I had a Department of Transport plane, and I had to make it very clear to him that this would not be paid for out of public funds, because he was very strict about those things. As a matter of fact, the Conservative party paid the $6000 for the plane as it eventually turned out. I took my family, my wife and my two daughters, and I went down. He was to go to Prince Albert at Christmas time and then the plane was to go out and pick him up and he would come down to Nassau. When we were down there, I put my views before the prime minister – why I thought we should have an election. I think it is fair to say that the prime minister then decided that we were going in March. This was not an easy decision because in Canada we had normally not had March elections. Finally, when the prime minister suggested to the cabinet that this was the date, March 18, then, of course, we had all the arguments against it. 'What is going to be the turn-out?' Because obviously the prime minister's forte was his ability to draw crowds. They said, 'Oh no, people won't come out in March. You know, the cold weather and so on.'

Anyway that was the decision. There was not very much in the way of strategy because we had been in office and the government had introduced quite a number of measures. There was a good deal of legislation on the books, on its way through, or in some cases through Parliament. So there was a record to go on. I remember saying, 'We want to carry on. We can implement our election promises. We need a majority to do it.'

Despite Grosart's pursuit of an early election, he suffered from some uncertainty at its outset. He was worried that Pearson's 'dreadful performance' in Parliament might get a sympathetic reaction. After all, Pearson was a Nobel Peace Prize winner. Grosart pleaded with Diefenbaker to treat Pearson gently. As an experienced campaigner, he was afraid of a sudden sympathetic swing in the votes. This was before the 1958 campaign had really begun.

Allister Grosart, whom Diefenbaker had named the 'architect' of the 1957 upset, was born in Ireland but grew up in China, where his mother was a medical missionary, and had studied at the China Inland Mission school in Chefoo before attending the University of Toronto. Subsequently he joined the Toronto Star, *and then entered the new profession of public relations. He worked for McKim Advertising Agency and later became its vice president.*

As a public relations man, Grosart became involved in Conservative politics. He started an information radio program for George Drew, then premier of Ontario, and organized the publicity for Drew's successful campaign for the federal leadership. He was an admitted image-builder and one of the first Canadians to adapt motivation studies to influence thinking and action. He went on to serve Premier Leslie Frost, and is credited with dubbing him Old Man Ontario. As a political organizer he came to be regarded as a miracle man associated with repeated Tory victories. One reason for his success was the thoroughness with which he tackled a job. He approached political problems in a deliberate, scientific manner, setting down pros and cons, and always weighing the cons. The balance he struck through this process in March 1958 made him apprehensive at the outset, but his worries were dispelled by the opening campaign meeting.

ALLISTER GROSART

I didn't usually go out in the field during an election campaign because I was supposed to be at headquarters, running the show from that end, mostly by long distance telephone calls. But this time I did go to the opening in Winnipeg. We paid a lot of attention to the opening of a campaign because if you get off to a flying start the momentum stays with you.

I was inside the Auditorium there an hour or so before the meeting was to begin and I well remember the manager coming up to me and saying, 'We've got a problem. They're forcing the doors open.' We went to take a look at the doors, and you could see the pressure on them from the crowd outside. They had been closed because the place was full – jampacked. They had big three-by-six boards that they could put across the doors. The manager said, 'We'd better barricade the doors or this crowd is going to break in.' I was going to say, 'Yes, do,' and then I thought to myself, 'Can it be all that bad if they break down the doors?' Just then, they did break down the doors, and I said, 'Well, that's the election campaign – don't worry.'

That was the story that went right across the country: 'They're breaking down the doors to hear Mr Diefenbaker.'

GORDON CHURCHILL

We had the opening meeting in Winnipeg, in the Auditorium, and the people came in and filled the place, and hundreds upon hundreds were outside milling around hoping to get in. They wrenched the doors loose from the auditorium, great big heavy doors, in an attempt to force their way in. It was a tremendous outburst of enthusiasm and that carried on throughout the campaign wherever Mr Diefenbaker went.

There was no diminution at all. It just kept building up, building up, building up. It wasn't really a contest. It was a walkover, the 1958 campaign. Two weeks after it started, in my own constituency, in Winnipeg South Centre, my people were forecasting a sweep, and I forecast it myself.

WILLIAM HAMILTON
There is no doubt that the rally in the huge Craig Street armoury in Montreal was one of the great political meetings. I remember Pierre Sévigny, who introduced Diefenbaker, just churning that crowd over and finally challenging them: 'Levez-vous, levez-vous, saluez votre chef! Rise, rise, salute your chief!' And that whole place, thousands upon thousands of people, jammed into that auditorium, just tore the roof off in a frenzy. I think it was probably one of the few times when Diefenbaker's quality of oratory met a real challenge.

> It was a joyous, triumphant campaign for the Conservatives. Allister Grosart had two-and-a-half times as much to spend, $2,500,000, as he had had in the previous campaign, and he was able to double the allotment to each constituency to $6000.
>
> One of Grosart's most important responsibilities in the campaign was scheduling the leader's tour of the country.

ALLISTER GROSART
You go twice over each area, not necessarily each particular city. In a national campaign in Canada the geography lends itself beautifully because if you are going west you can go out by the north route and come back by the south. Everywhere you have got a north town and a south town, a major centre north and south. In Ontario of course you can do the same thing, and in Quebec you can take the north and then the south.

I'm talking about the train which Mr Diefenbaker used almost exclusively in 1958. There is something about a train pulling in which isn't the same as an airplane dropping into an airport. Of course, the train stops at a lot more places than the airplane. The whistle-stop type of campaign was particularly suited, I think, to Mr Diefenbaker because he loved people. He loved the intimacy of people. Not every political leader does. But Mr Diefenbaker was one who simply loved main-streeting, as we used to say. He was never happier than when he was walking down Main Street in Prince Albert or Woodstock.

It was in Quebec city, driving down there in a slow cavalcade just after five o'clock, that I knew we had a sensational one in '58. People were coming out of offices. They weren't cheering but they were putting their hands up, almost with clenched fists. It looked as if they were saying, 'All right, you aren't going to win alone. We are going to be with you.'

MICHAEL STARR

That was the most fantastic election. We ministers were crossing paths back and forth like it was never done before. I spoke at five meetings in Saskatchewan, starting at ten o'clock at Cutworth. I said, 'Who in the world is going to be there at ten o'clock?' The place was jammed, 550 people. It was fantastic.

I went into little places. Smoky Lake, Alberta, where nobody ever saw a minister. Canora, Saskatchewan. Every meeting was jammed; outside there were speakers for those who couldn't get in. It was just fantastic, the most extraordinary experience that I have ever had.

I would go into a place like Smoky Lake, and they would have the mayor standing outside the town to welcome me and the women had been cooking all morning to feed me a big luncheon.

I got the biggest thrill in some of these small places out west. The halls would be filled with people, and sitting there in the front would be the first Ukrainian immigrants with shawls and hands gnarled from work. I would speak for about twenty minutes in English and then I would switch to Ukrainian and the tears would run down their faces. A man came to me one day and he said, 'Now I can die, I have met a minister of Ukrainian extraction.'

This really swept the West. I don't care who says what won the election: it was the emotional aspect that caught on. Diefenbaker used to come to meetings in that election and the people would mob him, virually mob him, and he would have to back up. They would be swarming at him just to touch his hand. You never saw anything like it.

T.C. DOUGLAS

There were large audiences, enthusiastic. They came up to me in droves after the meeting to say, 'Tommy, you know we have always voted for you provincially, and we will vote for you again.' The best proof of that is that two years later in the provincial election in Saskatchewan we cleaned the boards, and not one Conservative, for instance, was elected, and we put the Liberals away down. But in 1958 they said to me, 'We will vote for you provincially, but, you know, you will have to understand we are not going to vote for you federally. We are not going to take any chance on Jimmy Gardiner and C.D. Howe coming back.'

They had nothing against Mr St Laurent, but C.D. Howe and Gardiner, they were going to have no part of. They cleaned us out, defeated Coldwell, you know, who held the Rosetown-Biggar seat for twenty-three years, took out everyone of our members on the prairies except Argue and later took him out when he became a Liberal.

GEORGE HEES

Everybody realized that this next election was called at the time of our choosing and we were going to be a government with a big majority. So everybody climbed aboard. Everyone was our friend. Meetings were tremendous. I did a great deal of campaigning in Quebec. Meetings of 1000, 1500 people; you couldn't get the people in the halls. They stood, they didn't even sit; they were packed shoulder to shoulder. If you even coughed they cheered; no matter what happened they just wanted to be known as being for you because they wanted to be on the right side.

Everywhere you went in Canada, the meetings were very large, very enthusiastic. It couldn't have been more fun. Nothing is more fun than winning, and we were certainly winning in a big way. It was a lead-pipe cinch. There was nothing against us. We had gotten in, we had done all the good things, we hadn't tackled any of the tough ones. 'Now,' Mr Diefenbaker said, 'give us a majority and we'll handle all these other things as we go on.' The people said, 'That's what we would like to see you do.'

J.W. PICKERSGILL

I realized very early in the 1958 campaign that, for the first and only time when I was a politician, I had a contest in my own constituency. The Tories nominated a man, Jed Winter, a very respectable businessman in St John's with a good family background and a good name, who expected to be elected and had been promised a portfolio. People told me that they had some concern about this. I thought, 'Well, you know, I'm not going to have much influence on anybody if I don't keep my seat.' So I spent a good part of the '58 campaign in my constituency and I put on a real campaign. I astonished myself.

I remember one day, we hired a boat in Louisport and went around Westernhead on our way to Twillingate. It was a terrible day, and we were hurled out of our bunks, and the Newfoundland attorney general gathered himself up on the floor, looked at me, and said, 'What am I doing here when I could be sitting in my comfortable office in St John's?' I never forgot that. I have always been grateful to him.

Even a party that is riding to victory on emotion requires an election platform and a campaign strategy.

ALLISTER GROSART

You have to look at the position of the campaign manager this way: the

campaign manager doesn't make policy. Certain policies are decided in cabinet. The campaign manager's job is to take that package, if you like, and
sell it, to put it in its crudest terms. This is it, the government is going to
the public on this platform.

Once again, I concentrated on the leader. Here was Mr Dienfenbaker
who had won an election for the Conservatives for the first time in twenty-
two years, in amazing circumstances, having been elected leader on December the 14th and in June he was prime minister. Obviously the public believed
in Mr Dienfenbaker. People believed in what he stood for: his concept of the
supremacy of Parliament, a vision of Canada, something that almost inevi-
tably dies when a government is in power for a long time. The government
gets entangled in the nitty-gritty of everyday responses to day-to-day problems, and it is almost inevitable that it will cease to look at the on-going
policies that are necessary for the future of the country in creative and
imaginative terms.

I think that everybody would agree that at this time Mr Diefenbaker had
raised the level of policy-making, policy-thinking, policy decision-making to
a highly creative and imaginative level that caught the imagination of the
public.

PIERRE SÉVIGNY
Diefenbaker was anxious to find something on which he could tie his political destiny. He was asking everybody to give him ideas. Some of the ideas
made sense and some didn't; some were just plain foolishness. But Diefenbaker, being Diefenbaker, was asking everybody's opinion.

One day we had a big meeting on this matter and were sitting around
discussing what the slogan should be – some of us felt that this was rather
futile and could not be decided at a big meeting. Anyway, at one point,
Diefenbaker was talking in his inimitable way about Canada, the dream of
a greater and better and bigger Canada. I told him: 'Well let's leave it as
this. One Canada where everybody will live together in harmony.' I remember the word 'harmony.' My God, it was as if I had put a bomb under his
seat. He got up and said, 'That's it! Yes. One Canada.' Then, he started
right there in front of us all and he said, 'One Canada! What we can build
around that slogan!'

To launch the One Canada slogan, he chose the opening meeting in
Winnipeg. I will never forget that meeting. It was one of the most incredible
meetings I ever saw. He got there and the arena where the meeting was held
was packed to the roof. I mean there were kids sitting on the rafters. Dienfenbaker was in his finest form and let go with a speech where he saw that big-

ger, that greater Canada, where he saw high-rise buildings in the north, and all kinds of incredible things all over the place. Then, he started with this One Canada which he repeated – One Canada where people will live in harmony, One Canada where everything will be great.

The people were stirred up by this magnificent flurry of eloquence of his. When the meeting ended, the standing ovation that he got must have been music to his ears. It was certainly music to all the Tories because we could see that this was grasping the people. When he had finished that speech, as he was walking to the door, I saw people kneel and kiss his coat. Not one, but many. People were in tears. People were delirious. And this happened many a time after.

ALVIN HAMILTON

We had put through cabinet a development program before we went to the country in 1958. There were some twenty points, but Diefenbaker took only half of them. That was all he would talk about, and nine out of ten of this ten-point program came from my department [northern affairs and national resources]. This was the program that became known as the Vision of the North. A fellow who worked very closely with us in the preparation of these plans was a close friend of mine, Dr Merril Menzies, who was in Diefenbaker's office. He was really the originator of the whole program.

Diefenbaker himself realized its significance, and there were unbelievable contributions that he made because my summaries and memorandums were so long-winded. He just cut them down – three words in the case of Roads to Resources, that was his name – and left out all the rest.

Nine of the ten points came from my department but I would be wrong to take the credit myself. I borrowed from every source. For instance, I had a vague objective on how I wanted to tie the North up to the road system of the provinces, and then I found the answer hidden in a file in my own department where somebody had prepared a study twenty years before. Who is the unknown civil servant? I don't know. But somebody had been thinking along this line long before I got there.

When I presented the program in the House, I gave credit to a man who had been a minister in the Borden Administration in 1911. His name was Lougheed. He was a senator who was the interior minister [and grandfather of Premier Peter Lougheed of Alberta]; he was the one who actually introduced a bill to set up Roads to Resources. This was passed in the Commons in 1911 but defeated by the Liberals under Laurier in the Senate. Laurier took the traditional Liberal position that roads should only be built from one big community to another big community where most of the votes were. You don't build roads where no one lives.

When Pearson called this program a program of roads 'from igloo to igloo,' I got in touch with Mr Diefenbaker on the campaign trail and pointed out that this was what Laurier had said at the time of the building of the CPR. He had said, 'Who is going to ride on that railway, Indians and buffaloes?' Diefenbaker paraphrased that; he changed it a bit and had the Liberals saying that the CPR was a railway from 'wigwam to wigwam.' This is where it helped to have a knowledge of history.

J.W. PICKERSGILL

The landslide was inevitable. One must remember the landslide was not just against the Liberals. We did a lot better than the Social Credit which came back with zero, or the CCF which only had eight, having had twenty-five in the previous Parliament and losing Coldwell and Knowles and all these people. It was a tidal wave! It was just that the people decided they wanted something new and something different and I don't deny that Dienfenbaker's own campaign had a big effect on them. I don't think his campaign in '57, except in one or two places, had very much effect. I think people just voted against us. In '58 there is no doubt that they voted for Diefenbaker. He had already become a folk hero. But I didn't see so much of it because I was down in Newfoundland saving my own skin – and I saved it pretty well.

I met Diefenbaker in the cellar of the House of Commons just after the election, and he said to me, 'Weren't you the only Liberal in the whole country who increased his majority?' I said, 'Well, I don't know, I haven't checked, but I can tell you this, that I got more additional votes in '58 over '57 than your candidate got votes.' I increased my vote by 5000 and his candidate got 4000, altogether. But my percentage went down. In '57 I got 87 per cent of the votes and in '58 I only got 76 per cent.

LIONEL CHEVRIER

It was quite easy to see what was happening. The short time that we had in the opposition, we were not very good because we had had no experience, and there were only three or four or five who were doing most of the work. So, it became clear that the people of Canada wanted a majority government; and it also became clear in the province of Quebec: 'Well, now, look, Diefenbaker's going to be elected, so we might as well send some members on the Conservative side.'

Perhaps the most extraordinary result of the 1958 election was the Conservative victory in Quebec. Never before had the Tories won fifty seats in that province; the closest they had come was the forty-eight seats that Sir John A. Macdonald won in 1882 (that was a higher percentage, however, as Quebec

had only sixty-five seats then, compared with seventy-five in 1958). Premier
Duplessis turned his formidable 'machine' over to the Conservatives, and
there was a suspicion on the part of some that he had done so because he
hoped to gain control of the Diefenbaker government.

JACQUES FLYNN

It was so obvious that the Conservatives would win, that Mr Diefenbaker
would win a majority, that I used to tell the candidates, 'Talk about anything,
but conclude, when you speak on a given matter, "Whether you like it or
not, the Conservatives are going to win, so why not be with him?" ' I had
the students working for me, quite a large group in '58, and I told them, 'I
know that people describe Mr Diefenbaker in such different ways. Even if he
was a devil, don't you think you would do a good thing to elect people to
keep him – to circle him in other words?' People agreed. They said, 'That's
true, and the Liberals have been there for such a long time.'

The question is often asked whether most of the successful Conservative
candidates in Quebec weren't Union Nationale members. I would say yes,
because after all the Progressive Conservative party in Quebec was absorbed
by the Union Nationale. It all depends how the question is put. It may mean,
were the candidates more of the Union Nationale mentality than of the Progressive Conservative federal party? I would say that you had, of course,
strong supporters of the Union Nationale who were candidates for us, but,
generally speaking, the candidates were people who were more attracted by
federal politics than by provincial politics, and therefore I would say that
you have to consider most of them as Conservatives more than Union
Nationale.

It's generally true that the Duplessis machine was behind Diefenbaker in
'58. There's no doubt that the 1957 result had convinced Mr Duplessis that
Mr Diefenbaker would win. Therefore, he wanted to be in a good position
to bargain with him eventually. I think that was the viewpoint of Mr Duplessis. For that reason, he told his supporters, 'Yes, go ahead.'

WILLIAM HAMILTON

I am completely convinced and I think all the evidence indicates that Mr
Duplessis, at that particular point in time, saw a way by which he could
dominate and control the federal Parliament. No one in his right mind
could have conceived of the Conservatives obtaining a majority without
Quebec. They would have a minority without Quebec; then, twenty or thirty
seats in Quebec would make the difference. Now, it's pretty clear that if you,
as a provincial leader, can put twenty or thirty people who really believe that
they owe their presence there and their allegiance to you, rather than to their

federal leader and federal party, your power on the federal level will be tremendous.

I think there's ample evidence to show that this is the course of action which Duplessis set out to follow. Because, previously, the Union Nationale had certainly been anti-Liberal and sympathetic to the Conservatives, but it was sideline sympathy – it was standing on the sidelines and cheering and shouting while somebody else got battered on the battlefield of football or hockey or whatever. Then, suddenly you found in 1958 that anything you wanted was there. Candidates were springing up all over the place, and they were well funded where there had been a problem of obtaining funds before. Many of these people were very clearly within the National Union. I would say most of them were, very clearly, not only within the National Union's sphere but owed almost everything to the National Union.

The thing which blew Duplessis' plans to smithereens, fortunately, was the landslide, the 208 Conservatives elected. Even if you extracted the 50 Quebec names, you still had a clear majority of a few seats in the House over the Liberals and the other parties. That, as I say, destroyed his plans. Had things gone a little differently, had they had the normal 170, 160, there's no doubt that I think the course of legislation, the agreements that would have been entered into with Quebec, would have been of a vastly different category.

ALLISTER GROSART
There was no deal with Duplessis in '58. I was in the position of knowing whether there was a deal or not. What happened was that in '57 there had been a suggestion, in which I was involved, that the Conservatives could have UN support in certain conditions. This looked good to me but I simply said, 'I'm not in a position to make any deals.' This was actually just after the leadership convention. I said, 'Those of us who had been supporting Mr Diefenbaker asked him, not as a condition but as part of the climate of that support, that he would not make any deals, commitments, with anybody, and he asked us to do the same.' So I was able to say, 'Well look, none of us can make a commitment. I can't make any commitment, so that is the end of it.'

Now, it's no secret that there was support given to Conservatives in '57 through UN members in certain constituencies. It is a matter of record that in '58 this was greatly increased. I think the UN people, particularly Mr Duplessis, saw that there might be a tremendous turnover. They did put support behind the Conservative candidates. There is no question about that, money and other kinds of support. Their UN members went on platforms supporting the federal Conservative candidates, but there was never a deal.

This I know for a matter of fact because nobody would be in position to make any such deal but me. I was the one to talk to. It was made very clear there was no deal. It was part of Mr Diefenbaker's philosophy. He was absolutely adamant that at no time would he come into office, or stay in office as a result of a deal.

On election night 1958, the Diefenbakers were in Prince Albert. So was the prime minister's press secretary, Jim Nelson.

JAMES NELSON

Usually we stayed at a fairly modern motel on the main drag. But on that occasion the Diefenbakers stayed at an old hotel. That was where he received the returns. And the returns! We got them by long distance phone line from Tory headquarters in Ottawa. It was just amazing, the sweep that was on. It was almost impossible to comprehend.

Then – television hadn't reached Prince Albert – he flew late at night to Saskatoon to make a speech on the results of the election. I remember vividly getting back to Prince Albert very late that night – Prince Albert airport was on the flat prairie, and you could look as far as you could in every direction, and it was Tories except for one, Hazen Argue in Assiniboia. At that time, it couldn't be comprehended how great a sweep it was.

It was too great a triumph. Everyone I interviewed agreed that there were just too many Tories, that they would have done much better and lasted much longer if there had been fewer.

GEORGE HEES

I have come to the conclusion that the worst thing that a party can do for itself is to win with an over-large majority, because leaders have a tendency to believe that they are a little higher than God. This goes for all leaders of all parties who get these big majorities, provincial or federal. It's human nature. Leaders have a tendency to get a little fat, a little sloppy, not listen to people except the ones who tell them the nice things and how great they are and how well the party is doing. The net result is that after a little while you begin to slip because you haven't been working hard enough and doing your job well enough. It was a great lesson for me, just looking at it as a student politician.

The best thing the government can possibly do is to win with a slight over-all majority, that's all. Then you are on your toes. It's like an athlete who has somebody just about as good sitting on the bench ready and willing to take his place if he doesn't play well. That keeps him on his toes and he plays like he never played before. If there is nobody to take your place, you think you've got it made, you get sloppy, you don't play well, and the next thing you know you are out.

That was the 1958 election. We won it easy. We won it too big. It was a great thrill. It was exciting. But again I wish we had won it with fifty less members. It would have been a lot more healthy for us.

J. WALDO MONTEITH

I recall Dief, himself, saying in one of our first caucuses, after the election in '58: 'There is no place left to go but down. Now, everybody, please remember that. Act accordingly.'

But, of course, we had so many new boys they thought they were there forever, and some of them just became over-confident. I'm not talking about the cabinet at the moment, I'm talking about the average member. It was a hard caucus to control, undoubtedly.

R.A. BELL

Something happened when we became the majority government. The capacity to take firm decisions, which had been no difficulty prior to the 1958 election, suddenly seemed to disappear. The Messiah attitude invaded the prime minister's office, and the government, in my view, was far, far less effective. They consulted their colleagues in caucus almost not at all after the election, whereas prior to the election there had been very considerable consultation. All details, for example, of the old-age pension bill that was brought in in 1957 were fully discussed. No suggestion of, 'Oh, we can't let privy council secrets out to you poor fellows,' which was the whole story from then on. Caucuses became John Diefenbaker telling of his readings from Mackenzie King. At every caucus, we were regaled with something from Mackenzie King, who had become, for some reason or other that nobody could quite understand, John's great hero.

HOWARD GREEN

One of the great handicaps actually was our huge majority. If we'd had about fifty fewer members, we would have been a very much stronger government because you simply couldn't give all that number of private members adequate attention, couldn't give them sufficient responsibility. You couldn't organize the caucus on a close-knit basis such as we had from '57 until the election of '58. We were a very effective fighting machine during that period. But with an overwhelming majority, it really was very difficult.

ALLISTER GROSART

None of us, I think, anticipated that we were going to wind up with 208 seats. In retrospect, I wish we hadn't. I sometimes said that if I ever wrote my memoirs, which I don't intend to do for personal reasons, the opening paragraph would be, 'The worst thing that could have happened to any political party in Canada was to win 208 seats.'

You see even today the backbenchers' problems of being heard with 208 seats. With 50 from Quebec it was a very difficult situation. To be quite frank, the Conservative party was not structured culturally, politically, or any other way, to suddenly integrate 50 members from Quebec, the majority of whom were not English-speaking. The majority of the 50 members from Quebec spoke French only.

DOUGLAS HARKNESS

This very large majority, in my view, gave Mr Diefenbaker a case of megalomania. It persuaded him that he was in an unassailable position. He was able to persuade himself that his views were always correct and that he could carry the Canadian people with him. This attitude, of course, I think unconsciously seeped out to the general public and a large number of people came to resent this more and more, and this was one of the reasons for the decline in his popularity and the decline in the popularity of the government generally.

Now, from another point of view, the general public, I think, felt again, to quite an extent perhaps unconsciously, that this was too big a majority, and that you didn't get as good government with a small and weak opposition as you would if the opposition were stronger. So a lot of people came to think, 'Well, the next election, we better cut that majority down.'

T.C. DOUGLAS

I think that a government that has too large a majority suffers on several scores. First, it suffers from the fact that the opposition is so weak that it can't keep it on its toes. The opposition has neither the personnel nor the people of stature to go over the government's proposals with a fine-tooth comb and to draw attention to some of the flaws that are in it. I think secondly that a government with a big majority has a lot of members with not enough to do and they either become completely lazy and do nothing or they begin to fight among themselves for the perquisites of office. I think thirdly, psychologically, there is no place to go but down. So when they come to an election, the question isn't what seats are you going to win, but what seats can you keep from losing.

I don't say that just in theory. In the first government I headed in Saskatchewan in 1944 we had forty-seven members out of a House of fifty-two seats. We had five members in opposition and that was the worst four years I put in in the seventeen years that I was premier of the province. First of all the five in the opposition just didn't have the wherewithal to go over the legislation carefully, and ministers got sloppy in drafting their legislation, got sloppy about referring their presentation of the estimates. The job was to try to keep forty-seven members in the House when there were only five sitting on the opposition. They knew they couldn't be outvoted, and the tendency was to go off to do something else, to look after some constituency matters, to be overseeing a department because someone needed a bridge built, something of that sort. When we came to the next election, 1948, everybody knew we weren't going to increase; we were bound to come down. So you start on the defensive.

LIONEL CHEVRIER

When we got back into the House, here was our little group of forty-five or so [Liberals] with Tories in front, Tories on the left, Tories on the right, and even at the back of us, because there were two rows of backbenchers behind me who were Tories. We were well surrounded.

G.W. BALDWIN

Of the 208 members, I think that 110 of us were new. We arrived in Ottawa starry-eyed for the first meeting of Parliament. You know, when you are newly elected, you have suddenly climbed up to the skies, you are a great big frog in your own pond and you become something of a celebrity. You are asked for your views, you are suddenly being translated into someone who is supposed to know everything.

Your first experience of Parliament is being told that you are going to share an office in a little room with another member and two secretaries – as a lawyer in Peace River, I had a fair sized suite; I had two partners, and a student, and a staff of six or seven. You are given a copy of the standing orders, which is Greek to everybody new, and I suppose still Greek to a lot of other people. You are sent questionnaires about what committees you are going to be on and so on.

I think the trouble was that Diefenbaker was really embarrassed by all this wealth of people. I think what must have been passing through his mind is, 'What am I going to do with them to keep them busy and out of mischief?' There was the first great caucus and just imagine the first time Diefenbaker meets 208 members – a tremendous scene, enthusiasm, support. He of course probably had felt since the election those twinges of immortality which I am afraid afterwards led to the problem. We are all human beings and who can blame him for it? Not that he showed it; he never was condescending in that way.

THIS SCULPTURE, SYMBOLIC OF THE
COOPERATION OF THREE RACES IN THIS
COMMUNITY AND IN THE NORTH, WAS
ERECTED BY THE GOVERNMENT OF THE
NORTHWEST TERRITORIES IN HONOUR OF
THE OFFICIAL OPENING OF INUVIK. THE
OPENING CEREMONY WAS PERFORMED BY
THE RIGHT HONOURABLE
JOHN G. DIEFENBAKER, P.C., M.P.,
WHO WAS THE FIRST PRIME MINISTER
TO VISIT ANY PART OF CANADA NORTH
OF THE ARCTIC CIRCLE.
JULY 21, 1961.

7

Vision and reality

Before the last hurrahs of the greatest election triumph in Canadian history had ended, the prime minister and his cabinet were settling down to the business of government. They faced several difficult problems that could not be ignored by a government with such an overwhelming majority. Unemployment was growing and the economy was suffering from a slowdown, if not a recession. The confidential report prepared by economists in the Department of Trade and Commerce, which Diefenbaker had charged the Liberals with hiding, had warned the St Laurent government early in 1957 of a decline in American investment after the great splurge of the early fifties, and of a decrease in housing starts and farm income. These were some of the indicators of the hard times that hung like a cloud over the bright horizon.

Diefenbaker had campaigned on a program of economic expansion, the 'Vision' of northern development, but he was to find that a majority of his ministers – those who were more Conservative than Progressive – had the same restrictive mentality as the St Laurent government and the academic and civil service establishment. Merril Menzies, who was the prime minister's economic adviser in the early years of the Conservative government, said that the country had had no clearly defined national goals or priorities except during the war and the immediate postwar years.

MERRIL MENZIES

It's true that the goals and priorities they had then were relatively short term but very specific and related to overwhelming requirements: (1) to win the war; (2) to reconvert a wartime economy to peacetime with a minimum of dislocation and disruption. I must say they did a tremendous job, a fantastic

The Diefenbakers at Inuvik

job, and I know of no criticism of any serious nature against the really effective way in which they carried through their tasks. But in the 1950s all this disappeared, and we were back to a market economy, slightly modified by the Keynesian theory of maintaining short-term economic stability. This was extremely congenial to the government of the day, and, of course, to the man who really dominated economic policy, Mr. C.D. Howe.

They had an outstanding person in Mr Howe, extremely honourable, unusually able, a fantastic administrator. When these goals were clearly defined during the war period and the reconstruction period, he did a tremendous job. But in the 1950s when they were replaced by the policy of relying on the marketplace to dictate where we should go, what our national priorities should be, given the need for large aggregations of international investment capital, clearly our goals and priorities were going to be determined by the interests largely of others. Except for the limited application of what was then known as the Keynesian approach to the control of national economies, there were no national goals, however you wish to define them. They simply did not exist.

Indeed, it was always very painful for an academic or a politician to challenge what was an overwhelming consensus during this period. If he did, he was considered either rather deficient in mental capacity or possibly dangerous. This was due to the very success – we'll put it this way – the very success of the government and of the public service. During those years there was a great interchange – interaction – between the academic and the public service that possibly made it difficult, if not impossible, for that generation to adjust to the quite different demands and priorities of peacetime.

One of the unfortunate things at this time was that there was no strong political opposition. I think I've heard it said that many years in opposition had not led to any positive restatement of national goals and objectives by the opposition. The very fact that they had become so ineffective simply insured not only a complete lack of credibility as an alternative government, but reinforced what was a very profoundly held consensus at that time, that the government policy was not only right – it was the only possible policy. Any country that gets into that type of situation – looking at the fact that history is a very dynamic process and the only thing we're sure of is change – is going to be facing trouble before very long.

Another aspect of the problem: by following this policy [of concentrating on the marketplace and American or foreign investment], the massive rush for foreign takeovers was inevitable. It was a logical process, an inevitable process. And one could see this developing early in the 1950s. The

Canadian dollar became worth $1.10 American, and an over-valued Canadian dollar worked seriously against our major exports, such as, for example at that time, wheat. It reduced or undermined our competitive position as an industrial economy, vis-à-vis the US, Europe, and other industrial countries. The strength of the Canadian dollar was due to American investment. There is simply no doubt about that. Actually, there was no way that we could maintain our rate of growth and standard of living under that policy regime without this tremendous inflow of foreign capital.

On the other hand, if we had been looking ahead to our own needs, I think that we would have adopted entirely different policies with respect to exchange rate, with respect to laying down phase development programs for our major natural resources and, in particular, energy. But, in point of fact, this was against the whole tenor of both academic and political thought at the time. There were certain things that C.D. Howe could see – certain projects. Before the war, it was Trans-Canada Airlines, really a creation of his. In the 1950s, it was the Trans-Canada pipeline. He could see the value of this project, and certainly it was needed. It could have fitted into a broad concept of national development, and indeed it will fit into such a development. But he didn't modify essentially this reliance on the marketplace to decide where we were going. We just didn't know.

It used to be called the gross national product. So you said it was going up. Fine. The quality of the GNP, or the directions that this was leading us, made, in the longer term, the best economic and social sense.

While the Trans-Canada pipeline, as a project, had enormous validity, ironically it became the occasion for the downfall, not only of a government, but the breakdown of a period of consensus that has never been restored. As far as I'm concerned, I get worried when we have too much consensus because we have too little thought when that happens.

I suggest that the blame for this very unfortunate period in the first part of the '50s is pretty evenly spread. The government in power didn't in fact provide us with what I would call the leadership in terms of broad economic and social objectives which would prepare us for what the future was bound to bring. The opposition clearly had to share in that because they provided, in my view, literally no alternative at that time.

The feeling that developed quite strongly, and particularly during the pipeline debate, was that the government had become arrogant. The culminating point was the use of closure, which had almost died out as a parliamentary weapon until that time. There was a gradual build-up of frustration that went through the country. I think people, without really knowing very deeply or consciously what we should be doing, became frustrated about this ever and onward and upward move of the GNP, without knowing where this was leading.

This really brings us to the point at which this overwhelming consensus, and the government that had been in office for twenty years, was challenged for the first time. I could not see that anyone other than Mr Diefenbaker could have led a challenge to something that was so overwhelmingly accepted in the public service both political and the non-political, and also in the academic community.

Menzies was the originator of the Conservative policy of northern development. His brother-in-law, Dr Glen Green of Prince Albert, was a strong Conservative and a personal friend of John Diefenbaker. Just before the 1956 Progressive Conservative convention, Menzies received a letter from Dr Green asking him for some ideas on economic and national policies.

MERRIL MENZIES
I intended to reply to Dr Green. Certainly, I did not imagine a letter more than five or six pages long at the most. However, when I got into it, many of the ideas that had been generating over the previous five or six years seemed to demand re-expression in more popular and non-academic terms. In the end, the letter as written was between thirty and forty pages long, single-spaced, typewritten. In effect it was a major thesis or a re-definition in more popular language of the thesis I had already developed in large measure in an academic way when I was at the University of London.

My main theme was the overwhelming need in Canada for a much more positive government, in terms not just of effective administration but of setting national priorities and national goals, and not just short-term economic stability which seemed to be the prime pre-occupation of the government of that period, but looking ahead to the problems which clearly were going to arrive sooner or later. We could plan for them. I think it was Frank Underhill who years ago wrote an academic article in which he raised the need for a moral equivalent of the CPR. Well, it was something of that concept.

Both in my academic thesis in the early fifties and in this paper I raised the need for a very early development of a national energy policy encompassing not just petroleum or hydrocarbons but all sources of energy. I think, if my recollection is correct, I expressed the belief that technology either was available, or soon would be, by which we could develop an effective national energy grid, which would include electrical power lines, pipelines – the entire sources in use. I take no credit for great originality on this. Indeed [M.W.] Max Mackenzie, who had been deputy minister of trade and commerce, had written a very excellent paper in which he raised essentially the same issues. Unfortunately, this was running against the current of the times.

Out of that letter grew the program which became known as the 'Vision.' For a time, it was called the 'New Frontier Policy' – a title Menzies suggested after the leadership had changed hands and he was working for Mr Diefenbaker in the leader of the opposition's office.

MERRIL MENZIES

I think it was in December of '56; it might have been early January of '57. I wrote Mr Diefenbaker a letter – of which I have no copy, although, looking back at some old papers, I have seen some fairly current references to it – trying to describe in political terms the concept I had. I realized how the academic language was not adequate for public speaking, so I came up with the slogan which I called the 'new frontier policy.' This was not only designed to incorporate Professor Harold Innis' idea of the investment frontier, but it seemed to provide a vehicle to incorporate my ideas of a national energy policy, a national development, and so on.

The slogan was included in most of my early drafts of speeches for Diefenbaker, and he used it briefly in passing in the first major speech of the '57 campaign in Toronto. For some reason it didn't get a response. It was used just once or twice thereafter, with, I must confess, the same results. So it didn't become part of his political repertoire.

But it was used, and it was used years before by some strange coincidence it became the basis of Kennedy's political message to the American people. Diefenbaker has a fantastic retentive memory, and even if he discards something he doesn't forget it. The story has it that he, in fact, mentioned it to Kennedy in the early days before some differences of opinion developed between the two of them.

ALVIN HAMILTON

From 1957 to 1960–1, there wasn't enough room on the agenda of each session for all the things we were fighting for. There was, for instance, the Productivity Council, the Economic Council of Canada, and the Development Corporation – they had been accepted by cabinet but had different priorities.

Actually, the Productivity Council came in in '61, and the Economic Council in the fall of '62. The Development Corporation was supposed to have come in the fall of '62, but didn't. This is the one that I developed as the resources minister, and I was very disappointed that the Development Corporation that we had in mind wasn't enacted. It got such a bad name under Walter Gordon's concept of the corporation that it never really got off the ground and the present Development Corporation is still suffering from that. It was an altogether different philosophy. Walter was thinking in terms of trying to buy back existing companies, which I looked on as a loser's game. I wanted to collect money and give Canadians a chance to get at these big returns that there are in resource industries.

In October 1960 Alvin Hamilton became minister of agriculture and Walter Dinsdale, MP for Brandon-Souris, succeeded him as minister of northern affairs and national resources. Under Hamilton the department formulated the national development policy of the Conservative government, which included the plans for a National Energy Board, the Roads to Resources program, and the Resources for Tomorrow Conference. The conference, held in Montreal in 1961, drew together representatives of the federal and provincial governments, as well as of the universities, business, and industry, to develop a program for the better conservation and management of the nation's resources.

WALTER DINSDALE

I still remember the first meeting that René [Lévesque] attended. He was late. He came in with his entourage. We were meeting over in the East Block. I was chairing and we had the seats arranged in proper pecking order: Wilf Spooner was the Ontario minister on the right, and the empty chair on the left was for the minister from Quebec. I stopped the meeting, introduced Mr Lévesque all around, and invited him to sit down.

He said, 'Who are you?' I introduced myself and he said, 'Are you chairing this meeting?' I said, 'Yes.' He said, 'I won't participate. Ottawa has no resources.' So right there is the old confrontation technique and you had to bypass him. I said, 'Well, I am also the minister of northern affairs and we have all the resources north of sixty.' He shrugged his shoulders and said, 'You can preside as minister of northern affairs, not a resources minister.' That is the way you had to handle him all the time, walk around him because he has a very brilliant and keen mind.

But René Lévesque worked throughout the preparation for the Resources for Tomorrow Conference. We set up this Continuing Conference of Resource Ministers which was supposed to meet regularly, devise plans that would be mutually acceptable for provinces and the federal government, and he became the chairman of that committee. He was the first provincial minister to become a chairman, so he has gone a long way since that time.

That committee, that conference of resource ministers, has been completely neglected by succeeding Liberal governments. They had no interest in it, and it has now been abandoned at a time when this close consultation in resource matters is so badly needed.

Something that is not really known is the fact that it was the Diefenbaker government that anticipated the present oil shortage. We supported the first wildcat well in Winter Harbour on Melville Island in the winter of '61. They thought that we had gone completely bonkers then, to think that there was oil under the frozen tundra of the high Arctic. But we had the famous Quirin Report, which pointed out crystal clear that by 1975 the world would be faced with an energy crisis.

He [Quirin] was an authority on the geology of the North and he pointed out that it was the same as the Middle East. The geology of the Canadian archipelago was identical with that of the Middle East – so there must be oil there. The Dome Petroleum Company and a consortium of Canadian independents got the funds together. Peter Bawden Drilling Company accepted the contract. It was a million dollar contract. Peter is now a Conservative member of Parliament, but then he was just a young businessman in the drilling industry. He took his equipment to Montreal by train. He couldn't find a Canadian boat to take it up to the Arctic – there were no Canadian boats, they had been phased out. So the *Thorodan*, a Danish boat, was chartered and started off for Winter Harbour – this is way up in the northwest passage. They got within a hundred miles of Winter Harbour – I was keeping closely in touch with this thing because it was a risky proposition – and they got stuck in the ice. So we sent up the *John A. Macdonald* to get them free and they started drilling that winter.

They had a telephone communication system. I could talk at my desk with the men who were on the drilling site. They went down to about 11,500 feet. They had gas showing but no oil, but they proved the geology. If Prudhoe Bay had been discovered at Winter Harbour that winter, the history of Canada would have changed, but we didn't get it.

After the change of government, the program wasn't continued until, at the initiative of the oil companies – again the Dome Petroleum people were very active in this – they finally formed Panarctic and got going again; but we lost some very important years. Jack Gallagher, the president of Dome Petroleum, deserves a lot of credit for pushing northern exploration. We could have made our discoveries first if we had carried on, and now everybody of course realizes that the best hope of petroleum is in the Arctic.

To make sure that this northern development would be a Canadian development, we had to give fairly generous concessions to the people to go in to explore. It's risky in the North and we gave them fairly generous terms during the exploration phase. But once they were going into production they had to meet some very stringent regulations. The regulations insisted that shares go on the Canadian stock exchange, that 50 per cent of shares had to be available to Canadians, and that the company be a Canadian company and a good corporate citizen. This was the first attempt on the part of any government to insist and to insure that the resource industry is developed in the best interest of the public.

We had a Prospectors Assistance Program that was to encourage the men who really find the rich mineral deposits, the prospector with his pick and his axe. He was grub-staked by the government to encourage development. He had an assistance program for landing fields in the North too. North of sixty is our total responsibility. We have the resources there. We worked with Canada Tungsten in opening the Tungsten Mine in the Nahanni Valley, on the border of the Yukon and the Northwest Territories.

We opened negotiations with Japan to find a market for the Yukon minerals. John Diefenbaker was very popular in Japan. We started the trading regulations which have made the Japanese market second to the American market. I remember I made a trip to Japan to negotiate with the Japanese government for the sale of minerals. Since that time they have opened the new Imperial Mines in Whitehorse. There again is a copper deposit that had been known since the gold rush. The Anvil Mine had opened, and Japan is taking the total production. It's the basis for prosperity in the Yukon today.

The Roads to Resources program included a railroad to the Pine Point lead-zinc ore mine in the Northwest Territories. The railroad had been long promised to run through the Peace River Valley and this would be a logical route because the area was well populated, but the new member for that area found there was powerful pressure for another route to the east, through Fort Smith.

GERALD BALDWIN

A lot of things were involved. British Columbia was then coming ahead with northern development and Edmonton feared, 'If they build this railroad on the western route through Peace River, Bennett will build a railroad extension to join in at Tupper and drain away all that money and that wealth that should come through Edmonton, which is entitled to it as of right.' Northern Affairs at first was strong for the eastern route. Gordon Robertson was the deputy minister then and came from Saskatchewan, a Rhodes scholar, quite a brilliant man, and he exercised very strong influence over Alvin Hamilton. Alvin was pushing for this eastern route at the time, as I discovered later.

I forget how it first came about that I discovered exactly what was going on, and that the CNR wanted to build the railroad because they wanted expansion – this was another great venture, a 750-mile railroad into the North. Consolidated Mining and Smelting [who operated the mine] didn't really mind. (You know the CPR is a big element in Consolidated.) Consolidated wanted the railroad. They were aware of the geographical and engineering errors that were to be committed by building it in the eastern route but they said, 'We want the railroad. If we buck the establishment down here we won't get it at all.' Doug Harkness, through his friends, business connections, Alvin Hamilton, all the people in the city of Edmonton, the Chamber of Commerce in Edmonton, Donald Fleming. The only people in the government who held out on my side were the BC ministers, Davie Fulton and Howard Green, and they didn't dare say too much.

The first speech that I made was on the railroad. It was a pretty good speech. My time had run out and the speaker had cut me down and Jack Pickersgill said, 'Let him go. He is making a good speech; let him finish it.' I have always had a soft spot in my heart for Jack after that. Some people came to see me after that, and I mentioned the Peace River route and the promises. I had the letters, I had the statements made in the House of Commons and outside by people like [Sir Edward] Beatty and [R.B.] Bennett and D.M. Kennedy, a former member, and Jack Sissons who later became a judge and used to be the member for Peace River. All of these were commitments.

Then, I was told – I don't remember how I learnt it, it was late in '58 – that they were going to build a railroad but it was almost virtually certain that it was going to go the other way. So I started agitating. I was just shocked and I didn't care. I had told someone who, I knew, would get it to Diefenbaker that if I didn't get a fair chance, that if there was going to be a decision made in advance without proper discussion and debate, then I felt free to take any course of action that I wanted. Which was my freshman way of saying that I could cross the floor, not necessarily become a Liberal, but I would be free to take a different attitude.

I made speeches. We formed an organization with all the Chambers of Commerce, and the whole of the Peace River country got behind me. I got on the radio. We put pressure on, and I had some help from Senator [John A.] Buchanan. Buck Buchanan was from Edmonton, but he was an engineer and a surveyor and he knew something of the geographical problems as well as the political. I spoke to Diefenbaker about it, and my recollection was that he said he was aware of the probems. I think his gut reaction was that I was right. But he had all these people, especially Alvin Hamilton who was pretty close to him, and Gordon Robertson, and probably 75 per cent of his cabinet and the city of Edmonton in favour of the eastern route – it was linked up in part with the tar sands at that time – and he said, 'Well, you know there might be extensions of the tar sands north of McMurray.'

So Dief did the thing which all governments do and he appointed a royal commission which was a lightning conductor. He probably did it in the belief that they might well come out in favour of the McMurray route, but at least it shifted the burden. He announced that and I think I thanked him. I felt that we had a chance.

Actually, the commission decided nothing. [John] Anderson-Thomson came out 100 per cent with cogent good valid reasons for building the railroad to the west. [W.D.] Gainer, who I think was tied up with Edmonton people, came out for building it by the east. The chairman [M.E. Manning] said "If a railroad is going to be built at all, of which I have some doubt, I don't know which way it ought to be built.' It was a most unsatisfactory report, not only for us but I am sure for Diefenbaker. It threw the thing right back into his hands. It stayed there for some time. I have a hunch that Diefenbaker consulted a number of people, and I am sure that he consulted Anderson-Thomson and I am sure that he consulted people like Senator Buchanan. I am sure that he was subject to the continuous pressure of Edmonton, of Alvin Hamilton, of all these other people. Ultimately, there was a cabinet decision to build it, and to build it by the Peace River route, and they tied it up with a very good agreement with Cominco and they built it that way.

The only postscript that I'll add to this is that some years after it was built, the CNR held a showing called 'The Building of the Railroad.' All the people were there – Gordon Robertson and the CNR people, the Cominco people, and some cabinet ministers. This was a chronicle of their achievements, how they had built this great railroad, one of the best railroad construction jobs in all Canadian history: they built it for $10 million, less than what we had appropriated for it, and all the great things that had been done. Here were all the people who had been so opposed to it, and I say that it shows that when chips are down, Dief's political antennae were right on in the judgment that he made. He had to go in the face of strong opposition. I quarrelled with Dief about other things – and he didn't do this just for me. His judgment was sound. It is a tribute to his sagacity. There is no doubt also of his feeling that when it comes to a choice between people and other things that the people count.

Merril Warren Menzies was born near Melfort, Saskatchewan, 31 October 1920. His father was a pioneer farmer who had come to the prairies from Peterborough County, Ontario, at about the same time as the Diefenbakers.

His mother, Laura Lobb, taught school at Canora. Merril graduated at six-teen from a one-room high school in Beatty, where all four grades were taught by a single teacher. He worked on the family farm because there were no jobs to be had, and at nights he took a business course.

The war provided him with the opportunity of higher education. On several occasions, he had tried to enlist but could not pass the medical exam. He was working in a men's clothing store in Prince Albert when the Sixth Division was being organized in 1942. He got to know the recruiting officer and helped him with his accounts. This time there was no difficulty in enlist-ing – the doctor hardly looked at him – and he joined the Prince Albert Volunteers. A year later the division was broken up, and Menzies, now a commissioned officer, went overseas with the South Saskatchewan Regiment. He was wounded in Normandy.

On returning to Canada after the war, Menzies took advantage of the Veterans' Rehabilitation Act to go to the University of Saskatchewan. By 1949, he had received an MA and had won a Memorial Scholarship to the University of London where he studied for his PHD in economics. By accident more than anything else, Menzies then found a job as executive assistant to Stuart Garson, Liberal justice minister. Two years later he returned to London to write his thesis on the Canadian wheat trade. Most of the ideas he later developed for Diefenbaker were contained in his thesis. Shortly after Diefenbaker became Conservative leader, Menzies became his economic ad-viser. One of his first jobs was the 1958 conversion loan, which converted the war loans, bearing about 3 per cent interest, to higher interest.

MERRIL MENZIES

I am aware that a substantial number of people had to know about the con-version loan before it was announced – certainly the cabinet, the Bank of Canada, senior officials in the Department of Finance – and I would suspect that the financial community in Canada were not entirely ignorant of this proposal. But I can say that, although I was economic secretary to the prime minister, I did not hear a word about it. I had no idea that this was being considered until the morning that the policy was announced.

When I came to work that morning, I had a call from Mr Diefenbaker. He asked me to come down to his office because he had something that he wanted to talk over with me, that concerned him very much. I went in and I realized immediately that he was in an unusually thoughtful mood. He was looking out of the window, and after quite a pause, he turned to me and he said, in effect, 'I want to tell you about a policy that has been decided upon. It's going to be announced today. It's too late to reverse it, but I'm extremely concerned about it.' In effect, he was very worried that it had been a wrong policy decision.

Then he told me about the conversion loan, an $8 billion loan, and I was literally staggered. He said, 'We can't change this. I can't change it. But I'd like you to go away and think about it for a few hours, and then come back and tell me what you think about it.' Well, I had to come back and tell him that his worst fears were justified, because essentially this was a program that greatly intensified the restrictive policies that both Mr Fleming, the minister of finance, and Mr Coyne, the governor of the Bank of Canada, believed in so strongly, and were pursuing by various means. At this time, and well into at least 1960, there was no basic difference in policy between Mr Fleming and Mr Coyne. This is my personal view and personal observation.

In any case, I considered that this conversion loan was a calamity. The only positive argument that could be advanced for it was simply a sort of a housekeeping argument – a matter of convenience in terms of managing the public debt. But against that was the enormously restrictive implications at that time in terms of the economy and the fact that it could only result in a substantially increasing level of unemployment.

To give you the background to this, the last real inflationary period was 1956. There was a tremendous investment boom that grew out of the very enormous foreign investments, partially related to the Trans-Canada pipeline but to other resource investments too, primarily by US capital. By the end of 1956, this was beginning to fade. Such inflation as there was, and I suppose the Consumer Price Index is a rough measure, was generally of the cost-push variety. It wasn't being generated by new demand in excess of supplies or supply capability. It was simply the follow-through of catching up in labour agreements and so on. But it was quite clear that even this was fading out in '57 and we were moving inexorably into a period of not inflation but high levels of unemployment, whether this was officially designated as a recession period or not.

The time that the conversion loan was in fact announced was a very pivotal period – whether the government would move into consistent expansionary programs, both fiscal and monetary, at a time when clearly that kind of expansion was needed, or whether it would become restrictive, as clearly Mr Coyne wanted it and, in my view, Mr Fleming wanted it. Unfortunately the wrong decision was made, and Mr Diefenbaker knew perfectly well that he had been sold a terrible bill of goods, very much against the interests of Canada. He did tell me some years later that I was the only one who had told him the truth about this conversion loan before the event, before it actually happened. I can only feel sorry for him, because I can well see that about 100 per cent of the advice that he got was just of one opinion, and completely for it.

This demonstrates something that I've often felt about Mr Diefenbaker – that when his experience and technical knowledge in the sometimes complex and very disputatious field of economics weren't quite adequate to analyse a problem or a policy, his instinctive feel about it was often right on. When he listened to his instincts, he was right. But when he listened to his advisers during this critical period of 1958 to 1959, he was almost entirely wrong.

One decision which had been postponed by two different governments – that of Louis St Laurent and the first minority government of John Diefenbaker – was the fate of the CF-105, *the Avro Arrow. This was a highly advanced supersonic interceptor aircraft, driven by a powerful new jet engine, the Iroquois, that was being designed and built at Malton, just outside Toronto. The test model was a thrilling and beautiful sight. But by 1958 more than $300 million had been spent in development costs, and much more money would be needed to complete the project. The government decision was difficult. Against the cost of further work it had to balance the investment to date, the pool of talent and jobs created around the Arrow – and the effect on national pride. For the Arrow and the Iroquois were the forefront of aeronautical technology at the time, and they were the work of Canadian skill and industry.*

On 20 February 1959, the prime minister announced in the House of Commons that the Arrow contract was being terminated immediately. On the day of the announcement, the Avro management dismissed the 11,800 employees in its Malton plant. Among them were 2000 engineers, many of whom went down to the United States and were lost to Canada for good. The backlash in Toronto was formidable. The United States had refused to buy the Arrow – one of the factors in the plane's demise – and there were charges that Canadian military leaders were in collusion with the American aerospace industry and gave the new government bad advice. Altogether, it was an ugly business.

MERRIL MENZIES

Another policy that was sold to the government without adequate consideration of the economic and political implications was the Defence decision to scrap the Arrow. This was bad enough, but if that had been all, one could have possibly accepted it, but reluctantly. However, tied to that was the related Bomarc decision, which ironically by a chain of events led to the final break-up of the government, the final disputes between what I would call the

Progressives in the cabinet and the Conservatives in the cabinet. The Progressives were few, the Conservatives were the rest.

What really happened economically from that decision was again – even if localized – massive unemployment, and of very highly skilled people. We destroyed a whole industry. It was one of the major reasons for the total disaffection of the Toronto area which showed up, obviously, at the next election.

Now, one of the factors involved is that Mr Pearkes was defence minister at the time. Mr Diefenbaker and Mr Pearkes were very close friends. Mr Diefenbaker had a great regard for Mr Pearkes, understandably, and this was a consensus view by the military establishment. Certainly it was painful. And he did not take that decision in the callous way that was ascribed to him by his opponents. By no means, because he made it clear to me in a private conversation that if anything were to be his political nemesis, it would be unemployment. This showed insight and shrewdness on his part.

I don't think he ever really quite understood the economic implications of his decision. But let me say one thing. It's sometimes very difficult to explain to laymen – sometimes laymen might be politicians in this area – the very simple principle of sub-costs. In order to sell this Arrow decision to the government, what they did – and by they I would say the senior defence officials who were making a case for this decision – they added virtually all the costs from the initial development right through, and they were enormous. But most of them had been spent under the previous government. Then they divided these costs by 100 planes. Naturally, they came out with a cost per plane that was outrageous.

Now, all that money was spent. There was no way of getting it back. It wasn't a dead loss. We had an important industry and a first-class group of scientists, techicians in what would today be called the aerospace industry – and, indeed, a great many of them went on to NASA and some are still there. So it wasn't a dead loss. Those costs were not recoverable. The only costs that were relevant were the additional costs, the marginal costs. If they had been calculated fairly and divided by 100, the cost per plane would have been very reasonable. This might be proved or disproved by other people or sources, but I had a very strong feeling that the influence of the US Defense Department, particularly of the Air Force, was extremely strong in the Canadian decision because they argued that the bomber was dead. Not only the bomber but the fighter too – in fact, they said that the manned aircraft was dead. That was the position they put to Mr Pearkes and the Canadian chiefs of staff. It was basically on that that this decision was taken. Since then we've bought at least three or four generations of US fighters – and at that time we were ahead in technology.

The Canadian government was sold an erroneous position, I think, and one doesn't have to enlarge upon the implications for our balance of payments and the more sophisticated portions of our aero industries as a direct consequence of this. It's meant a continuing annual payment to the US for these very sophisticated weapons which they said we did not need and were obsolete in 1958.

What was even worse, they sold us a dog in the Bomarc. They considered it obsolete in their own establishment at that time. The one benefit possibly that we're getting out of it is that the missile underground station at North Bay is being used by a new technical college. Let's hope something comes of that.

I know that it was a matter of considerable mental anguish for Mr Diefenbaker to make the decision to terminate the Arrow. I think the first really hostile reaction he got, either in terms of letters or in terms of rather violent press attacks, particularly by the Toronto press, really came with this decision.

The cancellation of the Arrow led to a confrontation between business and government.

GRATTAN O'LEARY

I remember being in Diefenbaker's office the day when he met Crawford Gordon [president of A.V. Roe, builder of the Arrow]. I was sitting in the anteroom when this fellow came out and he was white as a sheet. I was next in, and Dief said, 'I have just told him that the thing is off.' I said, 'Why did you tell him that?' Diefenbaker was quite right. He said, 'Look, this is going to cost a billion dollars. We have no market for them, we can't sell them. So why do we spend a billion dollars on a plane that we have no use for? We don't need enough of them. We have no export market and no domestic market for these planes. They are costing too much, and I had to tell him no.'

He did this on his own. He wasn't concerned with what poor George Hees thought about its effect in Toronto. He said, no. He was right. But this was one of the few times that I have seen Dief make a real decision on his own, a big one. He would put off, put off. You remember the case of the Cuban crisis. He didn't come out of that very well, and that helped to defeat him. We wouldn't make up our minds whether we were with the Americans, or against them, or what we were doing. Then there was the Bomarc thing;

we couldn't make up our minds about that. This was his fault really. Politically Dief was all right, but when it came to making decisions of an administrative character, he was hesitant.

DOUGLAS HARKNESS

I think the reason that there was so much said about the Arrow at the time and afterwards was that so long was taken to make a decision on it. I think it was a year or more after we had been in office before the Arrow contract was cancelled, and I think people who knew anything about the matter knew that it perhaps should have been cancelled within two or three months of our taking office. The fact that it went on as long it did, and that, therefore, the amount of money which was spent in the intervening period was wasted – this really started the lack of credibility in the decisiveness and the ability of the government, because, of course, it was used as a great propaganda weapon by all of the opposition parties.

WILLIAM HAMILTON

But Diefenbaker avoided and evaded wherever he could those issues which were essentially divisive and more and more, as time went on, his tactics became evasive. I date it really from the Arrow affair.

I remember at almost our first cabinet meeting in 1957 we were asked to approve a Canadian National Railways expenditure for $200,000 for an extension of the Nova Scotian Hotel in Halifax. We were the government that was going to be very economical and save money, so we jumped on this from a great height and said that, in our opinion, there really was no need for this whatsoever, and we weren't going to approve that particular expenditure. The only man who differed at that particular point was George Nowlan, and I can remember now his laughing at us when it came back about a month later, and the same expenditure was approved almost automatically. He said, 'Well, I guess we're all going to learn a lot about politics in a hell of a hurry, now that we're in the cabinet.' The difference was that in the month all the members from Nova Scotia had been besieging the cabinet ministers, and there had been an uproar in Halifax, and generally it sounded as if we, by not allowing this extension to be built, were going to tear Canada asunder.

These were the kinds of things that Diefenbaker preferred to avoid if he possibly could. I think that's good politics, too. But all through the piece between '57 and '58 he had been doing things that people wanted – increasing old age pensions, and family allowances, and the whole thing. All right. Besides that, there was the tremendous upsurge of the '58 election and the honeymoon period which followed that. Then, suddenly, came the crunch point where he did have a major decision to make that was fundamentally unpopular in a very wide area, that ran counter to the desire of Canada to be a leader, in so far as it can be, in a variety of fields. It had an infinite number of complexities to it. That, of course, was the Arrow.

The resultant agonies from that, and the criticisms and the misunderstandings, I think, just frightened him to death. He began to be more and more cautious until finally we came down, in the latter stages, the last year or so, to only making the decisions that one was forced to make rather than making the decisions that one should make. The government began to suffer from paralysis – and it was due to the Arrow.

During most of the time that Merril Menzies was in the prime minister's office, he was, as he said, engaged in a desperate fight against the establishment. He was seeking an expansionary policy to deal with unemployment, but he found the cabinet seriously divided.

MERRIL MENZIES

I realized what I was up against. The majority of the cabinet, the whole consensus of the official position in Ottawa, was really against the policies of the small progressive wing. That wing had an instinctive feel that we should be developing expansionary policies and dealing with the immediate problem of unemployment – and also dealing with problems such as the overvalued Canadian dollar and the difficulties this caused our exporters, whether they were in the forestry industry, or wheat, or whether they were simply manufacturers competing with imports.

It was a most trying and difficult time. I could see the way things were going because weekly I would get these policy or economic appraisals from Finance, and the message invariably was the same. The great problem facing Canada was inflation, destroying the economy. Ridiculous on the face of it if you look at the realities. But that was it, and it was like an article of faith. I would append my little comment, almost always the same – 'It isn't true,' and it wasn't.

Diefenbaker knew well the dangers of unemployment politically, and he was concerned as a person as well. Again, I think this is where he let the overwhelming pressure from his advisers, who were consistently of one opinion except for very, very few, override what I believe his instincts would have told him was wrong.

There's no question whatsoever, without going into details, that it was essentially on this issue that I finally resigned from the East Block in November 1959. The final straw was a speech that had been prepared in Finance for the prime minister. It was strictly anti-inflationary. So I called DBS, got the latest data on the Consumer Price Index worked out, the annual average, and it was so ridiculously small that you could almost dismiss it as a statistical error. There was no inflation. He was getting absolutely wrong information.

This brought to an end my year-and-a-half effort to stand in the way of what, to me, were pretty disastrous short-term economic policies which were getting in the way of developing the long-term policies that were needed. Dienfenbaker had to make a decision, and I could only sympathize with how difficult it was. Here I was saying one thing, and everybody else apparently was saying something else. How could I be right? So, in fact, I left with nothing but respect and admiration for Mr Diefenbaker and feeling very sorry for him. I don't think that his position in Canadian history, or his contributions, or the incredible odds that he was fighting against within his cabinet and within the establishment, have ever been given the conscientious analysis with the proper perspective that they deserve. I trust that history will correct this.

In any case, within a short time of my going, Diefenbaker began to get very concerned about this problem. He established a committee of officials of the major economic departments, and decided to chair it himself. This was a very wise decision because there were very few of his colleagues that he could have trusted to have undertaken this. But things did not progress quickly, as you can guess, through the committee method.

Fleming brought down his budget in the spring of 1960. It was the same. It was the standard type budget based on principles he'd held all along, that the problems facing Canada were problems of inflation. It was pretty restrictionist, certainly not expansionist. The whole idea was that the economy was getting out of control.

A friend of mine later told me a story which I can well believe true. Apparently, the second-quarter DBS review of the economy came out literally within weeks of Fleming's budget, which had been based on this inflationary myth. And it showed really exactly the contrary – that the economy was stalling or maybe even turning down slightly. In any case, the story as he had it was that when Diefenbaker saw this, he called Fleming over to his office. He picked up this DBS report, and tossed it over his desk at Fleming, and said, 'There goes your damned budget.'

From then on, the government's course was being strongly shifted in an expansionary direction. Fleming, perforce, had to go along reluctantly until his run-in with Coyne, and then, of course, it was all in the open. So in point of fact I'd say within about a year after I'd left the East Block, Diefenbaker did indeed force the government to adopt expansionary policies. In the end you might say that he and the very few progressives in the cabinet probably won. But he was the major political casualty in the battle. Quite apart from this terrific struggle – and I don't know of a prime minister who has faced the odds within cabinet and within the public service that Diefenbaker did, and fought so hard for so long – he really achieved a lot. You work through all the things that he did, and it's not an unimpressive record. But I think that, from the point of view of history, what is equally important, and maybe more so, is the things that he tried to do and failed to achieve. They are, in most cases, the longer term policies we have discussed.

Who formed the progressive wing in the cabinet?

MERRIL MENZIES
Diefenbaker was the leader. Alvin Hamilton was really outstanding. MacLean – he wasn't aggressive in putting his views across but he was one of the first to understand the nature of the establishment's attack on the policies of the progressive wing, which were expansionist and with long term implications of establishing priorities and goals. Gordon Churchill has to be in there, no question about that. There are a few that you have to qualify. There were two or three great Diefenbaker loyalists like Pearkes and Green. I couldn't call them progressives by any means – I don't think either really had clear economic views – but in most cases Diefenbaker could count on those two. They were, after all, his generation in the House. Michael Starr tended towards the progressive rather than the conservative position, and also really had a loyalty to Diefenbaker. David Walker, an extremely perceptive and able person – not all his views were progressive, but he was too intelligent and too clever to commit suicide at the behest of an establishment viewpoint, and so he added his strength to the progressive wing when the issue was no longer capable of being avoided. Again, I couldn't call Davie Fulton a progressive, but he was intelligent. I respected him, and in a good many cases he would be adding his support to the progressive wing. Without any doubt, the undisputed leader of the conservative wing was Fleming, and, as I say, it was possibly typical but somewhat ironical that he was converted to the government's expansionist, or the progressive's expansionist, policy by a one-man pension plan. That's about the way I saw the cabinet from close to it but on the outside.

8
From Saskatchewan to China

Two achievements helped to win and hold the West for the Conservatives. The first was the construction of the South Saskatchewan Dam; the second was the multi million dollar sale of grain to China.

The dam had been promised to Saskatchewan during the 1957 campaign, and its completion provided the Chief with an enduring memorial. Diefenbaker Lake, created by the dam, protects farmers against the recurring droughts that were one of the causes of the dust storms of the thirties. The shores of the lake were turned into a provincial park, named in honour of T.C. Douglas who, as premier of Saskatchewan, had been a persistent advocate of the project. The dam itself was named after James Garfield Gardiner.

The prime minister, his economic adviser, Merril Menzies, and the idea man among his ministers, Alvin Hamilton, all came from Saskatchewan and had survived the depression there. They knew the problems of the prairies and were determined to resolve them by developing policies that would help to stabilize the traditionally uncertain ̇business of agriculture. Their most spectacular achievement was the huge Chinese wheat deal. At a time of surpluses, when the elevators were overflowing and grain had to be stored on the farms, this was an extraordinary sale, and a diplomatic breakthrough that opened the door to Peking.

The South Saskatchewan dam was the first of the Conservative campaign promises to the West to be fulfilled.

T.C. DOUGLAS

When Mr Diefenbaker became prime minister, one of the first things I did was to phone him to congratulate him and to suggest that I would like to

Diefenbaker triggers the explosion to start work on the South Saskatchewan dam discuss with him the matter of the South Saskatchewan Dam. He said, 'Of course, we are going to carry out that promise.' I said, 'I would like to meet and discuss it with you.' He said, 'Well, any time,' and I said, 'How about Monday morning, 10 o'clock?' – the Monday following his taking office.

I don't think he had anticipated starting quite so soon, but he said, 'Yes, certainly.' So I came down to Ottawa and we met and began discussions on the South Saskatchewan Dam. There was considerable division in the cabinets. The two ministers with whom I was supposed to carry on most of my discussions were Donald Fleming, who didn't appreciate having to spend this amount of money, and Douglas Harkness, who was from Alberta, and Alberta wasn't at all keen about the South Saskatchewan Dam. But I must say that Diefenbaker stood firm. When I left him that first morning, after he told me the arrangements had been made for me to discuss matters with Fleming and Harkness separately, I said, 'You know, I may run into some difficulties, and am I at liberty to call you?' He said, 'Of course.' So I did call him and we had a decisive meeting in his office where we got the whole matter settled – the four of us, Diefenbaker, Fleming, Harkness, and myself.

The South Saskatchewan Dam had first been suggested in Parliament by M.J. Coldwell, who in 1938 asked that a commission be established to study the feasibility of the project. During the Second World War, the three opposition members from Saskatchewan, Coldwell, Douglas, and Diefenbaker, were generally agreed on this and other measures to help the farmers, including payment for farm-stored grain. At the time, there was a surplus of wheat, and Tommy Douglas remembered big posters on the country elevators saying, 'Help win the war by growing less wheat.'

Thomas Clement Douglas helped to found three socialist parties in Canada: the Farmer Labour Party of Saskatchewan in 1931; the Co-operative Commonwealth Federation in 1933; and its successor, the New Democratic Party in 1961.

Douglas was born on 20 October 1904 in Falkirk, Scotland. He came to Canada as a youth, worked in his late teens for a printer, won the lightweight amateur boxing championship of Manitoba, and then studied at Brandon College and McMaster University. As an undergraduate he won gold medals in debating, dramatics, and oratory. His studies were in religion, and at Brandon College he became a student minister in the Baptist Church.

His first pastorate was at Weyburn, Saskatchewan, in 1930. During the depression, a number of clergyman joined radical movements; those who ran for office and were defeated were often dismissed by their churches. Douglas was successful, winning a seat in the House of Commons as a CCF candidate

in 1935. For twenty-five years he represented Weyburn, first in Parliament
and then in the Saskatchewan Legislature. From 1944 to 1961 he was prem-
ier of the province.

There had been a good deal of popular support for building the South
Saskatchewan Dam even before the war, but Douglas had found it impos-
sible to negotiate, with successive Liberal governments, an agreement that
would provide the essential federal funding.

T.C. DOUGLAS

While Mr Diefenbaker, in the election campaign, talked about building the
dam, he was not going to let us off any easier than the commitments we had
made to the St Laurent government. He insisted that we carry out the original agreement: we would pay for the levelling, the lateral ditches, the drain-
age, the irrigation work, and 25 per cent of the main reservoir. The question
came: who was going to be responsible for building the dam? I took the
position that if we were going to build the dam jointly then we would take
our 25 per cent right through. But if the federal government was going to
build the dam – that's what both Mr Harkness and Mr Fleming preferred,
and certainly it is much simpler to have one government build the dam rather
than to have two governments trying to do it jointly   my contention was that
since we would have no control of the expenditures that there should be a
limit on our participation. I suggested that the 25 per cent should be limited
to the $100 million estimate which both the PFRA [Prairie Farm Rehabilita-
tion Administration] and ourselves had agreed was a reasonable amount. I
thought it was a reasonable position to take. As a matter of fact it turned
out to be quite good because the reservoir cost less than $100 million. The
officials then worked out the details and modifications of the agreement,
which I had brought down with me, and finally Mr Harkness and I.C. Nollet,
provincial minister of agriculture, and myself signed the agreement.

The dam was completed in the mid-sixties. We didn't have any illusions
that this was going to suddenly transform Saskatchewan into a paradise, but
it was going to do several things. It was going to create a body of water 124
miles long and 5 miles wide. This set up convection currents, and evapora-
tion from convection currents increases the rainfall and provides water for
farmers. It makes possible irrigation. Irrigation will not come easily because
our farmers are not trained in irrigation, but we set up a small irrigation unit
in the university to train agricultural students in farming under irrigation
conditions.

The advantages to agriculture will continue. If we ever hit a drought
again – and anybody is foolish to think droughts are over, all the records for

the Palliser triangle indicate that there will be recurring periods of drought – it would mean in Saskatchewan that we would be able to grow sufficient feed to enable farmers to keep their basic herds alive. Few people realize that the terrible tragedy of the thirties wasn't for the grain farmer – the grain farmer could stop growing grain and wait until the rains came back to start growing again – but for the cattle man who had to let even his basic herds go.

Then there is the whole question of water supply. The consumption of water for domestic purposes and industrial purposes is going up in geometric progression. There is just no hope for industry and no hope for having large towns unless you have water supply. Moose Jaw was a place where they just didn't have enough water. By diverting water down into the Souris River (the South Saskatchewan also controlled the Souris River), we made places like Moose Jaw and Regina viable communities because now they could get water. In time that whole Qu'Appelle Valley could have an increased water supply which would enable towns all along there to get water.

So, from the standpoint of agriculture, from the standpoint of industrial and urban development, in addition to the recreational aspect, the value of having a huge lake in the centre of what was a veritable desert is tremendous. Power was the fourth factor. Saskatchewan had only limited sources of power. Two possible sources of power were to put a dam on the South Saskatchewan River and to put a series of dams on the North Saskatchewan. This has now been done.

ALVIN HAMILTON

I was there [during the negotiations for the South Saskatchewan Dam], but my views were simply unacceptable to Clarence Fines [Provincial Treasurer of Saskatchewan] and Tommy Douglas on one side, and Diefenbaker and Harkness on the other. I wanted to set up a corporation where we took all the resources of the area, fishing, recreation, water, and power, and put them into a corporative type of set-up, whereby all the revenues that would come from that river being dammed would be fed into this corporation. The thing could have been a money-maker for both the provincial government and the federal government. But it was done on the old basis of just putting in the taxpayers' money and not setting up a system to draw all these future revenues.

The Diefenbaker government's agricultural policy was very successful and consolidated the support of the rural ridings. Other farm-oriented legislation included the Stabilization Act, the Farm Credit Act, and the Crop Insurance Act. Douglas Harkness was agriculture minister when all these bills were introduced.

DOUGLAS HARKNESS

It put an end, for a time at least, to the feeling of alienation which existed in western Canada in so far as the East was concerned, and gave to the people of western Canada a feeling that, for the first time, their point of view, their problems, were getting full attention at Ottawa, and equal attention to that of Ontario and Quebec and so forth. Another thing is that we managed – this was part of this same thing – to put an end to the extreme discontent as far as the agricultural population was concerned, not only in western Canada but in eastern Canada.

MERRIL MENZIES

In 1957, wheat, as it so often has been in the past, was in very deep trouble. At that time, surpluses or apparent surpluses seemed to be the problem. I spent some weeks, perhaps a month or two, doing a review and analysis of the current wheat situation, and suggesting certain shorter term policies. They dealt in terms of about a five-year period – how we could get our wheat economy in better balance. I think the analysis was pretty obvious, but it was shorter term. Quite clearly, what happened a dozen years later certainly was foreseeable by about the mid-sixties; that was that the world would be running short of food, and, as in the case of energy, the ceiling would come off, which it has done.

The immediate Canadian problems at that time were wheat surpluses, limited markets, extreme American competition through Public Law 480 and various other measures. And the cloud on the horizon was the development of the Common Market, which was obviously going to be very protective.

Quite clearly we had to get wheat supplies in better balance with the demand, taking into account the realities of world competition at the time. What I was proposing was that there was no quick solution – no quick solution through export subsidies, certainly no quick solution in terms of domestic subsidies, although clearly farmers, when they were under pressure, needed assistance. I suggested that we could, by a gradual process over five years, get wheat acreage, therefore wheat supply, in balance. And, as a matter of fact, that's pretty well how it turned out.

Now, I'm not saying that this policy was followed consciously or conscientiously as I laid it out. But in point of fact, we did get the kind of balance we have. At that time, wheat acreage was much too high in relation to apparent domestic and foreign requirements for some years ahead. I suggested if we had to in the meantime carry the surplus stocks we already had, and would have as we gradually phased out the surplus capacity, we should do it as a national cost.

There were two basic points of view. Obviously, they related to wheat, but generally to any agricultural commodity in surplus to our domestic requirements. Simply stated, if we didn't grow more than we needed, we were in a fairly strong position to influence the price to the advantage of the farmer, as most countries in the world do – and certainly this is the basis of the European common agricultural policy. But for those commodities exported, there were those who wanted to put the whole emphasis on a general agreement, a pretty broad agreement anyhow, that the farmers needed help, they needed subsidy, they needed support through public funds because they'd gone through a long, tough period of much below average incomes, certainly since '53, and they were facing really unfair international competition. Others simply came out for a very simple solution in terms of a domestic subsidy or two-price system.

Basically, our argument was that the farmers should certainly get this extra financial support, but there were obvious and distinct disadvantages to a domestic subsidy when you already had too much wheat. It would just add incentives to additional production unless one went into programs of monetary restraints, which not too many people wanted. What we were trying to get at was to expand international trade and to put all available financial assistance to farmers through the Wheat Board – if they were wheat farmers – and through programs to expand demand. Well, the domestic demand was pretty flat, but certainly there was international demand. So there were quite a number of points, and I forget all of them.

There may well have been the beginnings of the idea for which I would have to give enormous credit, the chief credit, to Alvin Hamilton, that is the whole ARDA [Agriculture Rehabilitation and Development Act] concept.

T.C. DOUGLAS

First of all, Mr Diefenbaker did a number of things that needed to be done so far as prairie agriculture was concerned: storage payments on the farms, assistance to farmers in various ways to give the farmer a greater stability of income, acreage payments to compensate for the fact that the farmer was in a cost-price squeeze, that the price of grain wasn't keeping pace with the rising cost of production. I think those helped to stabilize prairie agriculture which was badly in need of it.

Despite their agricultural programs, by 1960 the Conservatives were at their lowest ebb on the prairies. The farmers were angry – they were saying that they had given the Diefenbaker government the biggest majority in history and yet the wheat was not being sold and the price was low. There was grow-

ing concern about the discontent in the cabinet and caucus, and in time a change of ministers.

ALVIN HAMILTON

Now, I came from a rural riding and was very conscious of the discontent. We were also getting a lot of static from the experts who advised government about a theory they called supply management. This is where you turn over the decision-making power from farmers – to decide whether they grow wheat, oats, or barley or raise cattle, hogs, chickens, turkeys, vegetables, or strawberries – and you give it to a group of civil servants. That way they can get the price up. At least, this is the theory. This is the sort of nonsense that just sends me right up the wall.

I was getting very outspoken. I accused Harkness – I am not proud of it – of being the only guy in the world who could make both the city guys and the farmers mad in the same speech because he was telling the farmers there was no chance to get higher prices and he was telling these city guys that there was no chance of getting lower prices. I guess I was fighting then as an individual member of Parliament rather than as resources minister, I was warning the cabinet about what was coming up very clearly from the country and very clearly from the caucus.

Diefenbaker wanted to know, 'What do you do with all this wheat?' I said, 'Sell it. Get the price up by fifty cents a bushel. Go up to the top of the scale on the International Wheat Agreement.' Diefenbaker said, 'Who could you put in the department to do this?' I said there were lots of good men: the one who I recommended most strongly was Warner Jorgenson who was the only man I knew in the House who understood how the Wheat Board operated and was very knowledgeable about farm policy.

I was quite happy with the work I was doing in Resources but knew that I had to get a better man into Agriculture than Doug Harkness. Doug is a good farmer, and he just didn't have any use for the other guys who weren't doing as well. I had this very grave suspicion of these experts who were arguing to restrict production, because all they saw were the traditional markets in Europe where they couldn't see any improvement.

On the day of the big ministerial shake-up, I walked into the cabinet and Diefenbaker read off the list of changes. I was the first one on the list. Well, I just about dropped dead when I heard that I was moved to Agriculture. I was the last person in the world who should be in Agriculture. I didn't know anything about it. But then I said, 'If I am going to take Agriculture I will not take it without the Wheat Board because the Wheat Board is the name of the game. If you sell the wheat, everything else seems to solve itself.' To cut a long story short, I got it, and 60 per cent of my time was spent on the Wheat Board. I never did bother too much with the Department of Agriculture. I did things like the livestock and the ARDA programs but I concentrated on selling wheat.

Before he entered Parliament in 1957, Francis Alvin Hamilton had been defeated more often than John Diefenbaker. In 1938, while still in university, he was nominated the Conservative candidate for the provincial riding of Biggar, but the chances of any Tory being elected in Saskatchewan in those years were so slim that none of his sponsors would put up the $100 deposit to enable him to run. He did run in the federal election of 1945, as PC candidate for Rosetown Biggar. He was then serving with the RCAF in Burma, and he would not have got home to campaign had Diefenbaker not brought pressure to bear in Ottawa; in the event he did fairly well against the CCF leader, M.J. Coldwell, but lost. He was an unsuccessful candidate again in the federal elections in 1949 in Rosetown Biggar and in 1953 in Qu'Appelle, and in the provincial elections of 1948, 1952, and 1956. It was his boast that he never lost a deposit, and in 1948 he came within 200 votes of beating the CCF highways minister. Between losses at the polls, he was provincial leader and organizer of the Progressive Conservative party in Saskatchewan. He changed its image by bringing in members of many ethnic groups and making them officers of what had been an exclusively Anglo-Saxon party.

As agriculture minister, Hamilton was depicted as an amiable hayseed, and he seemed to go out of his way to look like a country boy, but he never was a farmer. As a politician he was primarily interested in Canada's great storehouse of minerals and energy and was co-author of the resources policy at the PC convention in 1956.

But he made his name as agriculture minister because of the sale of grain to China. Under an agreement that was renewed several times, the Chinese bought, during the first three years, approximately 240 million bushels of wheat and barley, worth about $425 million.

ALVIN HAMILTON

Gordon Churchil, who had the Wheat Board before me, said that there had been a guy in Hong Kong, C.M. 'Max' Forsyth-Smith, writing letters all the time, asking permission to go into China to see if he could sell wheat. Naturally, the civil servants would write back and say, 'You can't sell wheat to China because China raises five billion bushels – that would be like selling coal to Newcastle.' I asked for that correspondence from Trade and Commerce, and I sent out a direct request that he and a representative of External Affairs, a fellow by the name of Small [C. John Small], should go to China.

They went for six weeks and they got a very courteous reception – but that was all.

At least, the Chinese knew that we were peddling grain, and we didn't know at that time that they were in trouble with their grain and vegetable production. I would think that was the end of November, 1960. Then, just before Christmas there was a phone call from the Queen Elizabeth Hotel in Montreal, from an agitated clerk at the desk, to say that there were two gentlemen there from Peking who wanted to talk to me.

They had flown right through to Montreal, the end of the CPA run. I knew what that meant, that our throwing our hook into the water had caught us a bite. Our main concentration at that time had been on Algeria, Egypt and Italy; they all wanted our grain but were trying to get around the difficulties – protectionist elements in Italy and Algeria, and in Egypt it was a question of whether they could get it from us for nothing. We wanted to sell it to them. I wasn't for giving away wheat.

So we got this nibble. I stood up and was punching buttons calling in my staff, and telling the hotel to get these fellows into the best suite, and organizing a plane. I didn't go to Montreal, but a couple of fellows on the staff went there and entertained them and took them to Winnipeg to talk to the Wheat Board. Then, the first decision was whether to let anybody know that two Chinese were here and were negotiating with us. I knew the fat would be in the fire if that came out. The McCarthy period was just barely slowing down in the United States, and any person who had anything to do with the Communists was really labeled, so we decided to keep it quiet.

I never met the two Chinese, and I don't know how they arrived. They didn't come through government-to-government at all. They just came in as travellers. They were from the China Cereals Corporation, and they had $63 million in letters of credit. They wanted to know how much grain they could buy with this amount.

The Chinese finally agreed on so much wheat and so much barley – I think it was about forty million bushels, twenty-eight million bushels of wheat and twelve million of barley. They wanted volume. That only told me one thing: they wanted bellies to be fed. Within two weeks of that deal being signed, I sent the two top men in the Wheat Board, W.C. McNamara and W. 'Bill' Riddel, to Peking. They were to phone me, and we arranged for a code, a football language: the Winnipeg Blue Bombers were at the Saskatchewan Rough Riders. How are they making out? A play-off tackle here and we made a few yards; the blockers fell down and we lost a couple here. This is how we described the various moves. In essence, the situation was that they wanted wheat but they had no money. I said, 'Stay there and keep talking. How much do you want?' McNamara said, 'Fifty million to get the ball rolling.'

I finally got a hundred million, but cabinet took six weeks trying to decide. Diefenbaker did not participate in the discussion, but others did. You've got all the economic reasons, you've got all the political reasons why we shouldn't do it. I argued most extensively on the economic reasons, that we could reduce the payment on the Temporary Wheat Reserves Act, we could get the price up by selling that amount of grain, we could get more money. I said that all we were risking in any one time was $50 million in the revolving fund, and that we were spending that much money on storing wheat uselessly. Then, if we only got paid for one year, $50 million would be covered by the amount we saved on the Temporary Wheat Reserves Act.

I wrote my resignation out and the prime minister read it to the cabinet. In the letter of resignation, I said the whole argument was whether the Chinese would pay. The civil service said that we shouldn't give them credit because they hadn't paid for those Ming Sun ships, and until they paid back the debts of a previous government, we shouldn't have any dealing with them. This was the financial advice that we got. In any case, Diefenbaker just read out my resignation and said, 'I think if a minister is willing to put his portfolio on the line for something that he believes in, offering to resign in the case that they don't pay, we should back him.' That is what prime ministers are for. We are all equal, except at that moment. So Diefenbaker should really get the credit for making the political decision.

This, the political response, was the great fear that we had. I talked to Hungarian taxi drivers in Montreal, I talked to ethnic people whom I knew in Toronto about their reaction to wheat being sold to a Communist country without naming the country, and I didn't think that the reaction would be that bad. There is no doubt that there was mounted against us, at that time, the greatest whispering campaign among the ethnic groups, and in the editorials of the ethnic papers, that we were playing footsie with the Communists all over the world. But we took that political gamble.

I had an idea how big the sale was. We were aware that there was going to be great difficulty in getting the grain out of the country, and, in this field, the members of the Wheat Board were particularly astute. They were great diplomats in the Wheat Board. They didn't have any power to boss the railways around or the terminals or the stevedores or the men that work in the terminals or the government departments. You have to persuade everybody when you're on the Wheat Board. I got all these people who said we couldn't move it out of the west coast at a meeting. The Wheat Board arranged that they picked a chairman. In five days, those working men gave us all sorts of ways to move grain, and they guaranteed eighteen million bushels a month. That is all I wanted, and in one month they actually put twenty-nine million bushels through, so that productivity *can* be achieved – and *management* can't give you productivity – by the working man who knows how to get the job done.

That conference also produced a no-strike pledge. Since all the extra money that was coming into the hands of management was all buckshee, I insisted that 10 per cent, $1,500,000 out of the $15,000,000 a year, be given as a bonus to all the guys working. At least, there was no strike as long as that continued. There was no strike for five years on the docks because we gave them a productivity payment.

This was the biggest single deal ever made up to then. Furthermore, it was a brand-new market which gave hope to the farmers because all they were getting was brainwashing from the governments on the prairies and from the farm organizations and from the farm business that there was no future in growing grain. As we sold, we kept raising the price; we got the price up from $1.60 to about $2.10 to $2.19 a bushel. And then, to make the whole thing ridiculous, in the spring of 1962 the Wheat Board said that there was no more grain: we couldn't sell any more. The so-called 'tremendous' surplus wasn't there! Thank Heavens, before it all went we sold it at a good price. But I said, 'Keep on selling.' For the only time in the Wheat Board's history they sold below their level of 250,000,000 bushels in storage. I asked the farmers to grow all they could. That year was a good year for us and we made enough to get by that winter of '62 to '63, and the next year '63 was a good year – so we got away with five good years. That was the only good time that the farmers had known since the twenties – their income went up three times from $2000 a year average to $6000 a year. Now, $6000 isn't much of an income for a big farm operation but the farmers thought that was a heck of a lot better than $2000.

This was the story of that wheat deal. When I spoke in the House I gave the credit to these two junior civil servants, C.J. Small and Forsythe-Smith; but I also said that some of the credit should go to Gordon Churchill for telling me about it.

GORDON CHURCHILL

A small point, but, you know, the initial step of trading in wheat with China was taken in the spring of 1958. It coincided with the election of 1958 and hence was overlooked. A great deal of credit goes to our trade commissioner in Hong Kong, Mr Forsythe-Smith, who cabled that there was an opportunity of selling some wheat to China and asked what response should be made.

Although at that time there wasn't unanimous approval of trading with China, I thought, as we were trading with Russia and Poland in wheat and they were Communist countries, I couldn't see any difference in selling wheat to China. And then, we wanted to get rid of our surplus. So I authorized the sale of wheat to China. Eight cargoes were actually despatched and paid for very promptly. Nothing much happened for another three years, but that was the initial breakthrough, and Mr Forsythe-Smith was the man who drew our attention to it.

Had there not been an election campaign on, there might have been quite a bit of public interest in the sale to China. And there might have been quite a bit of criticism. But my job, being responsible to the Wheat Board, was to assist them in any way possible to get rid of the surplus of wheat, and I couldn't see anything wrong in selling wheat to China. So that was the small step that was taken and led eventually to the massive sales.

HOWARD GREEN

As far as the wheat deal with China was concerned, Canada was in a very difficult position. We were paying for grain stored on the farms on the prairies, not only stored in elevators but stored right out on the fields of the farmers, and it was costing us a great deal of money. It was a very serious situation for the economy of the prairie provinces, and, in fact, for the whole of Canada. It was one of the great drains on our finances. Canada, as you know, depends on external trade to a far greater degree than any other country in the world. So when there was an opportunity to sell wheat to Red China, we took it. The Chinese were very grateful to us for getting them the wheat. For about a quarter of them the basic staple food is wheat; for the other three-quarters it is rice. I remember an evening I spent in Geneva with Chen-yi, the foreign minister of China, in 1962. He was very profuse in his thanks to us for selling them wheat. He said, 'The Americans wouldn't sell us wheat. We couldn't get it anywhere. We didn't have facilities for storing it in China and we are very grateful to Canada for selling us wheat.' I didn't tell him how grateful we were to them for buying it! But it certainly worked both ways. I don't think anybody has ever objected to Canada selling wheat to China.

ALVIN HAMILTON

You know, the Americans knew about the Chinese wheat deal long before the Canadian people heard about it. We did this so they had no grounds to complain about being kept in the dark. Actually there was no complaint then. About two years later, in 1962, somebody in the United States raised a howl that Canadian companies were buying American grain pumps to put onto ships to speed up the delivery of the grain. At that time China didn't have the modern grain-handling facilities that she has now.

There is an American law which says that the executives of a company or a corporation in the United States can go to jail for ten years if they trade with the enemy. Kennedy was caught. He had to say that the law would be enforced. However, since we had bought the pumps, we could have the last three or four of them and that was the end of it. Diefenbaker was awfully tough on that pump deal. He said that they had been informed throughout and that we were buying these pumps in good faith. He said he didn't give a damn what their laws were – this was a business deal and they had been making pumps for us for two years. Anyway, the compromise was that we got our pumps from the last order but didn't order any more.

9
Public and official relations

The success of a prime minister depends in great measure on his relations, not only with his colleagues in the cabinet but also with the public, the party, and the press through which he reaches the country. Much also depends on how well he and his cabinet work with the civil service which advises on government policy and implements it.

Of all political leaders, John Diefenbaker was perhaps the most concerned with what the public thought of him and his government. His antennae were constantly tuned to the grass roots and he paid a great deal of attention – too much, in the view of his critics – to his mail. At the same time he was scrupulous in his relations with the Progressive Conservative party. He saw the national director, Allister Grosart, regularly, but the meetings usually were held in his official residence, rather than in the prime minister's office. At all times he kept government and party at arm's length. With the press, his relations had been warm throughout his years as an MP; but once he became prime minister, they began to deteriorate.

In its relations with the civil service the Diefenbaker government had some difficulties. All the deputy ministers had been appointed by Louis St Laurent's government and, in fact, most Ottawa officials had known only a Liberal government. It would not have been unnatural for them to adopt a contemptuous disregard for the rump of Conservatives who were always changing leaders and never getting anywhere: Canada was as close to being a one-party state as a Western democracy could be. As Senator Eugene Forsey, in an interview, said, there was a natural tendency for the civil service to identify itself with the ruling party. What shocked him was that this affected the brightest and best.

Corridor press conference outside the cabinet room in the East Block

Senator Forsey said that people who dealt with the government, such as officials of the Canadian Labour Congress for whom he worked, had more or less the same attitude as the civil service. They had become used to the Liberals and could not believe that they could be replaced. He recalled a conversation which he had with Claude Jodoin, president of the CLC, shortly after the Conservatives came to power. There was a vacancy in the Congress, and names were being discussed. Jodoin said that there were a number of positions vacant – labour attaché in Brussels, assistant deputy minister of labour, labour representative on the Unemployment Insurance Commission, and so on. Subsequently Forsey wished he had warned the CLC president that John Diefenbaker would not simply accept Congress recommendations; if he had given the warning, some of the subsequent coolness between the Congress and the Conservative government might have been avoided. But many officials did seem to think that they could go on acting as if there had not been a change of government; or perhaps they believed the 1957 results were just an aberration, and that in a short time the Liberals would be back in power.

EUGENE FORSEY

After the new government of Mr Diefenbaker had taken office early in July, there was a garden party at the British High Commissioner's residence. Donald MacDonald, who became president of the Canadian Labour Congress, happened to pass near two very high officials, one a deputy minister and the other of the same rank, and, without any intention of eavesdropping, he could not avoid hearing them say: 'Well of course during the interregnum, such and such and such and such. Naturally, we should be back in a short time.' They quite confidently assumed that the electorate would recoil in horror from what it had done, that it had merely intended to give the Liberals a mild reproof by reducing their majority and, on discovering that it had destroyed the majority, would repent in sack cloth and ashes at the earliest possible opportunity and put the Liberals back in again.

Senator Forsey described as cosy the relationship that existed between some portions of the civil service and such pressure groups as the Canadian Labour Congress and the Liberal party. He had heard of one deputy minister who passed on information to the Liberal leader, L.B. Pearson, as soon as it became available and 'sometimes before the minister had seen it.' And he recounted a ludicrous little incident which he considered illustrative of official attitudes when the Conservatives were in power. It had been told him by his friend, Gowan Guest, the Vancouver lawyer who had the longest service as executive assistant to Prime Minister Diefenbaker. The story was confirmed by Guest.

EUGENE FORSEY

One day, Gowan Guest and Mr Diefenbaker were coming out of the prime minister's office, and they looked down into the foyer of the House of Commons. There was Mackenzie King's portrait and Borden's, and Mackenzie King's was resplendent in a blaze of light, while Borden's was in half-shadow. Gowan was aroused. He said, 'This is outrageous, this has got to be changed.'

Mr Diefenbaker said, 'Gowan, you can try if you want to but I tell you the system will beat you.' Gowan said, 'Well, I am going to try.' So he went around to the Department of Public Works and said, 'This has got to be changed.' They admitted that there was a hundred-watt bulb over King's portrait and a forty-watt bulb over Borden's but they said that thin was it and that nothing could be done about it. Gowan said, 'I will give you until Thursday' – this was a Monday or Tuesday – 'to change that and if it's not changed by Thursday I will call in the newspapers and tell them the whole story.' He had been shuffled around from one official to another until he finally got to the deputy minister, and had got the same run-around from all. Well, they blanched a little at this ultimatum.

On Thursday, he and Mr Diefenbaker came out of the office, looked down, and there was King still beaming in a vast blaze of light and there was Borden still in shadow. Gowan hit the roof, promptly went to the telephone, and said, 'What's all this? I told you that you had to change that.'

'Oh yes, Mr Guest. We changed the bulb. Yes, yes. Sir Robert's got a – '

'Well, it doesn't look like it.'

'Oh, well, you can go down and investigate for yourself. Get a ladder and look at it.'

He did investigate and sure enough they had changed the bulb and put a stronger one over Sir Robert. 'But,' he said, 'there is still the same effect.'

'Oh, well,' they said, 'the frame on Mr King's picture had just been re-gilded.'

'But you didn't do anything about Sir Robert's frame.'

'No, the regilding comes once in so many years and Mr King's time had come for regilding and Sir Robert's hasn't.'

And Mr Diefenbaker said, 'Gowan, what did I tell you? You can't beat the system.'

Not all officials by any means were obtuse or obstructive, and some Conservative ministers had good relations with the civil service. But there was a general sense of lack of rapport which was evident to leading Liberals as

well as Conservatives and to such insiders as Gowan Guest and Roy Faibish
[Alvin Hamilton's executive assistant, who also worked for Diefenbaker].
Their explanations differed.

GOWAN GUEST

Certainly at my level, that is to say among the executive assistants, I ran into the frustrations that the Conservative party had with the civil service in volume. Diefenbaker had no idea, but I would have a couple of calls a day from the executive assistants to the whatever minister, practically all of them saying they had problems, that they were not getting cooperation, or they were having difficulty communicating, or that these people were giving them stupid reasons. I certainly saw a lot of that sort of clash. But those were small things, mostly.

I always felt the civil service did not really appreciate that the Diefenbaker Conservative group had a d'fferent feeling about what government was for and what it should be doing. They failed, in my view, in that. With rare exceptions, they made no effort to understand what the people who had been elected wanted to do.

There were notable exceptions. Basil Robinson, Bob Bryce, the people who were close to our operation, would spend hours talking with me and others – not the prime minister because they didn't use his time, but other people – in an effort to try to understand what it was that Diefenbaker was after, and how he conceived the government should be. And I know they spent hours among themselves trying to figure out what this guy was about. But that wasn't the general rule. The trouble was that most of them said, 'Well, these people don't really know what they want to do, or, if they do, it's the wrong thing.' They didn't really say it, they gave the impression that they felt it.

They weren't positively and partisanly and schemingly nasty, but they were in a position where they knew what was the best thing to do. It could be in connection with anything – the Seaway, anything. They had the position papers and the study and so on, and sometimes they'd be indifferent, and they'd let you fan the air and try to figure it out. They'd always keep coming back and saying, politely mind you, 'This problem has been analysed, and there it is.' 'You can't close that military camp,' or 'You can't do this.' Well, you can categorize the world into problem-solvers and problem-finders. The Diefenbaker government was constantly faced with the latter, and occasionally there were flare-ups.

I think the fault was, on the part of the senior civil service, that they never got on the team. On the other side, on the part of the government, the fault was that they never really invited them to be part of the team.

ROY FAIBISH

What I saw happening quite quickly was a conflict between some bureaucrats who had for many years been used to working at a certain style and a certain pace, coming in headlong collision with a bunch of politicians who had been out of power for a long time, and who wanted to really get in high gear, and move very quickly, and never mind all the legal niceties and the loose ends. It was a conflict between the established order, if you want to call it that, and a group of people who were impatient as hell.

When the civil service would say, 'Well, wait a minute, we'd better think this over twice,' or 'You'd better send it back to that specialist to look at it,' that, if you were frustrated and impatient, could easily be interpreted as, 'He's blocking me; he's not lubricating the system.' But really, it wasn't. They were doing what they had traditionally done all the time. There might have been exceptions, but, generally speaking, it wasn't motivated by political partisanship at all. It was a conflict between two bodies that were going at different rates and different speeds.

PAUL MARTIN

This was one of John Diefenbaker's greatest problems – that he hadn't been close to any of the officials. He knew few if any of them. Yet, these were the men who would be daily with him in the Privy Council office, in the office of prime minister, advising the other ministers in the various departments. These were the men that he would have to rely on. It was a very difficult situation. I can understand that. After all, Pearson and our colleagues of that time and St Laurent's time and Mr King's time were all well acquainted with the public service. They weren't all our supporters, as John imagined, but they were people whom we knew personally. He didn't know them, and it must have been very difficult.

He told me that it took him a long time to really have confidence in many of them. I think one of the first that he developed confidence in was Bob Bryce (who was then clerk of the Privy Council). I'm sure from my knowledge of the public service that he could have relied on any of them. I'm sure that any of them worked and did give him the same kind of loyalty and attention and service that we received, but it is understandable that John would feel this way.

GRATTAN O'LEARY

When Diefenbaker became prime minister, he thought External Affairs was against him. He told me so. He thought the late Norman Robertson was an enemy. Norman Robertson couldn't be an enemy of anyone. Norman was too much of a philosopher for that.

For some time, the communications from London were sent to me [by George Drew, then high commissioner] and I gave them to Howard Green. They didn't trust External Affairs, and they didn't trust some people in External Affairs.

I remember Dief calling me up on a Saturday afternoon and saying, 'I'm going down to the UN to make a speech and I haven't got a thing, I haven't got a thing.' I said to him over the phone, 'What about External Affairs? Surely they can give you something.' 'External Affairs, all they tell me is to be kind to Khrushchev.' He went to New York. On Sunday afternoon, Bunny Pound, his secretary, called me and said, 'We are in an awful way here. There is nothing but papers and scraps lying around the bed. The speech is tomorrow and we haven't got a thing. Give us something!' So I dictated for half an hour over the phone. I remember dictating his peroration.

GEORGE HEES

Everybody told me when I got into Transport: 'Now, you are surrounded by appointments made by the Liberals over twenty-two years, and what you've got to do is to clear them all out. Otherwise they will torpedo you, they will murder you, they will trick you, they will get you out of power.' I found that these people who were civil servants were out to do one thing – to help their minister, Tory, Grit, NDP, or whatever. They are proud of their charge and responsibility. I found this in all my careers of minister. I always got 100 per cent backing from all civil servants. My assistant deputy minister [C.S. Booth] was a previous Liberal member of Parliament, was defeated, and was given this job. He did a just wonderful job for me, along with everybody else.

GORDON CHURCHILL

I shifted a number of people in Trade and Commerce – about seven all told. I think I was the only cabinet minister who did. If the other fellows had done what I had done we might have been saved from some of our troubles. I brought in Jim Roberts, an outsider, and that wasn't considered cricket. You're not supposed to do that.

The reason why we made so few changes was to show that we respected the civil service and that no patronage prevailed. I think that was the basic idea. But I knew something about some of the senior men in the civil service and how close they were to the politicians, the Grit politicians, so I favoured shifting – not firing them, you know, shifting. That wasn't done, and I think it was a very serious error. One of the reasons was that our people didn't want to be ruthless. Secondly, they were inexperienced and they quickly came to rely on the assistance they got from the experienced civil servants who, the senior ones, were very experienced indeed. They found it easier to go along, and, although I passed warning signals to some of our ministers, they took no action at all.

There are some very able men in the civil service. I respect them, but their attitude in that early year, 1957, was antagonistic. I remember going over to Europe with the Wheat Board. I called in at certain embassies there, and they hadn't yet adjusted themselves to the fact that there had been a change of government – they still had the pictures of St Laurent and Mike Pearson in their offices.

WALTER DINSDALE

I recommended that three top people be changed and I did this – I came in as minister of northern affairs in '60 – on the advice of people who had been involved in the first three years of the Diefenbaker government and were aware that there was sabotage going on. They said, 'You must deal with these three people.' I contacted the prime minister, and he said, 'Wait until after 1962. We will not rock the boat at the present time.' I was asked to deliver a memorandum which indicated my wishes in this regard. I think that memorandum was lost and got into the hands of members of the top echelon of the civil service. From '62 to '63 the attitude was not only uncooperative, it was outright hostility.

Political booby traps were constantly being laid. I had been in Parliament long enough to know what political booby traps were. I would say, 'This is political dynamite.' The reply would be 'Well, we aren't concerned with the politics of the thing. We just go on with the principles of the policy.' Then, there were always negatives. We were trying to initiate something and a memorandum would come in outlining why it couldn't be done. I would say, 'I want to know how it can be done, not why it can't be done.' This was a real problem.

I have heard that there were meetings in Ottawa that were plotting the downfall of the Diefenbaker government. I know when I was on the campaign trail [in 1962] I was constantly being pursued by certain departmental officials confronting me with crises that I must deal with immediately. Such nonsense.

J.W. PICKERSGILL

A modern complicated government cannot be operated without experts, and it cannot be operated without a good relationship of confidence both ways, between the majority of the senior public servants and the ministers. That did not exist, with one or two exceptions, in the Diefenbaker government. They regarded the public servants, quite wrongly, in my view, as a collection of Liberals who were working against them. They didn't believe they were getting honest advice and they didn't understand it when they got it.

This is a reason for their failure – it may have been because they had been in opposition so long and because they didn't have much talent in Parliament.

Now they had all those Senate vacancies to fill. If Diefenbaker had been really clever he would have got rid of all those old stagers – they were good backbenchers and could be counted on to vote right but they weren't much – and got a collection of A-1 candidates to run in the '58 election and re-made his cabinet. There was a great opportunity there that was missed.

Even sillier was this whole business of Mitchell Sharp. He had no desire to leave the government. I remember very well talking to Mitchell right after the '57 election, and one couldn't escape the impression that he was looking forward to something new and something interesting.

I don't know – there may have been one or two people, but most of the public servants I knew behaved in exactly the way I told my staff to behave when I had a meeting with them before I resigned. I said, 'You have been very loyal to me and I expect you to be equally loyal to the new government. They are the government, I am not, and I don't want any tales from any of you.' I never listened to any gossip or any secret information or any leaks from the public servants during the whole time I was in opposition.

GRATTAN O'LEARY
The first thing I would have done if I had been prime minister would have been to fire Mitchell Sharp. Just like that. And two or three others.

The central figure in the confrontation of the civil service with the Conservative government was Mitchell Sharp, who had been appointed deputy minister of trade and commerce by the Liberals just before the 1957 election and took charge only under the Conservatives. His departure in the spring of 1958 was something of a cause célèbre. He resigned at the same time as George McIvor, chairman of the Wheat Board, and W.O. Bennett, head of Atomic Energy of Canada. All three had been closely associated with C.D. Howe.

Mitchell William Sharp was born in Winnipeg on 11 May 1911. He was forced to leave school at the age of fourteen but his education continued and in 1934 he graduated from the University of Manitoba. He became a grain economist with James Richardson and Son, studied for a year at the London School of Economics, and in 1942 joined the federal civil service. Clifford Clark, then deputy minister of finance, offered him a job, saying they needed someone familiar with western affairs. After the war, Sharp stayed on to head

the economic policy division of the Department of Finance. Then, in 1950,
C.D. Howe, minister of trade and commerce, persuaded him to join his de-
partment as associate deputy minister.

Two months after the 1958 election, Sharp went to see Gordon Churchill,
the new Conservative minister, and asked whether he should accept an offer
of a job as vice-president of Brazilian Traction, Light, and Power. Churchill
said, 'Yes.' Within two years of Sharp's leaving the public service his old
friend and colleague, Mike Pearson, asked him to organize a Liberal Thinkers'
Conference in Kingston in 1960. In 1963 he was elected to Parliament as a
Liberal.

ROY FAIBISH

One of the earliest cabinet committees, consisting of Harkness, Hamilton,
and Churchill, was set up to deal with the huge carry-over of grain of three-
quarters of a billion bushels. Mitchell Sharp was asked to prepare draft
legislation to help the farmers by giving them cash advances on their unsold
crop. He came back and said, 'The previous government asked our advice
on the same matter not very long ago. We considered it, and studied it, and
we gave them our advice, and the advice, in fact, was, "No." It was too great
a risk. You couln't police the thing. The farmers would steal it. When the
grain could be sold, they'd find it had disappeared. They'd have bootlegged
it across the border. And there'd be nothing there. And how would you ever
collect your money? The Federal Treasury would be out by –' A complete
misunderstanding of the whole wheat situation, no knowledge at all. Remarkable, for a man of Mr Sharp's background, who did understand something about wheat, and came from Winnipeg. But, anyway, the upshot of it
was: 'The previous government had asked our advice, we studied it, we
reported back to them, and Mr Ministers, they took our advice.' Now, he
didn't say that in a provocative way. Just a straightforward way. Mr Hamilton said, 'Yes, they took your advice and look where they are now! Now,
you people bring back the draft legislation that we want.' At the next meeting
they came back, and there it was. They had the ability to do it, and they did
it. That draft legislation, in the first speech from the Throne, became the
'cash advance' legislation, which subsequent governments, Liberal and Conservative, have even made more generous.

My point is that if you are paranoid and suspicious, you could come out
of that meeting saying, 'They didn't want to do it because they're Liberals.'
If you look at it another way, you could say, 'Well, based on their knowledge,
their experience, what had happened previously, they were recommending
against it because they didn't feel that it could be supervised and monitored

in such a way that the federal treasury wouldn't end up $150 million in the hole. And they're being, in narrow terms, quite responsible.' But another guy looking at it could say, 'Well, you know, okay, that's because they're out of touch.' That was the problem. They were out of touch with how the system worked, with the mentality of the farmers. Hamilton saw that it wasn't partisanship. He saw that they were simply out of touch.

You can see how easy it was for two men coming out of the same meeting to draw totally different conclusions – one, that Sharp was partisan, and the other, that he was out of touch. It was the latter.

Unfortunately, it's true that Mr Churchill had been in the House all those years when Howe had been in there. They had some scars, some battles. He didn't feel easy with Sharp, as an individual, as he should have. And rightly or wrongly, he gave Mr Sharp no encouragement to stay.

Sharp had no intention of leaving. He didn't want to leave. Had he stayed, if there had've been compatibility – not political compatibility, just compatibility – he would have done an excellent job.

EUGENE FORSEY

As far as Mr Sharp is concerned, I had the curious experience of talking, shortly after he resigned as deputy minister, with Dick Petrie, a professor at the University of New Brunswick. He was very close to Hugh John Flemming down there, and he was quite a power behind the scene in the Conservative party. He was a long-time close friend of Mitchell Sharp and also of Gordon Churchill. He got from each of them an account of the transactions which led up to Sharp's resignation, and the accounts were totally at variance. He said, 'I have no reason to think that either of them was not telling the truth. I have always found them both exceedingly truthful people, but I am completely baffled to make out what took place. Here are these two old friends, both of whom I trust absolutely, and they give me absolutely different accounts of what took place – so I don't know.'

At all times, John Diefenbaker tried to keep apart his twin roles of prime minister of Canada and national leader of the Progressive Conservative party. He was meticulous about this, even though, as Allister Grosart recounts, it hurt him politically.

ALLISTER GROSART

I didn't see him daily. I saw Mr Diefenbaker when he wanted to see me – that was when he called me. Sometimes I would go up to his office, more often I would see him at home because it so happened that I lived almost just across the road from him when he was at 24 Sussex.

Naturally he was always concerned with the state of organization of the party. Occasionally he would ask me my judgment on policy matters, but he was very careful to always keep a complete distinction between his responsibility as the head of government and mine as the man running the party. This was again a principle with him, that in no way he wanted the two confused.

There is a rather amusing story about that. Chubby Power used to drop into my office sometimes on his way up to the Senate. One day he poked his head in when, as every government does, we were starting to get criticism in the press for this policy and that policy. He said, 'Grosart, are you afraid to read the *Globe and Mail* in the morning?' I said, 'Yes.' He said, 'Well, things haven't changed. I thought you would, because it was just the same when I had your job with Mackenzie King. You know I have been down at Queen's' – he was a visiting lecturer – 'and I am lecturing on Canadian politics and the constitution. I have been telling them how superior our system is to the American and British because we don't have a politician, a party functionary in the cabinet. The Americans and the British do. I am going back and I am going to change my tune. I am going to tell them that their system is right.'

Now this was an interesting point. Naturally the man who is running a political party is getting a feed-in from 30 to 40 per cent of the electorate. The phone is always ringing. A policy decision is announced and you hear from Alberta or Newfoundland, 'How stupid can you guys be down there?' I said, 'Look, I'm not in the cabinet but I know what you mean.' As Chubby said, both the British and Americans have a politician in the cabinet. The Americans used to call him the postmaster general. I think the British use the chancellor of the Duchy of Lancaster. He sits there and says, 'I think this would be the public reaction to this.'

I don't think there is anything wrong with that because in observing any government the first thing that you notice is that they are out of touch so soon. How can they get out of touch with the public as fast as they do? But Mr Diefenbaker would never have had anything like that. He really believed that he was elected, to put it in the corniest terms, the prime minister of all the people. He really felt that he had to be very very careful – and he was careful, I think sometimes too careful – to make his decisions in the interests of all the people and not for political reasons.

As Grosart indicated, the honeymoon with the press ended. The attacks against the Conservative government were increasing, and in 1959 there was what looked to some like a concerted campaign against Gordon Churchill, which led to his downfall as minister of trade and commerce. Churchill told me that he had been marked for destruction at a Liberal strategy meeting at the beginning of that year. Judith Robinson, political columnist of the To-ronto Telegram, *had come to warn him of this meeting, which he said had been attended by two 'well-known Grits,' Blair Fraser of* Maclean's *and Grant Dexter, associate editor of the Winnipeg* Free Press. *He had been selected, he said, because he had been the mastermind of the 1957* PC *election triumph, because he was considered anti-Quebec, and because of his treatment of Mitchell Sharp whom he called the 'white-haired boy' of the Liberal estab-lishment. It was through him, Churchill said, that the Liberals hoped to get at Diefenbaker. The controversy centred around a brief interview while he was in a trade mission in the Soviet Union.*

GORDON CHURCHILL

I guess it is the most bitter memory that I have of my parliamentary experi-ence. I have mellowed a lot since then but there are some things that I don't easily forget. That Moscow incident was intended to ruin me and drive me out of political life. I wasn't driven out, but it was really a shocking thing.

In addition to having the Department of Trade and Commerce I had a whole series of Crown companies, one of which was Atomic Energy of Can-ada and the uranium development in Canada. Prior to the Moscow incident, during the course of 1959, we had run into trouble on uranium. The Ameri-cans and the British had entered into a contract with Canada several years earlier for the purchase of large quantities of uranium, and for a few years Canada was the great producer. The Americans had an option which they could take up for further supplies later on, but in the interval they had dis-covered vast quantities of uranium in the United States. The result was that they would not then take up the option and we had a series of conferences with them. I went down to Washington on more than one occasion. We got the Americans to stretch out the contract that was then in existence over several more years so that the mines could be kept in operation and the pro-duction of uranium would continue, but of course they refused to take up the option because they were developing their own uranium mines in the United States.

Elliott Lake, the model mining town in Ontario, was the sufferer. You may recall that employment was diminished, some of the mines closed down, there was grave difficulty keeping some of them open, and this extension that we got of time with the Americans helped us quite a bit. We tried to find alternative employment for Elliott Lake. We investigated various things, the Department of National Defence looked into the matter. We tried to get some other industries to come in there and keep the community going – but nothing substantial was accomplished. So there was a very great deal of dissatisfaction and unrest in Elliott Lake.

The people of Elliott Lake came down to Ottawa to protest and a group of women appeared in Ottawa headed by a newspaper woman of Elliott Lake who was an American citizen. They met with Mr Diefenbaker. He, in his usual way, was able to persuade them that things were not quite as bad as they appeared on the surface and then he shifted them over to me in Trade and Commerce. I couldn't give them the treatment that Mr Diefenbaker had given them. I couldn't give them any assurance that the situation would improve, and they were very disappointed with the conference they had with me and with John Pallett, my executive parliamentary assistant. They went back to Elliott Lake and the discontent and the adverse publicity continued and they wanted representatives of cabinet to visit Elliott Lake, so the prime minister dragooned Mike Starr and myself to go up to Elliott Lake. I didn't like to have to go because the problem was a problem of employment. It wasn't uranium, it was employment. I thought that the Ontario ministers were the ones that should look after Elliott Lake – it was in their province – but they all ran for cover. So Mike Starr and I had to go up to Elliott Lake and we spent Saturday and Sunday there and had a very rough time of it. The people assumed that they were being very badly treated and that I was quite unsympathetic. They said I was reputed to be an ogre, whatever an ogre is.

Shortly after that I left for Moscow to sign an agreement with the Russians with regard to wheat. They had been in Ottawa three years earlier and it was a return engagement, a courtesy. Prior to leaving for Moscow, while we were at Elliott Lake, we went down to Stanrock Mine and saw the operations underground. So far, so good.

I got to Moscow, preceded by Jake Warren, who was assistant deputy minister, got into the hotel, entered the elevator, went up to the second or third floor, got off the elevator, and Jake Warren came rushing up the stairs, trailed by an American newspaperman. He introduced him to me while we were getting our bags carried into the room. He mentioned Elliott Lake, and said that he had been there at an earlier period. I said, 'Well, I have just come from there, just been down in the Stanrock Mine.' We said a few things like that with regard to Elliott Lake and he said, 'Are you going to sell uranium to Russia?' Warren and I both thought that the guy was being facetious, because I don't know how many times in the House I had mentioned the restrictions on the sale of uranium. If anybody was going to buy uranium, they had to agree that it would be used only for peaceful purposes. The statement had been made time and time again. Everybody knew that. And Russia at that period was engaged in development of bombs, and uranium was the last thing that you would mention to the Russians. You certainly wouldn't sell it to them.

At any rate it wasn't a normal press interview, it was just a casual meeting, and this fellow, [A.I.] Goldberg [of the Associated Press], asked that question, 'Are you going to sell uranium to Russia?' I said, 'We have got plenty of uranium.' And Jake Warren said, 'We're for trade,' laughing. We didn't think anything of it. That was the end of that.

A day later, the embassy in Russia advised us that a despatch had been printed in Canada to the effect that the minister of trade and commerce was negotiating with Russia for the sale of uranium to Russia.

The next day we had a proper press conference. There were six or seven members of press there and Goldberg was there, and we discussed what we were doing in Russia. We were there in connection with the sale of wheat, the wheat agreement. Nobody raised the question of uranium. Nobody said a word about it. I met Goldberg afterwards. Warren told him that I wanted to see him. I was pretty angry, and I asked him why he had sent this article back to Canada. I said, 'We thought you were joking when you mentioned uranium to us, and in any case you know the restrictions on the sale of uranium.' He admitted that he did and we had a few words. It wasn't an angry confrontation, but it was serious enough. So he sent another despatch to Canada saying that I said the whole thing was just a joke.

Apparently, the editorial writers in Canada seized on this – the minister of trade and commerce making a fool of himself over in Russia – and the cartoonists got hold of it. I didn't know anything about this until, on my way back, we stopped at Amsterdam over the weekend to have a two-day rest. Mr Diefenbaker phoned me and read over to me some of these horrible stories in the press. There I was, and I knew that I was destroyed.

On the way back on the plane, I drafted an answer which I would give on privilege in the House of Commons. When I got to Ottawa, Jake Warren, who had preceded me, rushed up to the plane to tell me of the various developments. Three or four members of the press were there and they started to question me about the stories in the Canadian newspapers which I hadn't actually seen. How can you see these things when you are overseas? It was very unsatisfactory.

Over the weekend I revised my statement and talked it over with Don Fleming. Then, in the House of Commons, I immediately rose and presented it. Pearson, who was ready to jump on me, had to put away whatever he had to say. That appeared to clear the situation up. However, the issue was raised again, two or three days later, by Doug Fisher [of the CCF] who reopened the subject and stressed in his question that Mr Goldberg had been a war correspondent. I guess I got into trouble with the press over that because, although I praised the war correspondents, I mentioned that I hadn't seen a war correspondent in the course of ten years of active service with the army. Although some war correspondents had undergone great danger, it was slightly different from a person who had served in twenty battles in Europe. The editor of the Montreal *Star*, George Ferguson, who was formerly in Winnipeg, had apoplexy. He wrote a stinker of an editorial about this. That Goldberg thing was highly destructive and I knew that my period with Trade and Commerce was ended after that. It was a planned and deliberate assault.

If that was not bad enough, then an oil paper in Calgary, which was controlled and published by a former Conservative member of Parliament, Carl Nickle, had a short article to the effect that while in Russia I had been negotiating with the Russians for the sale of oil from Russia to Canada. This was repeated by another publication in Winnipeg. The subject of oil had never been mentioned. I was over there to sign the wheat agreement and solely for that purpose. Nothing else. But who planted that story? I don't know.

I never suffered from the normal problem of being misquoted, but I suffered from what I called the planted story. That was a planted story in Moscow. It was a planted story by whoever wrote that article for Carl Nickle's publication. And I had two other incidents of planted stories like that. I was once out in Vancouver talking about everything except the merchant marine, which was not in my field at all, and a planted story appeared to the effect that the minister of trade and commerce was opposed to the development of a merchant marine. I had never mentioned the subject to anyone. And in the city of Winnipeg they were building a bridge across the Assiniboine River, right in my own area, and a story appeared to the effect that I had sabotaged the building of that bridge because, under the dominion act with regard to navigable rivers, dominion authorities have some control over what you do with navigable rivers. I had never had anything to do with that bridge over the Assiniboine. At the time that story was printed I was out in Saskatchewan and had been there for three days, so I had to threaten the *Free Press* with a suit, as well as members of the Metro Council who were making accusations against me. I suffered from that type of thing in the course of my career and I attribute it to a deliberate plan to drive me out of political life. It was not successful but it came awfully close, awfully close.

Like many another leader, John Diefenbaker had been aided and abetted in his rise to the top by the news media. For most of his political life, he had the best of relations with the press. In his opposition days in Parliament, everybody remarked on the way that he got along with the Ottawa correspondents: his door was always open, and he was always ready to be interviewed or just to sit back and chat about current events. The correspondents called him John and he encouraged the practice. Yet, after the 1958 election this good will was dissipated. Reporters and journalists became enemies. To Victor Mackie, a member of the Parliamentary Press Gallery, this transition was inevitable.

VICTOR MACKIE

It would be the end of '58, middle of '59 that the press began to be disenchanted. I wasn't disenchanted, because I knew that there was no way that John Diefenbaker could carry on a friendly relationship with the press like he'd had before. No prime minister can. It's impossible. The prime minister has to be more or less detached from the press, and he can't be on a friendly first-name basis and confiding all the state secrets to cronies of the press. It just doesn't work out. It's impossible. But there were a lot of chaps in the Gallery who felt he was being unnecessarily distant and cold and trying to mislead them. They got mad about this and built up resentments. And things went from bad to worse.

Even his own personal friends began to notice a great change in his approach. George Johnson, of Everson and Charlesworth in those days, a public relations firm in Toronto with offices in Montreal, was probably as close a personal friend as Senator Brunt. George used to come up about once every two weeks to have a personal talk with Diefenbaker and give him advice. He told me that after the second year in office Diefenbaker was no longer as friendly, as affable, or as easy to talk to. He said he seemed to get a swelled head. I don't think it was a swelled head – it was problems of office.

When he became prime minister, he tried to carry on in the same friendly way. He saw a lot of the press. Naturally, he couldn't see reporters nearly as freely as he had before because he was too busy, but if a press man or a group of press men said they wanted to see him, he would tell his staff to try and make time for them. He was very free in his comments and very frank – unusually frank, more than he should have been, I think.

I twigged very early that one of the best things for a writing man to do was to go over to the East Block and stand in the corridor outside the prime minister's office or outside the Privy Council chamber. Mr Diefenbaker would come out of the Privy Council chamber after a cabinet meeting, and if you stopped him (we had quite free access to the East Block then), he would stop and talk to you, because he liked the press, and he liked to verbally fence with the press, always. If an important issue had developed, you could question him about it and he would either answer the question directly or he'd say, 'I can't give you a comment on that; you know better than to ask me what we decide in cabinet,' and grin and make a couple of off-hand comments and disappear into his office. Eventually the crowd grew until there were maybe two dozen people standing in the corridor. Diefenbaker would make his usual comments or quips, and they would be blown up into big stories. This began to get him into trouble. I guess probably Jim Nelson warned him that this sort of practice was causing more trouble than it was worth, because some of his quips were being misinterpreted. So he decided he'd better start playing down this close association with the press.

We began to realize that the relationship had changed when there was a railway strike on. We were all in that corridor, practically the entire Press Gallery, and Diefenbaker would go into his office and go down to the room where the negotiations were taking place – I guess it was the Privy Council chamber – and then he'd come out. We'd say, 'Is there any progress towards settlement?' He'd say, 'None yet.'

Jean Leblanc was there for the Canadian Press; he was their key railway and freight rates expert. Jean and I had known John Diefenbaker for years, and we'd a very close personal relationship with him; and we always called him John. When I was president of the Gallery, I realized that this was something you mustn't do, or at least you're not supposed to do, because you respect the office, and, in order to respect the office, you adopt the address of prime minister. But this was just nonsense as far as Jean Leblanc was concerned. He always called him John and he continued to call him John.

I'll always remember when he stopped. By this time, radio was covering Parliament and there were microphones in the corridor of the East Block. John Diefenbaker would come out of these meetings, those crucial meetings where they were trying to hammer out a settlement, and Jean Leblanc, who was more or less a spokesman for the group because he represented the Canadian Press, would step forward and say, 'John, have you arranged a settlement yet?' And Diefenbaker on this occasion made a reply, 'Well, we're still working on it.' Then he went into his office, but immediately came out, called Jean Leblanc over, and said, 'I want to talk to you.' A little while later Jean came out of the prime minister's office, and we were all agog. We thought, 'Well, Jean Leblanc's got an exclusive. He's got the settlement.' We crowded around and said, 'What happened?' 'He gave me hell for calling him John. He said he's prime minister and he should be called prime minister.'

I think what bothered John Diefenbaker were the microphones. He didn't mind talking to us privately because he knew that when we wrote our stories we'd say 'the prime minister said this' or 'the prime minister did that.' But he suddenly realized this was being recorded and 'John, have you arranged a settlement?' would go out on the air waves. John Diefenbaker has a high regard for the office of prime minister, and he thinks it always should be treated with greatest respect and dignity.

Still, this incident marked a subtle change. From then on, he was 'prime minister.' He was not the friendly John Diefenbaker any more. We began to realize that he was feeling a strain in his relationships. And it began to build.

He was running into a lot of problems, the problems were being written up in the press, and he resented some of the ways they were being written up. He thought they were misinterpreted. He thought there was misinformation being spread around, and he got more and more resentful.

Then there was the tea party at 24 Sussex Drive. The members of the Parliamentary Press Gallery and others had received formal invitations to a reception held on one of the hottest days of the summer of 1958.

ELLEN FAIRCLOUGH

When you're invited to a reception in Ottawa, you don't think you are going to a tea party, you expect to get a drink. If the press had been told that they were invited to tea they would have gone and expected tea. But to be invited to a reception and be handed a tea cup – I really think that the majority of the press felt that they were being ridiculed.

I remember Charlie Lynch writing a column about the famous tea party, saying that he could just see the PM, after the gang had gone, laughing so hard his tears fell in his beer.

VICTOR MACKIE

This reception was at a time in the afternoon when everybody expected to be getting a nice, cool gin and tonic. It was a sweltering hot day, in the middle of a heat wave in the summer, and I remember going home to pick up my wife. I changed into a lighter suit because I was terribly hot, and as I came out of the house my neighbour was sitting on his lawn, relaxing with a cool gin and tonic in his hand. He said, 'Have a drink.' I said, 'Oh no. I'm going over to 24 Sussex and I'm going to be having drinks there.' When my wife and I arrived, George Nowlan was behind us. He was then minister of national revenue. George quipped about the terrible heat and what a heck of a day it was. Olive and John Diefenbaker were standing in the receiving line. I commented on the heat, and John had a big smile on his face and he said, 'Yes, isn't it a terrible day?'

We moved on and, as soon as we passed through, Nowlan, who was a very abrupt man, said, 'Well now, let's have a good cool drink, Vic.' He saw a chap in a white jacket, carrying a tray, and he said, 'Bring me a long, tall, cool one – gin and tonic.' The fellow said, 'I'm sorry sir, there's only hot tea.' Nowlan said, 'What?' He said, 'We're serving hot tea, that's all, sir, or lemonade.' I'll never forget to my dying day: Nowlan turned to me and said: 'To hell with this,' and he turned on his heel and walked out. I didn't have the guts to do that. I stayed with my wife. I had a cup of hot tea with the perspiration rolling off my forehead. Then we beat a retreat.

I've often wondered why John did that. He did it as a lark, I think. This was his way with the press. He liked to play jokes. But he didn't realize that there were a lot of newcomers. This is the thing about the Gallery: it's ever-changing. New faces appear, and new people who don't know the man, and they react differently. I knew Diefenbaker and I knew this was a typical kind of thing Diefenbaker would do. He'd say, 'Oh, you fellows have got a reputation of being heavy drinkers. Well, we'll make sure that we protect your liver on this occasion.'

Senator Grosart said this was not his idea. He said, 'I knew we were in trouble over that, and I tried to talk him out of it, but there was no way. The Old Chief's eyes twinkled, "Give them hot tea; it will be good for them." '

The tea party was one of the contributing factors to the growing rift between him and the press because most reporters felt this was one more indication of Diefenbaker saying, 'Well, the press don't really matter to me; I don't have to worry about whether you like me or don't like me.'

10
For Commonwealth and trade

If there was any difference between the Conservatives and Liberals in external outlook, it was that the Tories were more pro-British, pro-Commonwealth. Prime Minister Diefenbaker was certainly pro-British, although the attachment seemed to be to the British connection, the Crown, and parliamentary government, more than to the British themselves, as they were to find out. His strongest feelings were for the larger body, the Commonwealth. Howard Green, who became external affairs minister following the death of Sidney Smith, said that Diefenbaker and he were the two strongest pro-Commonwealth men in the party.

Less than a month after becoming prime minister, Mr Diefenbaker had hurried off to London to attend a conference of Commonwealth prime ministers, and in November 1958, with a giant majority behind him in Parliament, he set off on a round-the-world tour to visit other Commonwealth partners. The trip included such non-Commonwealth cities as New York, Paris, Bonn, and Rome, as well as London, Karachi, New Delhi, Colombo, Kuala Lumpur, Singapore, Sydney, and Dunedin. Besides Prime Minister and Mrs Diefenbaker, the official party included: Elmer Diefenbaker, the PM's brother; Dr. P.B. Rynard, MP for Simcoe East, the party's physician; Basil Robinson, liaison officer with External Affairs; Gowan Guest, Mr Diefenbaker's executive assistant; James Nelson, his press officer; Marion Wagner, his secretary; an RCMP security officer; Don Longchamps, steward; an official photographer; and two pressmen, Alan Donnelly of Canadian Press, and Bill Neville of British United Press. There was a double air crew and a conducting officer, an RCAF wing commander who did some administrative work and acted as aide-de-camp to the prime minister.

Hees and the trade commissioners at the export trade promotion conference

JAMES NELSON

We flew in the c5, a marvellous old plane. There were berths. The prime minister's suite at the back of the plane was made up into beds for the three or four who were there. There were two or three berths that could be made up in the front of the plane if you were tired enough and bitchy enough to demand one, or if you weren't well. I came down with a fever and I had a berth for the last part of the trip, but other than that it was sitting up all the time.

London – I think we spent two or three days there. It would have been Prime Minister Macmillan then. There was a dinner at 10 Downing Street followed by a large reception. Mr Diefenbaker spoke in Royal Albert Hall. Then, on to Bonn, where he had talks with [Konrad] Adenauer. He was quite an admirer of Adenauer as a politician. Diefenbaker, being an excellent politician himself, liked other good politicians. In Paris, there was a meeting at the Elysée with de Gaulle. Next to Rome, where there were meetings with the premier, whoever he was at the time, but more particularly an audience with the Pope. This was Pope John (xxiii), who had just taken office. As a matter of fact, at the time we left Ottawa, it wasn't even clear whether Pope John would be ready to receive visitors. We flew overnight to Teheran from Rome, and arrived early in the morning at which time they had an official breakfast for us at the airport. I can't recall whether the prime minister went downtown, but I know the rest of us didn't leave the airport. On to Karachi, Peshawar, the Khyber Pass, where Elmer was very anxious to walk across the border into Afghanistan, but was deterred.

They are much alike, official tours. Dinners and banquets and exchanges of views, as they call them. No doubt they were very worthwhile but, as far as the reporters and myself were concerned, it was a delightful world tour. I wasn't particularly burdened – except in some cases we were not always able to stay in the same quarters. For instance, in Kandy in Ceylon five or six stayed at the official guest house. The rest, including the reporters, stayed downtown. So I had to brief the boys on what happened.

In India, there were visits with Nehru. The PM got an honorary degree at the University of Delhi where the recipient wears a brilliant red satin academic robe, the satin robe that Diefenbaker is shown wearing in the picture in the foyer of the Centre Block of the Parliament Buildings. Then we flew to Agra to see the Taj Mahal, and we flew on to – the name of the place escapes me. But it was to go tiger hunting on the river there which was lined by very steep cliffs. At the bottom of the cliffs there was a little fringe of shrubbery and then the water. The night before a tiger hunt, they would stake out a bullock in the shrubbery, and if during the night the bullock was killed by a tiger, the tiger was supposed to stay in the vicinity for the next night and a second meal from the carcass. So you floated down the river in a boat. There were runners out flushing the tiger out of the shrubbery, supposedly. The party was divided into two – one group in the very modern yacht, cruiser type, and the second in an old, gassy, exhaust-ridden thing that had been built for King George and Queen Mary's jubilee visit to India. We did not shoot a tiger. We didn't even see one. We were then told that it was the wrong time of year – the tigers were more interested in finding other tigers than staying around for a second feed on the carcass.

GOWAN GUEST

In the latter stages of the trip, it almost became a medical officer of health problem. Jim Nelson contracted Asian flu or something, and was in bad shape, and people were dropping off – 40 days and 40 nights of big banquets, and rich food, and no exercise, and so on. But Diefenbaker was incredible. The only time his health flagged at all was one morning in New Delhi. He cancelled one meeting and stayed in his room. Even then, he was working on a speech. But the staff people were falling off right, left, and centre, and I had to collect bodies and find local doctors and so on.

In 1960 South Africa became a republic and, since it no longer recognized the sovereignty of the Queen, had to apply for continued membership in the Commonwealth. The application was discussed at the Commonwealth Prime Ministers' Conference which opened in London on 8 March 1961. The question was originally whether to admit another republic to the Commonwealth but was quickly changed to one of extending membership to a country governed by white supremacists who maintained a colour bar as official policy. John Diefenbaker sided with the six Asian and African prime ministers in refusing to accept South Africa as a continuing member; as a result, South Africa withdrew its application. Diefenbaker's opposition to the membership of South Africa in the Commonwealth was an outstanding policy initiative; however, it was not popular. There were large Canadian business interests in that country, and residual sentiment for the old sense of Empire.

ALVIN HAMILTON

I don't think there is any question about it that when that issue of South Africa came up, the great majority – in fact almost all – the cabinet were against him. Before he went to the Commonwealth Prime Ministers' Conference, I took a strong stand on the racial issue. He didn't say what he was for, but I said to him that if he had done anything in his whole life, it was as a protector of minority groups, of ethnic groups, of any group of disadvantaged, working men, farmers, older people, younger people; his whole life had been based on that principle. He shouldn't give it up because, not the great majority, but almost all the cabinet felt that we shouldn't interfere and let this type of thing go on.

When the debate was going on in London, he called Ottawa and said, 'Has Alvin changed his mind yet?' It was Howard Green who took the call and asked if I had changed my mind. I said, 'No, I am not going to see him destroyed.' He said, 'That's all I want to know.' He went ahead and took that position and Pearson took it after him.

PAUL MARTIN

After the Prime Ministers' Conference, I attacked Diefenbaker as being the cause of South Africa's retirement from the Commonwealth. Of course, he denied this. I must say that I was wrong in my attack. Diefenbaker had not initiated South Africa's withdrawal. This story is well and fully told by Harold Macmillan in the third volume of his memoirs. But Diefenbaker could have played a more effective part, not in being untrue to his opposition to apartheid, but in recognizing, as a Commonwealth man, how important it was that she be kept in. Prior to that conference, when South Africa indicated that she wasn't going to stay in, I think that if he had got together with Macmillan and with Nehru in particular, they could have worked out some arrangement. But Diefenbaker fell in too quickly with Nehru and some of the others in making it impossible at that conference for South Africa to do anything but what she did.

Prime ministers, when they go to those gatherings, have to be prepared to find accommodations for situations without betraying their principles. No one could give in to their strong and legitimate opposition to apartheid in South Africa. No one can ever give in on that. But it would have been possible to keep South Africa in, and I think that South Africa in would be more amenable to suggestions for an improvement in its policy than she would be outside the Commonwealth. It's particularly ironic that this should apply to Diefenbaker, because there is no one in Canada in political life who is as strong a proponent of the Commonwealth idea.

WILLIAM HAMILTON

A sidelight on the great controversy as to whether or not South Africa should remain in the Commonwealth or get kicked out. There is a special postage rate for countries within the Commonwealth. My reaction [as postmaster general] was that when you're not in the Commonwealth, and South Africa was not in the Commonwealth, one doesn't enjoy that special postage rate. But it required a minute to come up to cabinet, and I thought I'd just better check it with the prime minister. I did. There was no way we were going to change that postage rate, because all the supporters of South Africa in Canada would be reminded of this again when they had to write letters, and it would be disastrous.

I think we were probably the last country within the postal union to change our rate. It was something between six months and a year after it should have been done before I finally told my officials to go ahead and do it anyway. The minute that went to cabinet slipped through without any great fuss. But his reaction when I brought up the matter originally was quite violent as to whether I wanted to reopen the whole South African controversy again.

The policy on South Africa was a radical innovation. Otherwise, the Diefenbaker government's foreign policy was pragmatic to the point of being commercial. Diefenbaker believed that trade was a constructive element in international affairs. He considered it the cement that kept the Commonwealth together, beyond the ties of similar traditions and political systems. He was to warn Prime Minister Harold Macmillan that if Britain ever joined the European Common Market it would weaken the Commonwealth. But not everyone agreed with the government's policy on this.

ALLISTER GROSART

It's difficult to gauge public reaction. Sometimes you think you are acting in the public interest and you find, for one reason or another, it is unacceptable. Perhaps the best example was the meeting in Accra about the then contemplated entry of the UK into the European Common Market. Two of our ministers, Donald Fleming and George Hees, went over there and understandably made a very strong pitch for the consideration of Canadian interests as a result of Britain going into the EEC – and there were very serious problems at that time.

The presentations they made to that meeting were publicized. Understandably, the newspaper correspondents picked out only the hard position they took: Canadian interests have to be looked after in agriculture, wheat, newsprint, and so on. Strangely enough the reaction in Canada was, 'Poor little Britain,' the very opposite to what you would expect.

I used to once in a while pick up Jack Pickersgill when I was driving downtown. When the first accounts came across of the statements that George Hees and Don Fleming had made there, Pick said, 'It's the greatest mistake since St Laurent's "supermen" statement. You have managed to get the Conservative party tagged as anti-British. You're crazy.'

That was the case. You couldn't say that those ministers were wrong in taking that position. That was what they were there for. But somehow people felt that we should have been very considerate – Britain was in trouble and so on. How do you guess this? I don't know.

> *George Hees was responsible for a most dramatic attempt to increase Canadian exports. He brought all the trade commissioners back to Canada for a two-week conference with government officials and businessmen interested in increasing their trade with foreign countries.*

GEORGE HEES

The main thing [about the trade drive] was that I put the trade commissioners on a brand new basis. They had not been paid any attention to, really, by C.D. Howe, who was a great man in every way. As a builder, as a great Canadian, as a war minister, he couldn't have been better. A tremendous man. I loved him, I admired him, he was terrific. But he wasn't a salesman. He had never sold anything in his life. He didn't understand the importance of selling. He didn't realize that selling is the key to the whole industrial picture because you can't make anything until you can sell it – and then you can make more of it, and sell more, and employ people. The prosperity of the country depends on salesmanship.

We had a lot of good people in the Trade and Commerce Department who had never been paid any attention to. Nobody wrote to them, nobody patted them on the back, nobody noticed if they had a good year, if their area sold a lot of stuff for Canada. They were just people off in the hinterland, and nobody paid any attention to them. I called them all back: I treated them just like a sales manager would treat his sales force in industry. This is the benefit of being in plain ordinary business, because you understand what business does. I told them they were the most important people in the country. Up till then they had been very much the number two in the foreign affairs set-up – it was the External Affairs boys who were always graded number one in the embassies; these people were the poor relations, the fellows that looked after trade. It was like people in England a hundred years ago: anybody who was anybody went into being a doctor or a lawyer and so on; somebody way down the line went into business or went into trade, and was very much looked down upon.

The trade commissioners were the people who really did the job for Canada and built the business and did the selling. So I said, 'Look, as far as I am concerned, you are the most important people in any embassy in the world. You are far more useful to Canada. We are not going to take second place to anybody in the External Affairs Department. You go out and sell. You are going to be rewarded in the future, like businessmen, according to what you sell, not the length of time you have been in the business. If you can get out there and do a better job than somebody who has been in the business twice the time you have, you are going to get the promotion, he isn't. You are on your own.' It was quite a jolt to them but they liked it. Of course they were all good fellows. So we got going on that basis.

Then, of course, the thing was to link them up with the businessmen of Canada. We had innumerable conferences all over the country each year to which we invited businessmen. We gave presentations. The first hour would be taken up with presentations by eight fellows from each of the various branches of the department. They would say what the department could do to help the small businessmen, to sell produce in Canada and overseas. We had rehearsals and they were trained to get up and say, 'My job is to do so and so. Here is what I can do for you, one, two, three, four.' They had to do it exactly within five minutes, not one minute over. We would rehearse and it was just like a theatrical performance. I would say, 'Cut it. Who do you think you're talking to? How long do you think we can sit and listen?'

So we got a real theatrical performance. The first hour was eight of these fellows, each with an introduction from me, and then we would stop for coffee. Then the people would come back and question them as to what they could do: 'I have got this problem.' 'Can you help me here?' It brought businessmen into Ottawa. Most little businessmen were scared stiff to come and try to get through a labyrinth like the Trade and Commerce Department. 'We're too busy to see you.'

With this arrangement they made contacts. They weren't coming to look around the building to try and find somebody who would look after their problem and it would take them two days to find who was the guy. They made an appointment to see Mr John Jones in room 324 in the Trade and Commerce Department on Thursday the 24th of September, and then they would meet. The start of the whole thing was a big meeting with the businessmen where we had about 1500 businessmen who came for a week in December 1960 and had some 13,000 interviews with other people.

To sum it all up, we brought the trade commissioners and business together. We put a new attitude in our trade commissioners' minds: 'The sky was the limit.' They had the complete support of the department. We would back them against anybody. If they got into trouble, I would back them. The hell with whoever they were up against, I was going to fight for them. They would be paid and rewarded according to the results they obtained. This worked rather well because it was a straight business approach.

Besides the Commonwealth, which had such an emotional appeal for the Diefenbaker government, and the trade drive, on which so much energy was expended, there was the United Nations. Canada's support of the UN peace-keeping and peace-making function was continued. The minister of external affairs, Howard Green, saw eye to eye with his leader on almost all issues. In fact, it was said at the time that many of their attitudes were interchangeable.

HOWARD GREEN

Mr Diefenbaker was very much interested in foreign policy, but in effect he left me a free hand. We had been old friends, and we saw things very much alike. We were what you might call left-wing Conservatives. We had been in all sorts of battles, side by side, in the House. I hadn't asked for the job of foreign minister; I was perfectly happy in my other portfolio [public works]. I think there was complete confidence between the two of us and we were able to discuss anything. I doubt if we ever had any cross words at all during my whole time as foreign minister.

At the time of his appointment as external affairs minister, Howard Green seemed an unlikely choice. He was, however, the senior minister and acted as prime minister when Mr Diefenbaker was away. In time his homespun manner came to be accepted as an earnest of his integrity. He summed up Canada's role at the United Nations by saying it was to keep the big boys from rocking the boat, and he told the House of Commons, 'Canada has only friends and no enemies.'

Howard Charles Green was born on 5 November 1895 and grew up in the British Columbia mining town of Kaslo. He graduated from the University of Toronto in 1915, in time to go overseas with the 54th Kootenay Battalion. After the war he studied law at Osgoode Hall in Toronto.

Like his younger colleague, Davie Fulton, he came from a pioneer and political British Columbia family: an uncle, Senator R.F. Green, (federal MP for the Kootenays during the First World War) had served in Sir Richard McBride's provincial government with Fulton's father, Fred J. Fulton. He was also a good friend of Leon J. Ladner and succeeded him, one Parliament removed, as MP for Vancouver South in 1935. He was re-elected in the general elections of 1940 and 1945, and, after his riding was redistributed, was elected in Vancouver-Quadra in 1949, 1953, 1957, and 1958.

He was a tall, spare man, amiable and at the same time austere, a non-drinker and non-smoker with a strong sense of integrity. In his portfolio as minister of public works, he told Conservative MPs who were besieged by supporters demanding jobs that patronage was out – and he meant it. Nevertheless he retained his colleagues' affection. During his four years as external affairs minister, his principal interest was with nuclear disarmament; he was the successful sponsor of a UN *resolution calling for more adequate world-wide radiation detection. But with all his idealism he proved practical and hard-headed in negotiations.*

HOWARD GREEN

At that time the question of recognizing Red China was not very much to the fore. The British had recognized Red China some years before and they got nowhere with it. They weren't even allowed to put an ambassador in China. Our relations with China had always seemed to me to be much better than the Chinese relations with the British, although they had recognized China. I don't think Red China was worrying one bit about whether or not Canada recognized her.

I believe that during the St Laurent government the Liberals had been about to recognize Red China at one stage and then something happened and they decided not to do it. During our time, of course, China attacked India in a very unprovoked attack. The Chinese were being very, very war-like and there was no particular reason why we should rush to recognize them. We had very friendly relations with Taiwan and, mind you, the people of Chinese origin in Canada were almost unanimously opposed to recognition of Red China for fear there would be Chinese agents brought into the Chinese centres, particularly in Vancouver, my home city, where we have the largest Chinese population in Canada. They were very keen that Red China should not be recognized at the time.

There was also the problem of getting Red China into the United Nations and giving her the permanent seat on the Security Council. The tension between the Soviet Union and the United States was very, very severe. The Russians were making enough trouble in the United Nations with their veto on the Security Council without having the Chinese in there vetoing things too and making it even that much more difficult for the United Nations to function.

PAUL MARTIN

I remember once attacking Howard Green for his lack of a foreign policy in a particular area. It had to do with disarmament. Howard was going to a disarmament conference in a few days, and I wanted to know the policy that Canada was going to put forward. Howard said to me, quite correctly, 'The Hon. Member for Essex East knows perfectly well that I cannot tell the House now what position in every particular I am going to take. This is a conference of negotiation. Canada has a policy, and I am going to state that policy; but a good bit of it will be as a result of the negotiation that goes on before. We have general principles that we have agreed to in the government, but beyond that I cannot go. I've given the general principles.'

Howard Green was right. A foreign minister can't disclose before there is an agreement the particular position that he will take in negotiations. But we hammered this home. We were the opposition, of course, and while he was correct in principle we did our best to disarm him as much as we could to get him to reveal more of what the policy was than he had. He simply said it was not possible.

I know that we scored in this debate. We created the impression in the gallery and in the country, I suspect, that the government didn't have a policy, and the public are not always quick to accept the judgment that you can't disclose all of your positions prior to general agreement with other countries. So it looked at six o'clock as though the government had been placed in a very vulnerable position. At eight o'clock, Diefenbaker got up and spoke, and he did the very thing that Howard said couldn't be done. He exposed what the policy was, at least what he believed the policy was. I've since examined that speech, and I know that what John said that night was not the policy as it eventually was presented by Howard Green. But he gave the impression that Howard Green should not have been so secretive, that he should have been more generous in exposing what the government's position was, and if he, his foreign minister, wasn't going to do this, he, the prime minister, would. I thought that that was a great weakness, and everybody else did. I saw John do that on a number of occasions.

Paul Martin, who was to succeed Howard Green as external affairs minister when the Liberals won the 1963 election, was critical of a speech that Diefenbaker made in the UN General Assembly.

PAUL MARTIN

He went to the United Nations – I think it was in '57 – and he asked for the liberation of the Ukraine. He asked that the people of the Ukraine be freed from the slavery and the restrictions the state imposed on them by communist Russia. He spoke of the violation of human rights, and, in a direct way, he knew damned well that he could do nothing about it – that to get up in the United Nations and to complain about the violation of human rights in the Ukraine was not going to improve the lot of the Ukrainians. It wasn't going to influence the Soviet Union one bit, any more than General de Gaulle's speech on the steps of the Montreal City Hall improved the lot of French Canada.

What Diefenbaker was doing was to use the United Nations for political purposes back home in an obvious and irresponsible way. The effect of that is still apparent. The Ukrainians and the Poles and other people who live in this country and who come from these suppressed lands regard Diefenbaker as their great champion. But he didn't do any more than Pearson did or I did at the United Nations in complaining about the violation of human rights, but without directing it to the situation in any particular country. The copies that were made of the United Nations speech went all over this country and still do, and have a big effect on ethnic groups in this country.

I say that a man who is prime minister, while he must always look for political advantage, really lowers himself, lowers the office, in doing that kind of thing.

Canada's most crucial foreign relations are with the US. *In order to improve Canadian-American relations, the Diefenbaker government took the initiative of proposing regular discussions between elected representatives of the two countries. The Canada–United States Inter-Parliamentary Group was formed.*

Although the group had no powers, its value has been in bringing together legislators from both sides of the border.

Personal contact between the heads of government also has been important. Prime Minister Diefenbaker got along well with President Eisenhower. They were of the same generation, and the Canadian leader admired the way that Eisenhower could get people to work together. But Diefenbaker never appreciated John F. Kennedy. When, on a visit to Washington, he was shown a collection of steel engravings of naval battles on the Great Lakes during the War of 1812, he noted that they depicted only American victories. He asked where the pictures were of battles the British won and told President Kennedy that he would get him copies of these so he could hang them in the White House alongside the others. By this time John Fisher had succeeded Gowan Guest as the prime minister's executive assistant.

JOHN FISHER

When Diefenbaker got back he ordered Dr Kaye Lamb, the national librarian, to comb the galleries of New York and find pictures that would depict the British seizing American ships of war. Dr Lamb obtained several and had them out at the National War Museum. About every couple of weeks, he would phone me and he would say, 'John, can you get the prime minister to make up his mind which painting he wants to send to Kennedy?'

I said, 'I wish you'd send them all back, Dr Lamb, because it's only going to upset Kennedy. It's terrible.' On many occasions I pleaded with Mr Diefenbaker, 'Don't send that to Kennedy, sir. What are you trying to prove by sending down something a hundred years after the event?' 'Oh, we must teach him history. History must be taught,' he would mutter. I could tell from the twinkle in his eye that he was enjoying this devilish exercise.

Finally they were sent to the prime minister's office. He kept them behind the chesterfield and any time a delegation, like the Kiwanis, would come in, he'd pull them out and give a lecture in history, and how he was going to really put this young Kennedy in his place. Finally he said, 'Well, one of those two.'

So I told Marion Wagner and Bunny Pound, 'Send these out to be cleaned.' And then I just stalled, stalled, stalled. Anytime that Dief would ask, I'd say, 'They're still being cleaned.' And I said to the girls, 'Look, if I'm not around here, don't ever let those go to Washington, please, I beg you. It will only upset our relations.' We stalled for weeks, and he knew what we were doing.

Gradually relations between Canada and the US *soured. Washington complained about the way its notes were ignored and the length of time it took to get anything done in Ottawa.*

ROY FAIBISH

Where we could be charged with being dilatory was in the area of defence and foreign affairs. Often there was a consensus in cabinet, but there was a long time before action was taken. That was because his [Diefenbaker's] attitude towards Washington was such that he would do it in *his* time and not when *they* wanted it. So there was a delay, and Washington would be puzzled why it was taking so long. It wasn't because a consensus didn't exist. It did exist, but he wanted to move his own way.

JOHN FISHER

He'd receive confidential letters that would come from President Kennedy by special courier from Washington. They wouldn't go through the US embassy or the Canadian External Affairs Department. They would come straight to the prime minister's office and right in to him. He'd open them, look very mysterious, and usually shove the letters into his pocket, or under the blotter, or in a drawer. A few days later, the US State Department, through the embassy, would start to make some enquiries. The embassy people would be shocked too that there were such letters. They'd enquire of External – I guess that's the way protocol goes – and External had never heard of these letters. And there'd be all hell breaking loose.

The girls got used to this, and they were very smart about it. Usually they'd say, 'Well, they're either between his mattresses at home or they're in one of these deep drawers, or they're in a pocket in a clothes cupboard somewhere, or under the blotter.' Sure enough, we'd usually find the notes in one of those places.

That was a real hang-up with him. He did the same with Macmillan. He wouldn't answer these letters. Now, why? Who knows? Whether he didn't want to touch the problem, whether he was snubbing them – I don't know what reason he had, but he would avoid answering those special letters by courier. It was a great joke around the prime minister's office. Whenever the pressure was on, we knew where to go – even had the maids briefed. We would phone to 24 Sussex and get the maid to go up and do a little feeling in between the mattresses and usually pull out some secret documents.

Relations were such that at one point a story went the rounds of Ottawa that President Kennedy had pencilled an obscene and insulting reference to Diefenbaker on the margin of a memo when he was on a state visit to Canada. The memo, according to the story, was incautiously left behind and got into the hands of the prime minister. However, Senator O'Leary says it was all a mistake.

GRATTAN O'LEARY

An office in the East Block had been put at Kennedy's disposal, and this became American territory once he was there. [Walt] Rostow put in a memo about the speech Kennedy was going to make the next day to a joint session of Parliament. One of the things that he wrote in the memo was, 'Be critical, be tough about their failure to join the Organization of American States, OAS.' He wrote OAS in pencil as a marginal note. Now, this was sloppy, but Kennedy dropped that memorandum in a waste basket. It was picked up and turned over to Dief. I submit that it should have been sent to our ambassador in Washington to give to the secretary of state of the US with a note: 'Here, this was found; it is your property.' For some extraordinary reason – I have seen this document – Dief thought the pencilled note was SOB. He believes this. He is writing his memoirs and he believes he is going to shake the world with this.

11
'Stuff' and cabinet meetings

The Diefenbaker image changed as the euphoria of 1958 gave way to the practicalities of dealing with a declining economy and rising unemployment. The first grumblings of discontent were heard in the metropolitan Toronto area after the cancellation of the Arrow contract. The newspapers began complaining that Diefenbaker was high-handed, that he didn't listen to advice, that he ran a one-man government. Later they were to charge him with being indecisive and procrastinating, as well as dictatorial. There were apparently distinct differences in his two tenures of office: during his first minority government, Diefenbaker was vital, decisive, a man of destiny; but with an overwhelming majority in the Commons he became cautious to the point of always searching for a consensus.

An outward aspect of the majority government's difficulties was the interminable length of cabinet meetings. There were understandable reasons: the Tories' inexperience and their distrust of officials, the growing complexity of government, and the seriousness with which certain questions were treated. The Conservatives spent much time reviewing the death sentences that came before them, and the abolitionists among them, including the prime minister, agonized over each. Only Senator Grattan O'Leary, among those I interviewed, believed that Diefenbaker ran a one-man government, and he was never in the cabinet. The other former ministers denied this.

HOWARD GREEN

I thought those reports [of a one-man government] were very unfair. Mr Diefenbaker always gave the ministers ample opportunity to discuss the questions which were before the cabinet. On occasion I felt he gave them

Part of the Government benches in the House

too much opportunity. Very often, when there was a difference of opinion, he would defer consideration to the next cabinet meeting. I think this is one of the reasons he was criticized by the press for being slow in reaching a conclusion. But he was very, very good about letting everyone have his or her say.

You must remember that, under our system, the prime minister has very wide power. I think this is a weakness of the British parliamentary structure, that the prime minister has a veto on all the members of the cabinet. While he isn't given it legally, in fact it works out that way. I know, because I acted as prime minister whenever Mr Diefenbaker was away, and could take a hand in the business of any particular department. All the real power is concentrated, in the final analysis, in the hands of the prime minister. So that when the prime minister is accused of being a loner or being an autocrat or anything of this kind, it's necessary to remember that under our system he must accept the responsibility for making the final decisions.

ALVIN HAMILTON

I know about the myth of a one-man government. To me it is patently untrue for the simple reason that he never interfered with those of us who were busy developing policy and in getting this through Parliament and setting up the administrative framework. The only thing that he watched was the political repercussion of any of our actions. I can honestly say that, during the five and a half years that I spent as a minister, I don't recall a single instance of him interfering with any of my departmental responsibilities.

On some of the things that I did politically he had lots to say and there is no secret what they were. I deliberately started a fight with the farm organizations in western Canada. No prime minister is going to let one of his ministers go out publicly and pick a fight with ten farm organizations in three prairie provinces without asking, 'Why? What are you trying to do?' When I explained my position, I think he saw the point. I said, 'There is an election that has got to be faced and we have got to win it and you naturally pick on somebody to fight. These fellows are wrong, they are fat cats, and I just took the side of the people against them. That's all; it is a natural political stance.' After I explained it to him, he thought it was very astute.

DOUGLAS HARKNESS

Mr Diefenbaker, in my view, spent far too much time in cabinet asking the opinion of every member in connection with most questions. He would frequently have a series of meetings, with the result that ministers spent far too much time in cabinet and were not in a position to devote the amount of time that they needed to their own departments. At some periods, when matters of considerable importance were up for discussion and decision, we would have two cabinet meetings a day almost continuously for a week or more.

PIERRE SÉVIGNY

Diefenbaker, in 1958, was surprised by the extent of his victory, and the first really big mistake that he made as prime minister he made right after that. He never realized that the Canadian people, as never before in history, had given him *carte blanche* to do exactly as he pleased, to really create that One Canada he had been talking about. Diefenbaker was given a mandate of such strength that he should have ruled by decree rather than submit even the most minute decision to parliamentary debate.

But immediately after that sweeping victory he changed. Instead of making these rapid decisions which had marked his administration between June 1957 and January 1958, he decided to rule by meetings. He started having endless cabinet meetings. He insisted on giving back to Parliament the full power which he claimed Parliament had been deprived of by the Liberals. He insisted that each issue, however tiny it was, should be submitted to Parliament. The sessions which in the St Laurent days would last roughly about seven months were prolonged to nine and even ten months.

The opposition was completely shattered really when Pearson came back after the 1958 election with his 48 members and the NDP with 8 – I mean they looked somewhat ridiculous on the left hand of Mr Speaker. But they realized that they were given the opportunity to express their views and fight back on each issue, and each issue was being submitted to Parliament. It was apparent that the Diefenbaker of decision had become a man who had decided to push the democratic way of government to excess.

ROY FAIBISH

The late Blair Fraser said in his articles many times: 'The essential problem with the Diefenbaker cabinet was that it was a one-man government.' I wish that that was so. I know, on occasion after occasion, that we prayed that that were the case, because, over and over again, what he wanted to do was the right thing, and it was his colleagues in his cabinet, usually with legal or financial background, who stopped him. If he had been left alone, as a dictator, I think things that didn't happen would have happened.

I was never in cabinet, of course, but I saw him on some cabinet committees, and I was told by ministers that he was the same in cabinet. If there wasn't a consensus and he didn't think the person holding out was a fool, to the exasperation of those of us who knew we were on the right course and wanted to get on with it, he would roll it over, bring it up another time, try to bring him around, almost like a lawyer trying to bring a jury around so you've got all the twelve heads nodding. In the end he usually decided, but he took so long that he was accused, properly, of procrastination.

Parallel with the accusation that he was a one-man government was the charge that he was indecisive. He wasn't indecisive. He took a long time making up his mind because he had difficulty being arbitrary.

DAVIE FULTON

One of the things that stands out in my mind about John Diefenbaker is that, while he had great concepts, he was not strong on an actual program by which they would be implemented. Perhaps this was a result of his training as a defence counsel. It was not his responsibility to build a positive case, it was his responsibility to destroy the Crown's case. I think maybe that this training, this whole background and attitude, made it difficult for John Diefenbaker to sit down and plan out step by step the positive program. Although he always wanted to see such a program, it was difficult to get him to agree to it in detail.

Another reason is that as head of the government, in my experience in any event, he rarely if ever interfered in the details of departmental administration, or even in a minister's own legislative program. If you went to him with a well-conceived project, such as the initiation of the program on penal reform, which had an instinctive appeal to Mr Diefenbaker, he rarely interfered. He would say, 'Okay, put it before cabinet, and God bless you.'

But when it came to a political decision, where anything had a political connotation in the broader sense of the word, he seemed to reserve judgment there to himself alone. Rarely, it seemed to me, or increasingly rarely, he took the judgment of his cabinet as to whether there might be some political problems involved, but the benefits of the program outweighed and would override those political problems. Mind you, a prime minister has to be able to make decisions: but the decisions seemed to be not so much that 'I think this is wrong for these reasons' but rather that 'This is just wrong' and so no decisions would be taken. That's where the frustration came in – lengthy cabinet meetings at which we would go over the ground and come to the point of decision-making, but if the prime minister sensed that the decision on a consensus basis would be a majority against him, then he would adjourn the discussion and say, 'We'll have another go at this.' So he would go back over the same ground.

That was the history of the nuclear arms decision: endless discussion and debate in cabinet until finally the thing exploded in Harkness's resignation. That was the atmosphere of the Columbia River Treaty – not so much the treaty as the method of implementing it. The arrangements to be worked out with British Columbia got into the same sort of rut and endless discussions of the same ground, the same issues and an unreadiness to have the government enter into a confrontation as it were with Mr Bennett because, I think, in the prime minister's judgment, we wouldn't win such a confrontation in the political sense. So, in effect, no decision.

DONALD FLEMING

Mr Diefenbaker chose as his models, in his role as prime minister, Sir John A. Macdonald and Mr King. Both men had the reputation of deferring decisions that were thorny and troublesome. Mr Diefenbaker did not have the quality of decisiveness. This became more apparent as time went on. He found it more and more easy as the years passed to defer decisions – even those that needed, in the view of most of us, to be made.

As to administration, Mr Diefenbaker did not attempt to run the departments of government. It's quite wrong to say that he interfered in the operation of departments. He deliberately sought to avoid this. This was an accusation that was made against R.B. Bennett when he was prime minister. Mr Diefenbaker made very certain that no one would ever be able to say that he had interfered in the internal administration of any department.

HOWARD GREEN

I would think that he would be classified as a man of ideas. I don't think his strength was in the administrative field. It's almost impossible to get a man who is good in both fields.

ANGUS MACLEAN

I think he was an excellent presiding officer but I don't think he was decisive enough. When you had a situation where there was one of his colleagues whom he admired and had a high respect for in disagreement with the rest of us, he would go to any extent to try to get unanimity. I don't think he was brutal enough as a prime minister, or callous enough, or decisive enough. Even Pearson, you know, had various cabinet ministers resigning or leave, or somebody would get kicked upstairs, but this never happened with the Diefenbaker government.

ALVIN HAMILTON

In the cabinet he rarely said anything. He would introduce the subjects on the agenda. We all had copies. Then he would go around the table and, almost invariably, he didn't put his views out until the whole viewpoint was accepted. Then, if there was general consensus, he rarely said anything. The point that I am making is that he did not say what he thought, but he listened.

ELLEN FAIRCLOUGH

Even in the most serious times, funny little things crop up. The prime minister was always indulging in witty asides, sometimes delightful and sometimes pretty caustic. There was a journalist by the name of Robert Moon. He had written something criticizing Murdo MacPherson's appointment to the chairmanship of the royal commission on freight rates and his criticism was based on the assertion that Murdo was known to be pro-province and anti-railroads. Someone said the article was so vicious that he could be sued for libel. With a perfectly deadpan expression, Diefenbaker said quietly, 'That would be the height of lunacy.'

GEORGE HEES

Mr Diefenbaker did not ever like to make a decision himself. If something went wrong, he didn't want to be the person that had made the wrong decision. If a thing went right he took the credit for it, but he never took the blame if it went wrong. He didn't want to be the person who said, 'I have listened to everything. This is what we are going to do.' So we had to wait until we came to a clear consensus, and we would argue and argue. People were dying to have somebody say, 'I have listened to the evidence. This is what we are going to do.'

If the boss says that, everybody says, 'Thank God. I put forward my point of view, I have been conscientious, but if the boss says this is what we are going to do, my job is to do it.' Everybody, including Donald Fleming and Howard Green who had great Presbyterian consciences, would have been very glad to stop arguing and go along. But as long as they were expected to keep arguing, they kept arguing. Donald and Howard and perhaps others. We felt that we had to keep on going, and we just argued ourselves into exhaustion.

Gordon Churchill says, and he is a pretty wise guy, that the reason the thing broke up in the end was because we were all completely exhausted men, and exhausted men don't make rational judgments. I think that he is 100 per cent right. That's why we took so long, the cabinet meetings went on and on and they went on.

Mr Diefenbaker didn't like to go away for weekends: he wasn't a skier, or he wasn't somebody who liked to go off and play golf and things like that. Really, I think he was never happier than having a weekend of cabinet meetings. He was happy as the devil to have a meeting on Saturday and another meeting on Sunday. This just about killed us because if you are working hard you know perfectly well that you can only work hard for five days. If you try to work six and seven days a week, sooner or later you break down.

Or if you don't actually break down, the production of your mind is not nearly as good as it should be.

In later years, when the prime minister's office had grown to million-dollar proportions, Diefenbaker would boast that under his administration it cost no more than $50,000 a year, about the same amount spent by St Laurent; but this figure did not include the salaries of staff members seconded from other departments. A bureaucratic structure was not the Diefenbaker style. In fact almost two months elapsed between Derek Bedson's departure in 1957 to become an aide to Manitoba's Premier Duff Roblin and Gowan Guest's arrival to succeed him as executive assistant to the prime minister. This in itself was a sign that there was no very clear definition of jobs in the prime minister's office. According to John Fisher, Guest's successor, an executive assistant could be everything from a valet to an adviser, speech writer, researcher, hand holder, father confessor. The same was true of other members of the small staff. When James Nelson became press secretary, his first job was to accompany the prime minister to Toronto. On the plane he was given the PM's briefcase and told to guard it; later he found that all it contained was a clean shirt.

However, everyone who worked in the prime minister's office was expected to provide him with newspaper clippings, research materials, memoranda, correspondence, etc. Diefenbaker called it 'stuff.'

GOWAN GUEST

I tried to find out from him just exactly what he wanted me to do, and he as much as said that if he knew he wouldn't have appointed me. That was my problem. There were twenty-six people in that office who were working for him, at least he thought they were working for him, but he wasn't sure what they were doing, and they weren't sure what they were doing. My job was to make the twenty-six people function as required in the prime minister's office. As far as budget or money was concerned, that would be primarily Bob Bryce's problem, but any decision which would put us in danger of spending more than one dollar more than St Laurent had had in his budget for the year ending March 31, 1957, had to be very carefully reviewed.

There was no really defined regime. I think that was the nature of the man. I tried to structure an organization but it didn't work. I always felt that Diefenbaker deliberately refrained from holding anybody out as his agent with his authority to unquestionably wield his power. I think that was deliberate. He didn't want to get into a position where I would ever walk into the office of the governor of the Bank of Canada and say 'Close the bank' and the governor took it for granted that this came from the prime minister, and closed the bank.

JOHN FISHER

Somebody gave Mr Diefenbaker a new dog and he came into the office one morning and told us about it. He said, 'Now, I want a name for that dog. Get your brains together and see what you can come up with.'

I said, 'Mr Diefenbaker, first of all, I think it should have a bilingual name that is pronounceable and understandable in both languages of this country.' He kind of looked at me a bit and he didn't say anything. I went home that night and I whipped out, on my typewriter, thirty different suggested names for this darned dog. The next morning, I handed the list to him. He was a bit grumpy, and he just scanned it. Of course he could scan very rapidly – he can read a page in just a flash. He put it down on his desk, and reared back in his chair, and said, 'I have decided to name the dog Prince.'

I said, 'Prince! Mr Diefenbaker! Royalty isn't too popular right now, and in Quebec that won't go.' He said, 'You wanted a bilingual word.' I said, 'Yes, but what you gain on the bilingualism you lose on the royalty aspect of "Prince."' He said, 'Prince' (using the French pronunciation). I said, 'Well, they'll think that's Prince Albert.' He said, 'That's what it is.' I said, 'I don't know. My recommendation would be that you could do better that that.' 'Well, you're so bright, give me some more names.' I said I would bring in some more names in the morning, because he was busy all that day.

That night I prepared another list of names. I really worked hard at it too. I came in and I gave him the list; he scanned it and refused to comment. He said, 'I have a name that Allister Grosart has given me.' I said, 'What's that?' He said, 'Tory.' I said, 'Oh, Mr Diefenbaker, you must have lost your senses! Tory! For a dog? Can't you picture every cartoonist in this country. They'll say the Conservatives are so convinced that they've chosen a dog and they've gone to the dogs.' He looked a little alarmed. I said, 'No, that's the last name you should have for a friendly dog.' He looked at me again as if I'd taken leave of my senses. I said, 'If you don't believe me, ask your dear faithful courier out here, Gilbert Champagne. Ask him.'

So he pushed the buzzer, and he never could remember which buzzer he was supposed to push, because mechanics troubled him. Anyway, Gilbert was summoned to the throne, and he came in and he stood at attention, because I think he was always a bit intimidated by the Chief. The Chief said, 'Gilbert, what does the word Tory mean to you?' Old Gilbert said, 'That means George Drew. It means the striped pants, something what you in

English call "stuffy." ' Dief thought that was great and he had a roar of laughter. He said, 'That's what you think it is, eh?' Gilbert said, 'I would not be happy with that word.' Dief said, 'That's it! "Happy!" You said it. Thanks, Gilbert.'

And that's how the dog was named 'Happy.'

MERRIL MENZIES

I consciously avoided having an office on the second floor of the East Block (where the prime minister's office was) to avoid the day-to-day issues and politics. I was either located on the first floor or, later, on the third. This isolated me, and I think fortunately, from these immediate pressures to think about broader policies. It's fair to say that this is the way Mr Diefenbaker saw my role too, and, in fact, the way he employed my services during this period. He usually asked me to concentrate my efforts on more major policy issues, and so I did a series of studies for him, and I tried at all times to relate this to the broader concept of development that I had. This worked fairly well.

There was one aspect, however, in which I was involved in a more routine or continuing way. There used to be weekly assessments of the economy transmitted from the finance minister's office to the East Block. Sometimes they were in the form of draft speeches, sometimes just an assessment. My normal procedure was to read and attach a very very brief memo to it indicating my view of the document and simply send it on to Mr Diefenbaker's office.

JOHN FISHER

I was appalled to find that there was no lock on the door into his office. Any crank with a gun could just push someone aside and walk right in and mow him down. I thought that there should be one of those electric locks that he could control from his own desk. I asked him about it, but I don't think he knew what I was saying. Anyway, we had it installed, because there was a guy sending threatening letters to him and I saw him a few times out on the lawn. I was getting a little apprehensive, and so were other members of the staff.

We had this electric lock installed. Someone important like Senator Brunt would come, and we would then press the buzzer outside for Mr Diefenbaker to press his buzzer, which would release the lock. He'd always get mixed up, and he'd think it was the telephone ringing, and he'd grab the red phone to Moscow or Washington, and he'd knock over pens and everything. He never could seem to get on to this mechanical lock. It would make him furious. Finally we'd have to bang on the doors. And we had another secret – we could unlock it from our side. So that only lasted a few days, and it was out.

Mechanics really troubled him. We tried to get him to use the hearing aid so he wouldn't miss things, but he would either turn up the volume too high, and it would nearly drive his brains in, or he wouldn't use it at all, or he didn't have it in right. It was just a waste of money – anything mechanical.

The status of the parliamentary assistants was as obscure then as it is now. The appointment of these so-called 'junior ministers' carried with it a small extra stipend but no power. There could be a great deal of work or nothing to do – the job depended on the minister. It is significant that Gowan Guest could not recall the parliamentary assistants to Diefenbaker. Among them only Paul Martineau had an office in the East Block; the others were not even that close to the prime minister's suite in the Centre Block of the Parliament Buildings.

PAUL MARTINEAU

The routine was that every morning I would meet with Mr Diefenbaker somewhere around eight o'clock. He was, of course, as everyone knows, an early riser, and I had to be there around eight o'clock, quarter to eight. He would rapidly go through his mail and he would discuss various things. He would ask me if I could think of any questions that might be asked for in the House, and to prepare possible answers on these topics, which I would do. My work also consisted in ghost-writing speeches, some of which were used and some were not. I would meet a lot of the people who wanted to see the prime minister for something or another, and make a memo on what they had in mind, or their suggestions, whatever the problem was, and submit it to the prime minister.

I also had to go through all the years of Hansard and pick out the salient parts of the speeches of the four principal opposition members of that day, who were Mr Pearson, Mr Martin, Mr Chevrier, and Mr Pickersgill. We used to refer to them as the Four Horsemen of the Apocalypse. He wanted their words, speeches, thoughts, to be before him in readily consultable form so that should they make any suggestion or taunt or otherwise make an aggressive speech he would be able to reply.

Anytime he had to make a pronouncement in French or if he went somewhere in Quebec where he was expected to say at least some words in French, I would prepare it for him. On many occasions, I would read it in front of him, so that he would get the drift of the pronunciation. Sometimes he would read it himself, and I would correct certain imprecisions in pronunciation and so on.

Under Diefenbaker for the first time the cabinet gave strong representation to the East and West and, also for the first time, included a woman minister. Léon Balcer remarked in an interview that because of Quebec's secondary position in the cabinet, the real power of decision was, as he put it, 'off balance.' For the first time, the balance of power had shifted from central Canada.

LÉON BALCER

There was a Diefenbaker inner group. It included Howard Green, Alvin Hamilton, Dave Walker, and Gordon Churchill. Those were the people who understood Diefenbaker. These people – which is quite natural – were the friends of Diefenbaker.

WALTER DINSDALE

The Diefenbaker government of 1958 represented the first major breakthrough for the West and the Atlantic provinces. It was the first time that the balance of power had shifted to the extremities of Canada. Ever since Confederation it had always gone between Quebec or Ontario, Upper Canada or Lower Canada as we like to refer to central Canada out West, but it was true that for the first time the West and the Maritimes had the balance of power. Look at the portfolio structure – except Finance, the big portfolios were either in the Maritimes or in the West.

As the first woman cabinet minister, Ellen Fairclough was used to working with men; she had served on many committees where she had been the only woman member. There was only one incident because of her sex, and this was over the Truscott case.

ELLEN FAIRCLOUGH

There was a cabinet meeting called to consider the matter and whether this boy, Steven Truscott, should hang or not. We all gathered in the room and you could almost cut the atmosphere with a knife. Finally Dief said, 'Ellen, I am sorry, but would you please retire.' There was nothing on the table at this time. I didn't know why I had been asked to leave. I knew that it was a case supposedly of rape and murder and I thought, 'Well, the boys want to use language which they don't wish to use in front of me and they don't want to pussyfoot.' Léon Balcer is wrong to say that I was angry. I never wept. It is utter nonsense. I can't even say that I was annoyed.

As a matter of fact, if anything, it was the men who were embarrassed. They weren't big enough to look at it in an objective fashion. Now, I would have looked at it in an objective fashion. This wouldn't have embarrassed me one little bit. I had served on committees in city council where I listened to some pretty lurid things and this wouldn't have bothered me. But my reaction, I can say quite frankly, was one of puzzlement, wondering what it was all about, but also, subsequently, one of some amusement that men in a position of running a country should be so namby-pamby about discussing things in front of a woman.

There were a couple of inconveniences. The women's washroom was one. There was none on the second floor of the East Block. You had to go all the way down the corridor and up to the third or fourth floor. After three or four cabinet meetings, I got a little bit weary of this. The men's washroom, which was just outside the cabinet room door, didn't even have a lock on the door, so you couldn't go in and lock it. There was a steward who stood in the corridor all the time. I said to him, 'I am going in here, you stand here.' He said, 'Okay.' From then on, every time I went out there, I would just say, 'Hey, you, come and stand here,' and he would.

The other was being invited to a luncheon which one of the banks threw for the cabinet and which was held at the Rideau Club. Well, I just wrote a little note saying thank you for the invitation but for obvious reasons I will be unable to attend, and let it go at that. When I got back to my room that night I had the biggest basket of flowers you have ever seen in your life. Just like a funeral parlor. It was terrific.

Few changes were made in the Diefenbaker government, and most of the ministers served the full five and a half to six years the Conservatives were in power; some of them even retained the same portfolios for the entire period. Yet no Canadian government has had more scope to make changes if it wanted to, since its overwhelming majority provided many brilliant and eager backbenchers. The prime minister was being constantly reminded that he must do something for them or they would become frustrated and disillusioned. Furthermore, he was under considerable pressure to give Quebec more ministers and more important portfolios.

MICHAEL STARR

This is the time to be frank, and my opinion was that Mr Diefenbaker kept his cabinet intact for too long a period of time. There were people in that cabinet who had ambitions to be leader at the same time as he did and were hoping that they would eventually achieve these ambitions. If I had been prime minister, I would have got rid of about three-quarters of them after the second year. I would have put them in the Senate and made them judges and brought in all that beautiful material that was sitting behind, brilliant young men who would look up to you as a leader, who would relish your wisdom and political experience and do a good job for you. Because I think those who were there felt that they knew just as much about these things as John did.

I think this is the most important error that was made. They got entrenched. They had the opinion that they were indispensable because they weren't being replaced. They got to the position where they became strongwilled. They were defying the prime minister actually in respect to policy. This is when the government started to crumble.

LIONEL CHEVRIER

We also began to see the handwriting on the wall because of the discrepancies in the cabinet, because of the difficulties that the prime minister was having with some of his ministers, because of the lack of confidence that he had in some of his ministers, because of the statements that some of his ministers were making, particularly Mr Bulcer. It was during the sittings of the Public Accounts Committee that, for the first time, I noticed a division.

David Walker was the spokesman for the government in that committee, and [Noel] Dorion, who was a minister, wanted to have a say. He came to the Committee one day, hoping that he would perhaps be the spokesman. It was apparent at once that there was a division of opinion between Dorion and Walker. So that immediately raised in my mind [the thought] that if that were the case between those two, there was certainly bound to be division elsewhere.

At the end of 1961 there was a highly publicized move towards a major cabinet shuffle. There was much speculation as to who would accompany the prime minister when he travelled to Quebec, where the governor general was then in residence, to present his new ministers. But in the end only one minister was replaced and another promoted.

JACQUES FLYNN

Mr Comtois [minister of mines] was appointed lieutenant governor of Quebec in October 1961, and, around the 15th of December, Mr Diefenbaker called me and asked to see me in Ottawa. So I went, and he mentioned that he was thinking of appointing me to the cabinet. He had several things in mind. But also he said, 'What about becoming speaker?' I said, 'When?' He said, 'Now.' I said, 'What would you do with Mr Michener?' 'Well,' he said, 'I don't know.' He was thinking of naming him to an embassy somewhere. I said, 'If you want me to become speaker, I don't mind, but I suppose I would keep the office after the election,' because it was obvious that we would have an election in about six months.

Then later on he mentioned that he had a big reshuffling in mind; he spoke even of putting me in Justice. But nobody wanted to budge, nobody wanted to give up their jobs in the cabinet, so he phoned me and said, 'What about Mines and Technical Surveys?' I said, 'It's your decision, sir.' He said, 'Tell nobody, otherwise you're out.' I said, 'Sir, I cannot prevent people from speculating when everybody knows that there's a special train in the Ottawa station waiting to take you to Quebec city.'

The only appointment in that cabinet shuffle was mine. He did make Noel Dorion chairman of the Privy Council which, at that time, was just an honour, no responsibility. And he named as Privy Councillors Leslie Frost and Senator [W.M.] Aseltine. That was the extent of the reshuffling. From what I could gather, nobody wanted to move. Don Fleming didn't want to give up Finance, or Davie Fulton didn't want to give up Justice, or someone else thought that if he were put somewhere else that it would be considered as a demotion. I think that's what happened. It was too difficult to make the moves because of the interpretation that might have been put on the changes. Finally, he didn't have time since he was caught by the arrangements made to have that meeting at the Citadel.

LÉON BALCER

I attach a lot of importance to that trip we made to the Citadel of Quebec, where there was supposed to be the big reshuffling of cabinet. It was at the end of December 1961. Up to that date, Diefenbaker was on top of the world; I mean he was running the country. Then he had told the press that there would be a great show, and they all came down to Quebec on the same train. I remember we were a huge train; Diefenbaker had two private cars, and there was a parlour car for the press. The reporters were building up cabinets with one another, and the next day nothing came out, and Diefenbaker told them that he had never assured them of reshuffle. They didn't like it and they felt that they were let down. From then on, Diefenbaker changed. He lost his confidence and his authority over the key ministers.

On the train, we were all together and we were having a friendly drink. We were all relaxed and sort of joking about the future appointments; everybody in the room was wondering if he was the only one who was not being appointed to another post. One or two of them were summoned to Diefenbaker's car and came back saying that the boss was in a very very difficult disposition and was mad at everybody and so forth. Then he sent for another minister, and everybody was sort of trying to stay away from going to see Diefenbaker. Apart from his mood, there was no liquor in Diefenbaker's car. Many of our cabinet colleagues were enjoying the ride and didn't want to go and be confronted with Mr Diefenbaker who was in an awful mood. It was an interesting trip, to say the least.

PIERRE SÉVIGNY

There again Diefenbaker missed the boat, through his own fault. The idea to go to Quebec, to such a picturesque site as the Citadel, was good; but once in Quebec something should have been done for Quebec. The cabinet should have given a dinner for Quebec. There should have been a mass meeting where Diefenbaker would have spoken and the key Quebeckers would have spoken. Then the Quebeckers would have said, 'Well, isn't it nice to see the federal cabinet coming here and playing up to us.'

Something like this should have been done, which I strongly suggested, but Diefenbaker would have nothing of that. He said, 'We will go to Quebec, have our meeting, make my shuffle (which was no shuffle at all) and then we will come back.' I said, 'Well, what are we going to Quebec for, a train ride, have a meeting there, and then come back?' He said, 'We can't stay in Quebec, we've got to be close to Parliament and close to Ottawa.' Well, Parliament wasn't sitting to start with. He said, 'We have got to be back in Ottawa in case something happens.'

12
Diefenbaker and French Canada

It was the Conservatives' misfortune that they were in power when Quebec was in the throes of what became known as the Quiet Revolution. As a result, when they Introduced some long-needed reforms, such as simultaneous interpretation in Parliament, the moves were contemptuously dismissed as token gestures.

When the great Diefenbaker upset had occurred in 1957, Premier Maurice Duplessis was still firmly entrenched in power, his Union Nationale party having won another sweeping victory the year before. It was due to the assistance of 'Le Chef' that the Conservatives got fifty Quebec seats in the 1958 election, the largest number they ever had. In September 1959 Duplessis died, but it was not so much his death that hurt the Tories as the death of his successor, Paul Sauvé, a few months later. Diefenbaker had the highest regard for Paul Sauvé and believed he could have been the saviour of confederation; he spoke of him as a future prime minister of Canada.

PAUL MARTINEAU

At first, Mr Diefenbaker's attitude towards Quebec didn't enter into my concern at all. I'm talking about '56 – the leadership convention. I did not think for a moment that he would not be aceptable to Quebec. I believed in Mr Diefenbaker's conception of Quebec – of the Quebec problem, if you wish – of the problems of the relationship of Quebec to the confederation as a whole, or the relationship of the federal power to the provinces generally, the question of bilingualism, biculturalism, and all that. Mr Diefenbaker had a very simplistic outlook; it was rather typical of the then westerner's conception of Quebec. He believed that all he had to do was be a good fellow,

Prime Minister Diefenbaker and Premier Paul Sauvé of Quebec

slap a few of his friends on the back, say a few words in French, and make a few token gestures, and that all would be well. One of his phrases that he always liked to repeat was that there was one Canada, with rights to all and privileges to none. In other words, everything was rosy in the rosiest of worlds. We were all Canadians, and this question of French Canada – well, we should let them work out their own thing as long as they didn't interfere with the general conduct of the administration. And so on. Why worry about it? And I think that this was still his outlook and his attitude in '57 and '58.

> *If Paul Martineau was unconcerned in the late fifties, it is hardly surprising that Hugh John Flemming was unaware of the tensions beneath the surface in his own province of New Brunswick, which was one-third French-speaking. Flemming had entered the federal Conservative cabinet as the first forestry minister shortly after the defeat of his own provincial government in 1960.*

HUGH JOHN FLEMMING

During that period, from 1957 to 1960, after Mr Diefenbaker came in and when our government was still in office in New Brunswick, I was not conscious of there being any difference between the French and the English in New Brunswick at all. As a matter of fact, I thought that we were getting along extremely well. I always tried to make appointments and do things on the basis of qualification rather than of race, bearing in mind that on boards and things of a collective nature you should take pains to see that their viewpoint is represented so that there is a spokesman for them.

RICHARD BELL

I don't think that there was anything in Mr Diefenbaker's makeup that could be called prejudice or a desire to discriminate or anything of that sort. I am not sure that he ever really understood the hopes or the aspirations of French people; in fact I am sure he did not. He felt that in the appointment of General Vanier as governor general that he had gone a great distance. And it must be remembered that he encountered very great criticism over the appointment of a French Roman Catholic to be the representative of the Queen in Canada. I had trouble in my own riding. The president of my association at that time told me point blank that he would never cast another Conservative vote in his life as a result of this: unfortunately he died before he had a chance to change his mind. But Mr Diefenbaker certainly received privately very great criticism from elements in the community. There was simultaneous translation, and a number of things. He felt that he had gone a long distance and I think he felt hurt that he had not been shown the response to what he thought were magnanimous gestures towards the French.

WILLIAM HAMILTON

At one time, when Diefenbaker was prime minister on campaign, he was invited to go to City Hall in Montreal and address the city council. As the local minister, I went along with him. While we were waiting, he said, 'Would you put down just one or two sentences in French for me to start with.' So I put down one or two sentences in French, and then, because the pronunciation of French is so vastly different from English, and because I've always felt that it could be shown phonetically quite neatly, I put a phonetic version of this underneath. I handed it to Diefenbaker, and pointed out to him that I had given him a phonetic version of the sentences. His indignation at that was quite short, but rather frightening to behold. He suggested to me in no uncertain terms that he knew exactly how to speak French, and that he didn't need any phonetic version handed him, thank you very much.

I think one of the things that has been most noted about his attempts to get some kind of empathy with French Canada was not only his inability to speak French, but the quality of the French which he did speak. It suggests to me that his attitude was, 'As long as I use the French words, no matter how badly pronounced they are, they should be adequate. I am making my bow in the direction of French Canada.' No, there was a complete lack of understanding, as there was, I think, of a number of other areas in Canada.

LÉON BALCER

To this day Diefenbaker will tell you, 'I named the first French Canadian governor general, and I gave Quebec simultaneous translation, and things like that.' He feels that that was all right. But, as far as we were concerned, we interpreted his delays and the time he would take to settle any Quebec problems, appointments, and things like that, as keeping Quebec in its place.

It was always an up-hill fight [getting anything done] and he was getting annoyed. Time after time he told me, 'You and your Quebec!' because that was my role in Conservative politics: when we would all get together, everybody excited about a big plan, then I would say, 'Wait a minute gentlemen, what about Quebec?' 'Ah, here he comes again.' That was frustrating, and after a while when we had a heated discussion, there was always, 'This man is throwing a monkey wrench in everything that we do!' That was the expression Diefenbaker used.

Also, he was not always surrounded by very good advisers; he had some friends in Quebec amongst French Canadians who were not elected, who were sort of 'yes' men. Every time they met Diefenbaker they would say, 'Oh, you are doing fine. You are great. Everybody loves you!' Of course, you couldn't blame the man for listening to sweet talk that was very pleasant to hear, but it was not always the truth, and they were not always painting the true picture of Quebec. They were people like Paul LaFontaine, Yvon Sabourin, who were great gentlemen, very pleasant gentlemen, great Conservatives, but of another age. They were talking about Borden, and Meighen. Our fifty Quebec members had never seen Meighen and had surely never seen Borden. It was another generation in politics. The generation gap played a big part.

T.C. DOUGLAS

He had the same difficulty that any westerner has in dealing with French Canada. He didn't have enough daily association with it to fully understand it, to understand the nuances and the pitfalls that are all around the subject. Mackenzie King I don't think understood French Canada, but Mackenzie King had the capacity for delegating, and so he let the three Quebec ministers, [Ernest] Lapointe, [P.J.A.] Cardin, and Chubby Power, look after Quebec. Whatever they decided was best for Quebec, King would stand by that, and put it through cabinet, and put it through caucus, and put it through the House of Commons.

Unfortunately, Mr Diefenbaker didn't have that kind of lieutenant in Quebec, and I am not sure that, if he had, he could have worked with him. I think he had a tendency to feel he had to have all the stage , not only the centre of the stage; he ought to have allowed some people to get on to the stage too, even if they stayed back a bit. But this tendency to have everything around himself, and to be like a banyan tree, as someone said of Roosevelt, where nothing could grow close to him, would have made it difficult for him to have worked with a French-Canadian lieutenant. Unfortunately, he didn't have one and didn't appear to be encouraging one.

PAUL MARTIN

I don't think he knows Quebec at all. I don't think he has any feel for Quebec. Mind you, I don't say he's alone in this regard. Given his background, given the fact that he doesn't speak French, that he's never been part of that milieu, I can understand all this. But I can't justify it. Pearson couldn't speak French. Pearson was never happy in French company. This was not his side, this was not his milieu either. But Pearson, as prime minister, understood the place of Quebec in Canadian confederation. Pearson, as prime minister and as leader of the opposition, recognized the indispensability of Quebec and the French fact in the Canadian scene, and he took steps to meet it. I think this was Pearson's biggest contribution, in moving for a real *rapprochement* between Quebec and the rest of Canada, in the way that John never did and never understood.

I don't think he understands it to this day. And he's not alone in that. A lot of people in Canada don't understand it. It's a very difficult problem. But, you know, it's there. French Canada's there. The French factor's there. You go to Montreal or Quebec now, listen to the radio, to the television, and there is a durability of the French culture that is undeniable. We have got to accept that durability and find a place for it in the Canadian scene, and John didn't do that.

JACQUES FLYNN

Mr Diefenbaker was very open-minded as far as the French language was concerned, and still is. He had no problem in this regard. The difficulties which he had were due to the fact, first, that so many of the Quebec delegates were against him at the [1956 leadership] convention – he was a bit suspicious of the Quebeckers because of that. And he didn't know many of his new members elected in '58. Before he could make up his mind and assess each and every one of them, it took quite some time.

I would say that he did more to meet the Quebec aspirations at the time than Mr St Laurent had, because he made very precise moves. The simultaneous translation in the House, that was his. The appointment of Mr Vanier, that was something also. Later we had the bilingual cheques. There were other decisions of the same type that were far-reaching by comparison with what Mr St Laurent had done. But he wanted to be sure that he was not making a mistake; and by hesitating and delaying he lost much of the credit for what he did.

CLÉMENT BROWN

You know, the great majority of the Conservative members at that period were elected due to the Union Nationale organization, which I wouldn't say switched but lined up completely behind the Conservatives in '58. Before that, Duplessis always said publicly that he had given freedom to his party supporters to vote as they wished; but I remember that he did add the caveat that if you work for a party, work for the Conservative. That was his opinion and he put his machine behind Diefenbaker in '58 and got fifty members elected that time.

They were unruly at first and they didn't see eye to eye. They were complete strangers in Ottawa because they were used to Quebec politics. The atmosphere was completely different, and they had difficulty adjusting and seeing the problem as a national problem and not from the Quebec angle alone.

Mr Diefenbaker once remarked to me that he felt that he had been elected prime minister one election too soon, because in '57 he had only nine members from Quebec and his selections for cabinet posts were rather restricted. In fact he appointed only two or three and the Quebec press was rather hostile to that. But I don't think that there was any other choice, because he had Mr [Paul] Comtois, who was sixty and who was an experienced civil servant, and Balcer, but Balcer had some unfriendly relationship with Mr Diefenbaker before – he walked out at the convention, he resigned as president of the Association, and ran as a candidate and then withdrew. They were not on a personally friendly footing.

> *Léon Claude Balcer was the senior* MP *among the Quebec Conservatives. He was first elected for Trois Rivières in 1949, and was the president of the Progressive Conservative Association of Canada at the time of the 1956 leadership convention.*
>
> *Léon Balcer was born in Trois Rivières on 13 October 1917, and was educated at Laval University. His father was a Liberal, but his mother, Berthe Harnois, was a strong Conservative, the niece of Dr Louis-Philippe Normand, president of the Privy Council in the Meighen government. Balcer was admitted to the Quebec bar in July 1941, just before he enlisted in the Royal Canadian Navy.*
>
> *At the end of the war – he retired with the rank of lieutenant – he was, in his own words, 'anti-establishment.' The Liberals were the establishment then, and the Conservatives very much the underdogs, especially in Quebec. He was attracted to the Tories because, as he said, he 'wanted things to change.'*

LÉON BALCER

We had all been elected on a very strong autonomy platform, a sort of a special status for Quebec, and special recognition for Quebec. I mean it sounds pretty old-fashioned now, but the Conservative party was the party of confederation against centralization. At that time, Duplessis was in power in Quebec, and it was a strong autonomy policy that was coming from the Quebec government. We were all elected with the support of Duplessis' Union Nationale. That was the theme of our campaign in Quebec, more autonomy for Quebec and less centralization in Ottawa.

When we came to Ottawa, Diefenbaker took completely the opposite stand. He was always attaching that to the big cliché, 'All one Canada,' and there was nothing that should divide our group. But in practice you had the language barrier and this thing that Quebec is not a province like the others.

There were some grumblings among Quebec MPs because we couldn't hold a Quebec caucus, which is a tradition in Canadian political parties. We have always had provincial caucuses but Diefenbaker didn't want to have any; he decided not to have any provincial caucuses. Some Quebec MPs resented that very badly.

We were extremely busy as we had been out of power for twenty-two years. More and more pressure was put on me, as the senior Quebec minister, to get better recognition as far as Quebec was concerned.

WILLIAM HAMILTON

There was the continuing tension between Léon Balcer and the prime minister himself, and Léon Balcer and his French-speaking colleagues from Quebec. Léon was a tremendously low-key individual who had a capacity to get elected and re-elected and by seniority had achieved his position. In my opinion, he had a good mind and a grasp of what was going on, but a relative inability to direct the events or give leadership to the events which were happening around him. As a result, he never had the dynamic support of the group from Quebec. Yet, on the other hand, no one else ever seemed to evolve who captured their attention to the point where they would follow the alternative or dethrone Balcer.

A major complaint about Prime Minister Diefenbaker was that he did not have enough French Canadian cabinet ministers and that he did not give enough responsibility to those he had.

PAUL MARTINEAU

Now in '57, as there were only a very few members from Quebec elected, Mr Diefenbaker had a very good excuse for the small Quebec representation in the cabinet. He said to his members and he said to his candidates, 'Elect members from Quebec who are of cabinet calibre, and you will have plenty of representation.' We went along with that in '57. But in '58 there were fifty members, and I think a lot of material from which good cabinet ministers could have been drawn. Yet the representation remained small.

R.A. BELL

One must look at this from Mr. Diefenbaker's point of view, which clearly was that he had to work with the material that had been given him. He was not impressed by the quality or character of the material. Partly, I think, this was his own background and I don't think he fully understood the people he was dealing with. Perhaps if he had given a greater challenge to some of these people at an earlier stage and taken some risks of them not doing well, it might have been better.

His early appointments from Quebec were absolutely disastrous and I am thinking back to [Henri] Courtemanche and [Raymond] O'Hurley. Courtemanche was an orator and nothing else, and was known as that by his colleagues. O'Hurley was one of the most genial, delightful men I have ever known in my life, but away out of his depth in Defence Production attempting to deal with the business community. Then Sévigny – it seemed that the only French Canadians who came to Mr Diefenbaker's attention were those who sat in the deputy speaker's chair. If they were dreadful enough as deputy speaker, then they were bound to get promotion to the cabinet. Except for Martineau, the French Canadian deputy speakers were atrocious.

WILLIAM HAMILTON
For whatever reason, one of the great weaknesses of the Diefenbaker cabinet was the quality of the representation that it had from the province of Quebec. People can form their own opinion about me as an English Canadian, but my opinion of my colleagues from Quebec was that none of them approached a few of the outstanding ministers from other provinces.

I think you'd better be quite specific about this, because any cabinet is probably going to have two-thirds or three-quarters of its membership that are not particularly outstanding. Then you're going to have a few that are really notable, if you've chosen as well as you could. When you think back over the Diefenbaker cabinet, you have men like George Nowlan, who was not only a grand man, he had a good grasp. You had Donald Fleming, for example, who perhaps stood out notably. You had Alvin Hamilton, who was genuinely a brilliant individual and most imaginative. You might find two or three others – Davie Fulton, I think. But never did anyone of that kind materialize from Quebec. In some cases, you had, perhaps, people who were a little bit less notable than their colleagues. I'm not going to start ranking the bottom grouping, English or French, but I think this was one of the great weaknesses of Diefenbaker's French representation.

The greatest paradox in this regard was Pierre Sévigny, who had many of the characteristics of real political greatness. He was a magnificent orator. He was completely fluent in the two languages. He had a fine war record. All these things to his credit, but I think one is justified in questioning his quality of judgment. This was evident during his cabinet period, which tended to make people a little loath to take his leadership.

Of the Quebec ministers, Pierre Sévigny was the closest to Prime Minister Diefenbaker.

PIERRE SÉVIGNY
As matters stood, Diefenbaker had a violent hatred for Léon Balcer. Noel Dorion could not speak a word of English and never did learn it adequately and behaved in such a way in Ottawa that he did not really inspire Mr Diefen-

baker's confidence. Ray O'Hurley was a good man but he was a man who, because of his education and his background, was limited. He had an enormous job which he did well, considering once again his education and his background, but he was not a man really of stature who could influence the public at large. Comtois was an older man. He had been a civil servant for most of his life and, you know, once a civil servant always a civil servant. It is very difficult to become a leader once you have been used to taking orders and submitting to the orders of those above.

So I was really about the only one who was in full command of the English language and who could just as easily communicate with the French as the English, and who was so fanatically attached to our political fortunes. Furthermore I was always one who came forth with certain ideas, like the idea of Expo. I was the one who suggested, for instance, that Governor General Vanier be appointed. I am the one who more or less found a solution to settling the question of grants to universities, and Diefenbaker liked that.

There was another reason why I was the one being consulted most frequently. It's because Diefenbaker liked me and I liked him, in spite of the fact that we fought continually and he gave me more hell than I deserved – maybe I did deserve some, too. But the fact remained I liked him and he liked me. Eventually, though, we got to fighting a little too much.

Jacques Flynn was one Quebec MP *on whom Diefenbaker came to rely. He was from an old 'bleu' family. His grandfather, Edmund James Flynn, was premier of Quebec from May 1896 to May 1897, the last Conservative to hold that office.*

Jacques Flynn was born 22 August 1915 at St Hyacinthe, Quebec. He was educated in a seminary and took a BA *and a law degree at Laval University. After being admitted to the Quebec bar, he had his first taste of politics campaigning in Roberval for the Union Nationale candidate in the 1939 provincial election. The only place where he did not speak that year was the only place to give his candidate a majority. It was such a shattering experience that Flynn took no active part in politics for the next thirteen years. He did run in 1957, however, and although he was defeated on that occasion he was elected for Quebec South in the Diefenbaker sweep of 1958.*

While it may have been Pierre Sévigny who found the solution to the problem of the university grants, it was Jacques Flynn who was given the task of negotiating with Quebec the deal which was a proud achievement of the Conservative government.

JACQUES FLYNN

I had a meeting with Mr Duplessis in the summer of '59. I wanted to discuss with him the problem of the subventions to universities. The Union Nationale government had told the universities not to accept these federal subventions and was creating a problem for the Quebec Conservatives. I was looking for a formula to settle it.

In fact, the formula which was subsequently adopted was the one that I discussed with Mr Duplessis at that time. But Mr Duplessis was to die a few months later, and he was already a bit sick. He was not budging from his position. He was practically always repeating the same thing. When I argued with him, he would say, 'Oh, no, no, no!'

The funny thing is that the day after this meeting, I was at the wedding of a cousin. Duplessis was there too. Someone said to Mr Duplessis, 'You know Jacques Flynn.' He said, 'Oh, yes.' I said, 'Yes. We exchanged views yesterday.' He said, 'No, no, no. We each kept our own view.' No exchange.

The formula was accepted by [Paul] Sauvé in principle, and in practice by [Antonio] Barrette. It was worked out here in Ottawa, in part with Mr Fleming.

I think the amounts were given to the government rather than to the universities, and the government in turn was to distribute the amount among the universities. A sort of equalization payment.

The university grants formula was an important development in the relations between Ottawa and Quebec. This Conservative initiative became the basis for the Pearson government's so-called 'opting out' formula whereby a province (usually Quebec), if it did not wish to subscribe to a federal program, would get the financial equivalent from Ottawa to be spent on a similar provincial program; thus, provincial claims to rights under the constitution were satisfied.

DONALD FLEMING

We had a challenging situation where Quebec, with a third of the students of university age in this country and paying a quarter of the federal taxes, was receiving not a cent of the federal grants towards university education. The terms on which these grants had been brought into effect by the St Laurent government had made them entirely unacceptable to Quebec. I made this a matter of personal effort and personal responsibility. It wasn't possible to work this out until after the death of Mr Duplessis, but I developed very close working relationships with Paul Sauvé. It was really he and I who arrived at a formula that made it possible for Quebec to accept a form of fiscal assistance from the federal treasury equivalent to the assistance Quebec universities would have drawn from the federal treasury if they had been allowed to do so. In other words, the Quebec provincial government, exercising its constitutional authority and in fidelity to its view of the constitution, made equivalent grants available to its universities and we made equivalent grants available to the treasury of Quebec.

Paul Sauvé died in the middle of all this. It was a great loss to this country. I carried on the discussions to a conclusion with his successor, Mr Barrette. Mr Sauvé handled this matter altogether personally himself. Mr Barrette didn't have quite the same authority with his cabinet and so in his case I negotiated with him and two of his senior ministers, Mr [A.] Talbot and Mr [A.] Rivard, but at the end we arrived at a formula. What I regarded and personally lamented as a major injustice to the province of Quebec was righted and solved.

> *In comparison with the previous Liberal governments of Mackenzie King and St Laurent, the Diefenbaker government could claim to have done a great deal more for Quebec and the French language. However, the Conservatives – an unlucky party, federally – came to power at a time of great changes, not only in French Canada but in French-English relations, and the government found itself in the position of a man on a treadmill.*

LÉON BALCER

A matter like simultaneous translation would have been tremendous in 1955. That was the kind of thing that would have created enthusiasm in Quebec in the fifties. But you mustn't forget that in 1960, in Quebec, the Quiet Revolution had started. It was a brand new game, and simultaneous translation and bilingual cheques and things like that were just considered tokenism.

CLÉMENT BROWN

There was a good period when the Quebec caucus cooperated with Diefenbaker and tried to influence him in the sense of enlarging the role of the French language in Ottawa. You remember that simultaneous translation affair which came under the pressure of the Quebec caucus and which resulted in improving the relations between the government and even the party members on either side of the House. I remember very well in the old days when a member wasn't bilingual, especially one from Quebec, he couldn't ask any question of a unilingual English-speaking minister in the House. So he had either to wait until he saw the minister privately or he had someone put in the order paper a question that the minister could read in English and answer. Now there is a constant dialogue in either language and there is no difficulty. I think that is one of the major contributions to national unity and the improvement of the relations between the two language groups.

The other thing that was hard to swallow for some of the Quebec ministers was the affair of the bilingual cheques. It took two or three years before the cabinet decided that every cheque of the government should be printed in both languages. That was a trifling matter – but it was a matter of principle for the Quebec caucus members. This political gesture, which could have had a good effect in Quebec in '59, for instance, or '60, came too late, too close to the election to restore the reputation of Diefenbaker in Quebec – and at that time he was dealing with the major problem of unemployment, especially in Quebec.

WILLIAM HAMILTON

When you can spend endless hours in cabinet arguing over whether or not bilingual cheques should be instituted, and when that kind of a decision extends over a period of several months, and is then heralded and announced as a major step towards better understanding between English and French Canada, it seems to me you have an appreciation of just how little understanding existed at that time about the relationships between the two major races in Canada. I was part of all this. I felt that bilingual cheques were a good thing, and I couldn't understand why my colleagues from other parts of Canada didn't think they were a good thing. I suspect I also thought that this was going to be quite a major step toward better understanding between the English and the French. As I look back, I can see just what a piddling little thing it was.

LÉON BALCER

There were achievements, as far as Quebec was concerned. We had the national programs, the Roads to Resources and matters like that, the increase in old-age pensions. This is one of the facts that is very often forgotten, that the social security legislation of Diefenbaker was quite outstanding. We increased the old-age pension quite substantially. As far as the Quebec members were concerned, we were very happy about that. Diefenbaker, I must give that to him, was very receptive to all our ideas on that subject – and he did grand things. We settled the university problem beautifully with Paul Sauvé.

Then there were more valid matters, where we had to exert the pressure. For instance you had projects like the South Saskatchewan Dam that would profit the western provinces. Those were great: we wanted our share of those development projects in Quebec. Well, in that field, we had a pretty good record. I want to give you an example: we had the ship-building subsidy when I was minister of transport. This is something that has assured Canada's modern inland merchant marine. You see our lakers were all obsolete; we built them up and we have a brand new modern fleet, even now. That was a great thing for Quebec, because the ship-building industry in Quebec is of major importance. On that matter I got Diefenbaker's support all along, and in cabinet it went extremely well.

CLÉMENT BROWN

Some issues were solved due to the Quebec caucus. One is the Trans-Canada Highway and the other the financing of university education. They were settled after Duplessis died. Mr Diefenbaker told me that two days before he left for Schefferville, where he died, Duplessis called Diefenbaker and he asked him if it would be possible that they could meet. Diefenbaker never knew what Duplessis had in mind.

But Sauvé solved the two thorny issues that were dividing Quebec and Ottawa. Duplessis had refused any federal money for the financing of universities; he felt that it was ultra-vires of Ottawa. Sauvé took the other view; at least he came to a compromise. He settled for getting a larger share of the personal and corporate tax. Sauvé was prime minister only for a hundred days, in fact ninety-seven days, but we still talk of Sauvé's hundred days in Quebec, a complete turnabout from the Duplessis regime.

Anyway, the other problem was the Trans-Canada Highway. The St Laurent government had passed legislation, and the federal government was giving 90 per cent of the funds, providing that the highway would be built by the province according to Ottawa's specifications. Duplessis refused: 'The highway is a provincial jurisdiction, I don't want your money.' Quebec was behind $200 or $300 million on account of it, because Duplessis started and continued to build his own highway, linking it with the Trans-Canada Highway but refusing any federal funds for it. Sauvé said, 'We are going to settle.' Due to the Quebec caucus, Howard Green, who was public works minister at that time, agreed that the Quebec specification would be regarded as the national specification, which was in fact a very easy way to settle the problem.

Diefenbaker dreamed of making Paul Sauvé his successor. I think that he could have been able to persuade Sauvé, whose father had been the leader of the opposition for twenty years in Quebec and postmaster general under Bennett in the thirties.

LÉON BALCER

Sauvé had no interest at all in federal politics, and it was pretty hard to get Sauvé to give the Conservative party the same kind of support that Duplessis and Dan Johnson would give. Diefenbaker got along with one man, Daniel Johnson, who was a very good campaigner and was very close to all who were Quebec Conservative MPs, and Johnson was the real friend of Diefenbaker's in Quebec.

WILLIAM HAMILTON

I'm not being defensive here, but it was not only Diefenbaker that failed to realize the issue. It was the people around him. It was the government which had preceded him. Mr St Laurent's famous observation that Quebec is a province like the rest, which came only a year or two before the advent of the Conservative government, represented a patrician French Canadian from Quebec speaking about his own province and, it seems to me, clearly misunderstanding the feeling which was developing.

CLÉMENT BROWN

The Quebec Conservatives wanted a larger share in the cabinet and more French Canadians in the civil service. You must remember that when Mackenzie King left the government, there was not a single French-speaking deputy minister. There were some assistant deputy ministers but there was no French-speaking Canadian at the deputy minister level when Mackenzie King left. St Laurent started building, but you don't move people to the deputy minister level instantly. They have tò be put in the mold and so on, except for people with exceptional experience.

GORDON CHURCHILL

Mr Diefenbaker was respected in Quebec because he seemed to be a strong, capable leader, and not a weakling. He wanted and did treat Quebec on an equality with the other provinces. In political life you get critics who are never satisfied with things that are done, but, by and large, I think it was the best that could be done.

Quebec during our term of office was going through a rather disturbing period. The death of Mr Duplessis and the very sudden death of Mr Sauvé and then the work of Mr Lesage – all of these things were very upsetting in the province of Quebec. And they were making great advances. But we didn't lose complete support in the province of Quebec by any means, and I think Mr Diefenbaker is still highly regarded there.

Mark you, no government has found it particularly easy with regard to Quebec, and the demand for provincial rights has plagued Canadian political history right from the very beginning.

DAVIE FULTON

I don't think the Diefenbaker government can be singled out as having had worse relations with Quebec than any other government. One can certainly say that there was a great opportunity, one on which we failed to capitalize, in that we had a large number of members from Quebec after 1958 and yet we did lose our support there. I certainly wouldn't put it on the plus side.

ANGUS MAC LEAN

I think that the Diefenbaker government got along with Quebec as well as any other government did. There were a number of misfortunes which befell the Diefenbaker government which had nothing to do with anything it did itself. For example, I think the death of the premier, Mr Sauvé, as time has proven, probably turned out to be a tragic thing, not only perhaps for the Diefenbaker government but for the province of Quebec as well. I think the course of the history of Quebec and its roles and attitudes within Confederation and so on might have gone along a somewhat different course had Sauvé lived. He was an especially great man who was cut off just when he was reaching the position where he could have had an influence on the affairs of the nation.

JACQUES FLYNN

It's not so much the Quiet Revolution that hurt Mr Diefenbaker and the Progressive Conservative party, but the fact that the Union Nationale had been defeated. That was a change, a substantial change, in Quebec, and the Liberals were able to count on the support of the provincial government of Mr Lesage. It was not so much the climate as the practical situation created by the change of government which happened in 1960. That's where I think we lost a lot of support, and some went to the Social Credit. The Social Credit supporters are not people really affected by the Quiet Revolution – they were mostly rural voters. It was really where Mr Duplessis was strong.

You've got to remember that the difference between the Conservative party and the Liberal party was that the latter had a provincial party which was very close. They had always been in office, either in Ottawa or Quebec, except from '57 to '60, two years and a half. You always had either a federal Liberal government or a provincial Liberal government. The exchange between the two creates that difference.

We disappeared provincially, practically, with the absorption by the Union Nationale, and the fact that during the Second World War there was the problem of the conscription. Then you start again, and you have the Social Credit coming from nowhere, and taking most of its support from us.

J.W. PICKERSGILL

The Diefenbaker government's relations with Quebec were just a disaster. They were a disaster for the old and fundamental reason that basically – this is not as true today as it was a generation ago and not as true as it was two generations ago – but basically the rank and file of the supporters of the Tory party do not believe in equality between the two major races. They show it all the time. One of them who showed it the most all through his career was

Diefenbaker himself. I remember one day, and I'm sure Dick Bell wouldn't deny it, there was a by-election in Quebec during the war somewhere. I said to Dick, 'Why don't you send Diefenbaker out there? He's a stirring speaker. He could put on a great campaign.' He just looked at me. He realized that this would be sheer poison.

EUGENE FORSEY

In the first place, Mr Diefenbaker had a dreadful legacy from the Conservative party of the past. He had a wall of prejudice to try to break through or leap over. In the second place, he had virtually no real Conservative party in Quebec. He had to make do with the ragtag and bobtail. Some of them who were touted as quite considerable figures and experts in constitutional law and this kind of thing were mediocrities at best, a terrible crowd. I watched some of them at work and I had to sit for questioning by one man who was considered to be quite a constitutional expert. It was child's play answering him. His questions were piffling. I went in with some trepidation but I could have answered him in my sleep, easily and adequately. He had a terrible lot to pick from. There were very few people of any standing at all who would have come into his cabinet. Some who were supposed to be of some standing would have been quite useless to him, even if he had got them.

I think that he is quite right in saying that he has never had any prejudice against French Canadians. I think he is quite right in saying he has stood up for them and fought their battles on more occasions than one out in Saskatchewan in the face of great unpopularity, and he can give you chapter and verse on this. He knows a great deal more French than people give him credit for. He will give you at sight an excellent translation of any piece of French you put in front of him, I mean a newspaper article and that kind of thing. I have seen him do it. When he talks French his accent is something awful but he knows what he is saying and gets the emphasis in the right places, whereas Pearson went right through all the stoplights. So I don't think there was any prejudice, but, of course, he came from a part of the country where there were very few French Canadians, and he wasn't used to dealing with them.

Let's be honest about it. The French Canadian society in the province of Quebec, Quebec politics, are a tough proposition for almost any English-speaking Canadian. I have lived in or on the edge of Quebec most of my life. I have a great many French Canadian friends. I have a good deal to do with various French Canadian organizations. I speak French tolerably well. I preached eight sermons in French and a lady from France came up to me afterwards and wanted to know what part of France I came from, so I think I can say that my French is a bit better, my spoken French, than John's is. I think I am in a little better position than many English Canadians to know what's going on in Quebec and why and how, but even now, every now and again, I find myself quite baffled.

I think that the leader of the Conservative party, whoever he is, faced with the history of the Conservative party in Quebec almost since 1896, certainly since the turn of the century, faced with the disastrous history of the nationalist and conservative alliance of 1911, faced with the fact that there has been no real Conservative organization worth mentioning there for many many years – faced with all these things, I think any Conservative leader is up against it and may be forgiven for appearing to be rather at sea. I think John probably did his very best, but he had the most miserable material to work with and he was faced with a problem with which he had had no experience and which must over and over again have baffled, frustrated, and mystified him.

GRATTAN O'LEARY

The story of Quebec is a terrible story, as far as the Conservative party is concerned. When we hanged Louis Riel, tried him for murder and hanged him for treason, it was a hell of a thing. Mind you, Macdonald did this at the demands of the Orangemen of Ontario, because Riel had caused the murder of this poor fellow, Scott, who was an Orangeman. But once we hanged Riel, we have never recovered in Quebec. Even Macdonald couldn't.

There have been special occasions, like when Borden, in 1911, got some nationalists there who were real Conservatives, and when they got here they became Conservatives; and Bennett that one year got some of them. They don't stay, there is no question about it. The average French Canadians, looking at these two parties, feel that they are more comfortable in the Liberal party. I don't think there is any doubt about it.

Between the Conservatives and the Liberals, it is not the old case of the *Rouges* and the *Bleus*; the *Bleus* were strong in Quebec up to the days of Riel. After that we faded. We have never recovered, and this is understandable.

This is a great tragedy for Canada. As long as Quebec votes solidly for the Liberal party, the Liberal party is in trouble in the rest of Canada.

13
The wrong and the rights

By June 1958, when the Conservatives had been in power for a year, the number of unemployed reached 487,000. This was 7.9 per cent (seasonally adjusted) of the labour force, the highest unemployment rate since the depression. The following year witnessed a slight improvement, the unemployment rate falling to 6.5 per cent, but in 1960 and 1961 the number of jobless was back to half a million and the rate hovered around 7.5 per cent. Whether it was a recession, which was a relatively new economic term, or a depression — recession sounded better — there was no doubt about the hard times. The Liberal rump on the opposition benches were exultant: 'Tory times are hard times.'

The unemployment led to long and anguished debates in cabinet. There were recriminations and suspicions, openly expressed, that the ministers were getting the wrong advice from their officials. Unemployment obscured the Bill of Rights and other achievements of the Diefenbaker government.

Shortly after the Conservatives came to power, I had lunch with Davie Fulton. Even then, he was worried about the rise in unemployment. He had probably seen the secret report predicting a downturn in the economy, and he was haunted by the memory of the Bennett government's identification with the depression.

DAVIE FULTON
After the Bennett government, and the depression and the bad times the Conservative party went through then, it was a fair observation that we couldn't stand another depression. Indeed, unemployment probably did more than anything else to beat us in the end.

We made strenuous efforts to overcome it and to minimize the effects on people who were unemployed. We started a considerable expansion of the unemployment insurance program and a winter works program. Some of the grants to municipalities, in particular with respect to the sewage treatment plant program, had a dual objective: one, of solving the problem of pollution, and the other, of making useful work. We were charting, to some extent, ground that had never been charted before in Canada, even if the programs didn't work as well as we would have liked. Then there were the massive deficits that were incurred as a matter of deliberate budget policy. All these measures were a sign of the concern of the Conservative government, not just for its own welfare, for the welfare of Canada, but a recognition that we just couldn't ride with it and do nothing.

Mr Diefenbaker demanded, almost, of his ministers that they and their top civil service advisers produce measures and ideas that would counter unemployment. He was impatient with those who cautioned or counselled care because of the economic implications of some of the deficit programs. His impatience amounted almost to exasperation that he, John Diefenbaker, with his concern with this government, and with all his background, could not stem unemployment in spite of all the efforts that were being made. Here was a man who had come to power on the basis of a desire and appeal to do great new things, and then this economic recession got in his way. So there was, perhaps, in his mind, in his whole being, a sense of frustration. It made him difficult, and did make the arriving at clear decisions, especially in the area of economic policy and budgeting policy, pretty difficult.

DONALD FLEMING

I suppose, having regard to the history of the Bennett defeat in 1935 after Mr Bennett's heroic efforts to pull the country through the worldwide depression, we were sensitive on this question of unemployment – and not least of all Mr Diefenbaker. He always had a keen sensitivity on this question. He was determined that the party was going to have a different image from the one that was attached to it in and after the Bennett days.

Unemployment had begun to rear its head in 1957, even before the election, not on a large scale, but the seeds were evident. It began then. You will remember that Mr Diefenbaker used, with enormous effect in the House, in reply to Mr Pearson, the report which had been submitted to the government by the economic experts prior to the general election campaign in '57, when the government had been warned by its own advisers that they must make preparations for meeting the growing problem of unemployment. Instead of that the Liberal ministers in the 1957 election campaign busied themselves with denying that there was an incipient unemployment problem. Just as Mr Bennett in 1930 inherited the unemployment problem that had all of its seeds and its beginning in the Liberal regime that preceded it, so in 1957 and the later years we inherited the problem which had all its seeds and had its firm beginning before we came into office.

It didn't grow rapidly at first, but it began to grow in the winter of 1957–8, it was growing in '58, it was growing into '59; and it was only in about 1960 that a substantial dent began to be made in the problem. Our approach to it I think was a realistic one. We did take measures to increase direct employment by government programs. In some cases we were working in association with the provinces but in others we took on the fiscal responsibilities virtually entirely.

ROY FAIBISH

The Liberals had a very effective group in the opposition, Messrs Pearson, Chevrier, Martin, and Pickersgill. Immensely effective. Every day: unemployment, unemployment, unemployment, unemployment. And the figures weren't too good.

There were interminable cabinet meetings on economic policy, and the prime minister felt he just wasn't really getting the advice that he wanted to break through this thing. It was one of those occasions where, having listened to the ministers, he called a meeting of just the advisers. Left the ministers out. There were about twenty of them in the room.

He pointed his finger and he went around the room and said, 'Now, is that the advice you're giving me? Is that the advice?' About eighteen of them were going this way [nodding], which wasn't the way he wanted to go. [O.J.] Firestone happened to be one who was saying, 'No, that's all wrong; the fiscal policy's wrong that they're recommending; the monetary policy's wrong; and the general economic policy's wrong. It's wrong. I don't agree with them.'

In this case, Diefenbaker waited as long as he could, and went with the majority. That was catastrophic. Unemployment got worse, and a kind of panic developed, and it spread right into the early '60s. It was never effectively coped with. Mike Starr came forward with his winter works program and there were one or two other things. But, generally speaking, on a broad approach, there wasn't a coordinated fiscal, monetary, and general economic policy. It wasn't coordinated, it wasn't well thought through, and it didn't effectively meet the problems of the time.

MICHAEL STARR

This was the slogan, 'Why wait for spring? Do it now.' We pointed out how construction can be carried on in the winter months without any stoppage.

Bob Campeau was one of the first to pick me up on this, and he built the apartment building on Bronson [in Ottawa], where I turned the first sod in October. Now you can see construction going on year round, but that was the beginning – that slogan, and the research and the education for the builders that we promoted.

Then we started the municipal winter works program to help fight unemployment in the winter months by contributing to the labour costs. This was a result of a conference I had with the Canadian Federation of Mayors and Municipalities. They said, 'Yes, we'll do it if you'll alleviate that additional cost that we have to bear if we do this sort of thing in the winter months.' That's how it started. Another program was the technical and vocational schools program. We built 880 schools and additions. All these were innovations in the Labour Department which, prior to that, had been considered sort of a second cousin to all the other departments; now, it rose to an equal basis and became prominent because that is where the programs were emanating from.

We started these programs to relieve unemployment. Don't forget that in that period you found a high unemployment in the winter months and it tapered down to 300,000 in the summer, not as you find it now, where it is constant, a half a million year round. The truth is that we didn't create unemployment. It was just our tough luck to walk in when it was developing.

We couldn't avoid it because the opposition kept pounding at us like they don't do now. It was an everyday occurrence with the 'Four Horsemen' [Pearson, Martin, Chevrier, and Pickersgill]. I remember $35 million for the municipal winter works program. They debated it for eight days, eight solid days!

DONALD FLEMING

The winter works program was one of the many programs that we initiated to provide direct employment. This was something new actually, because the prevailing attitude in times past had been that work involving manual effort just couldn't be carried on in the municipalities in the winter. We thought this view was out of date. Our programs in this respect did lead to substantial local employment on local projects in the municipalities in the winter months when employment normally is acute because of seasonal factors.

The program wasn't developed in its entirety in any one year. We brought in additional measures in succeeding years as the nature of the problem as well as its world-wide impact became clearer. The United States was going through the same experience, and this reflected on conditions in Canada. I would say that, whereas in my student days we were taught that the trend of the US economy made itself felt in Canada with a lag of about six months, in more recent times, and certainly in the period we are speaking of now, the lag became reduced. We feel the result of trends in the economy of the United States sooner now in Canada than we used to fifty years ago.

Our fiscal programs were developed further in the years '59 and '60. On March 31, 1960, I brought in my budget and it was a balanced budget. I had achieved my long-sought goal of a balanced budget. If you look at the photograph that was taken in the Press Gallery that night, at the press conference following the budget speech, you will see a radiantly happy-looking minister of finance surrounded by three of the officials of the department. It was I think the happiest night I had in my more than five years as minister of finance.

We had high hopes that we had rounded the corner in 1960, but it was not to be. Within three weeks of the introduction of that budget, the economic indicators began to show a downward trend and they continued downward through that summer and fall. It threw my budget calculations out of joint and it became necessary in all fairness to the Canadian economy to bring in the baby budget which I did the December following. It was necessary then, as we thought, to resort to more fiscal measures to accompany any measures in the monetary field that the Bank of Canada might see fit to take. They were quite extensive, and designed to stimulate the economy, the product of several months of very earnest study.

Some sought to make light of my balanced budget of March 31st, but the fact was that that budget was based on the most up-to-date information and forecasts that were available at that time. But, within three weeks, as I said, the downturn started.

R.A. BELL

There was deep concern. In retrospect, I am certain that not enough was done until too late. The initial approach was on the basis of creating a stimulus for the economy through tax cuts, which occurred in a budget late in 1957, and a stimulus through additional governmental spending, first by direct payments as increases in old age pensions, and secondly by the winter works program, by the roads to resources program, by an attempt at development in the north country, all of which were started late in '57 or during the early part of '58.

An attempt was made to ease the money situation. The attempt, regrettably, was not successful. It will probably be for all time a matter of controversy, the extent to which the lack of success was due to Wellington Street becoming the widest street in all the world – the distance between the Bank of Canada and the Department of Finance was growing wider every day. But in any event there were attempts, and they were not sufficient.

Unemployment was the government's real failure. It put us into a position where we could be tarred with the carry-over from the Bennett days. Paul Martin was especially skilful in his daily questioning on matters related to unemployment. The breach between Diefenbaker and [Mr Speaker Roland] Michener really arose out of Diefenbaker's feeling that Michener was refusing to discipline Martin in connection with these questions on the Orders of the Day, that Martin was turning his back on the speaker, and that Michener, in Diefenbaker's view, was too weak to handle Martin.

ALVIN HAMILTON

We couldn't do anything about unemployment with the weapons that we used from 1957 to 1960. I spent more money fighting unemployment than any other minister because I was the one who hired them for all the bush work. My protest was that it was costing us so much per job that it wasn't worth it. I supported Mike Starr when he proposed turning it over to the municipalities to get work, because it cost much less to get each job.

The economy did start to improve slightly in '59, but that tight money budget stopped it. Now, the two programs, (a) the public works program and (b) the winter works program, were not really solving anything. My argument was: let's get the economy moving and let private enterprise, which I used to say was 80 per cent of the jobs anyway, do it.

This is where you run into trouble. You have a group of people in monetary and fiscal policy who want to tighten the thing down. One of them used to say to us, 'If only we had a government that had enough guts to make a half a million unemployed, then labour would be humble and wouldn't ask for so much money and the economy could grow.' That man's name is [Simon] Reisman, and Reisman knows that we all remember this because he finally found a government that would do it in 1969.

The minute we got going on the expansionist theory of getting the dollar down – George Hees was pulled into the Trade and Commerce Department because he had more zip and go than Gordon Churchill, and I was given the Wheat Board – there was a rise in exports, from 1960 on. There is no country in the world except Japan that exceeded that rise. The average growth of trade in the sixties was approximately 103 per cent around the world. Canada's growth during that same period was 160 per cent.

The keynote of that whole expansionist drive was, first, the big sales with China which brought $500 million of unexpected currency into our hands, and this had a multiplier effect of $1.5 billion. But the gut thing was the devaluation of the dollar down to 92.5 cents. That was the spark that made us competitive in manufacturing all over the world. The biggest percentage increase was not in wheat but in the manufacturing segment.

You have got to give the credit to Trade and Commerce – that was George Hees, yelling and shouting at the top of it, and a whole dedicated team which went out to help him. It wasn't only the thing of selling goods, it was the question of getting companies interested in selling. It was the expansionist concept that began to bring people back to work.

If you look at the indicators you will find that, from the period of '57 to '61, there had been one rise and one drop and one rise; in '61 the thing turned upwards and never stopped until February '66. Our expansion program started in the spring of 1961 and then we pegged the dollar: that program corresponded with the economic uplift. The wheat sale started it off, and the devaluation of the dollar the next year brought this country into the greatest growth period in its history, from February '61 to February '66. Sixty full months is the longest sustained growth period in Canada's history, both by quantitative amount and by percentage.

Perhaps because of the high rate of unemployment and the recession there were few serious labour disputes while the Conservatives were in power. Yet, John Diefenbaker as prime minister did not always step wisely in his dealings with union leaders.

GORDON CHURCHILL

One thing that impressed me when I look back is that no national crippling strike occurred during our term of office. There was a threatened railway strike but it didn't take place. I recall that the prime minister, Mr Diefenbaker, George Hees, the minister of transport, and Mike Starr, the minister of labour, and myself sat up all night while the CPR management and the labour unions were attempting to reach an agreement. The agreement was finally reached at 4 o'clock in the morning and the railway strike was averted, to the great benefit of the country. I think that our record with regard to labour relations was distinctly good during our term of office. We had the threats of strikes but they were avoided.

EUGENE FORSEY

It was at the government's annual meeting with the Canadian Labour Congress. We had put in a long memorandum as usual. I had drafted the sections dealing with unemployment and had listed a long stream of things that we felt ought to be done. When the memorandum had been presented, Mr Diefenbaker said, 'I will ask the minister of labour for a reply.' I thought,

'Now, this is very good, because this will help to give the quietus to these yarns that John is the whole government, that he never allows his ministers to do or say anything except by his leave.' Mike Starr got up and did a superb job. He took up our proposals one, two, three, four, five, six – there were ten or a dozen of them – and on each one he said, 'On this the government had done such and such; or, on this the government is doing such and such; I am introducing a bill this afternoon which will so and so; on this the government is about to do such and such; I am introducing a measure on Monday.' All the things he said they were going to do, they did, and he ran over things they had done and which were related to matters which we proposed, and it was a very impressive performance. The only slip he made was that we had said something about rationalization of industry and Mike confused it with nationalization, and he tut-tutted us for that. When he had finished, I think the delegation was quite impressed.

There were about six hundred trade unionists there in the Railway Committee Room and [Claude] Jodoin got up and replied in a somewhat casual fashion. Then, to my astonishment and horror, the prime minister arose and said, 'I have nothing to add to what the minister of labour has said,' and then talked for ten minutes and proved it. He not only had nothing to add, he had a great deal to subtract. It wasn't at all clear, it was all like Ramsay Mac-Donald's speeches in his later years, loud detonations in a dense fog. But out of the fog came, from time to time, 'free enterprise, the principles of free enterprise, the principles of free enterprise to which this government was devoted, the principles of free enterprise on which this government's policy is based.'

The impression left at the end of the speech, as I said in the letter I wrote to John, was that in his list of priorities pure 1830 Manchester Liberal free enterprise was right up at the top and the unemployed were way down at the bottom. I said, 'I think you did yourself an injustice. This is not true. Anybody who knows you knows it is not true. Anybody who looks at the record of your government knows it is not true. Mike listed a whole string of things that your government had done or was doing or was about to do, and everyone of them was an intereference with free enterprise, but so what? Presumably you thought they were right or you wouldn't have done them or wouldn't be proposing to do them. I think they were all right. I think they were perfectly good proposals and good Conservative proposals, and I am sorry that you, I think, did yourself a serious injustice before that trade union audience, and probably forfeited support to which you were entitled.' I said, 'I hope I am the last man in the country to want you to sacrifice your principles for votes, but I can't see why you should deliberately throw away votes by denying what are clearly your own principles and your whole attitude.'

I never got an acknowledgment, and, for the next two years, whenever I saw John, all I got was a curt nod of the head.

One of Diefenbaker's achievements was the Bill of Rights, which became law 10 August 1960. He also removed questions on racial origins from the census. In the 1960 census, for the first time, people were able to register themselves as Canadian. The first half-decade of Diefenbaker government, in the view of the participants, was one of numerous accomplishments in the area of civil rights and in other areas as well.

HOWARD GREEN

Mr Diefenbaker is a great humanitarian and always very much touched by hardship. He was a great defence lawyer. He was always on the side of the underdog, and he was that way as prime minister, particularly with regard to the prairie people.

The Bill of Rights may or may not be a valuable piece of legislation. I was never as enthusiastic about it as he was; in fact I used to tease him about it. But he meant business when he advocated the Bill of Rights and I am sure he would say that the highlight of his term as prime minister was its enactment.

I think also the fact that the government directed the attention of the Canadian people to northern Canada was very, very important and will be steadily more important as time goes on. People criticized him for that. They said that it was a lot of nonsense. I think the man had a real vision about developing Canada in the North and I think that will prove to be very much worthwhile.

There were various other matters. For example, the aid to technical schools, which has caught on, certainly in British Columbia. The Institute of Technology is now one of our finest schools – no trouble placing graduates – whereas university students have many problems. I think the aid we gave of that kind was very, very helpful. The same is true of housing. I was particularly interested in housing. Our housing starts in 1958 set a record which lasted until a short time ago. We brought in a small home plan.

PAUL MARTIN

The Bill of Rights was a very successful venture. He made a lot of that. It was a good thing to have done. I didn't give him all the praise that he deserved for it at the time, but looking back on it, that was an achievement.

I think that he gave politics a good, lively flavour. I think he was proud of Canada, and he spoke in a highly emotional vein about Canada's future, and all of that I applaud. He was the leader of the nation. Once he came down to Windsor to get an honorary degree, and he came out and spoke to the children in the high school in the town of Essex. And he was quite impressive. He did that all the time. That kind of thing was good and valuable. He worked hard at being a political leader, and he won acclaim and admiration from thousands of people.

His championing of the North was innovative. I think perhaps he was the first to do that. While we scoffed at it, our scoffing was obviously political. I think he did give the North a new meaning to Canadians, and that new meaning has evolved into our present Arctic policy, into the present attention that is being paid to the discovery of oil in the Arctic, into the development of the resources of the Northwest. He did give leadership there.

But in the sheer business of government, hard government, I don't think that he measured up. Of course, this is a very difficult country to govern.

JACQUES FLYNN

There's no doubt that the Diefenbaker government was starting a new era – no doubt. With Mr St Laurent you had very conservative government with a small 'c.' You remember how Mr St Laurent was. He was running the country as a corporation. There's no doubt that Mr Diefenbaker, with his totally different personality, his flamboyance, started something new in many areas. In social security, for instance, he went much further and faster than Mr St Laurent. With the Bill of Rights, he also created a climate. There was quite a lot of debate over that, and since then this has been a major preoccupation of Parliament. These two things marked a difference from the previous administration.

ELLEN FAIRCLOUGH

Certainly, I think one of the personal successes of Diefenbaker was the Bill of Rights. I don't think there is any doubt about that. It was something that he had had in his mind for a long, long time and had proposed many times from opposition. I think it gave him great gratification and justly so. It gave us all a great deal of satisfaction to have his success so pronounced.

PAUL MARTINEAU

I believe the Bill of Rights was an important accomplishment. It was the crowning of a life-long ambition by Mr Diefenbaker. While it was belittled at the time as having insufficient teeth and so on, it has subsequently been recognized as an important element in the legal economy of this country by the Supreme Court of Canada. It certainly must be considered by legislators, and in relationships between people generally.

I believe also that the Diefenbaker government was instrumental in a great degree in opening up new markets for Canada, especially for wheat-growers. It was during our government that the first important contracts with Soviet Russia and China were signed, and that the wheat was delivered. And under the emphasis of George Hees there was a growing movement in our trade relations abroad that resulted in substantial expanded trade, and this trend has continued, making Canada one of the world's top traders.

GORDON CHURCHILL

The Bill of Rights has become established now as one of the basic and fundamental protections for the individual in Canada. That certainly was an achievement.

I am of the opinion that we enhanced our position in international affairs due to the activity of the prime minister and the ministers of external affairs. We supported NATO to the full. We supported the Commonwealth and played a prominent part at the United Nations.

One of the major matters that engaged our attention quite early was giving financial aid to the provinces and that was done rather speedily. Vast sums of money were allocated to the provinces, reducing the amount available for the federal government, and special financial aid was given to the Atlantic provinces. We wouldn't have had a deficit of any size during our six years in office had it not been for the large sums of money that were allocated to the provinces.

DONALD FLEMING

I take a lot of satisfaction from what we did in federal-provincial relations. Part of the scheme of equalization payments had been devised by our predecessors, but we entered into this field and deliberately incurred deficits in order to assist the fiscal positions of the provinces on a scale never attempted before. I personally had the satisfaction of introducing the Maritimes adjustment grants. These went to the four Atlantic provinces, and were a special kind of assistance to them directly out of the federal treasury.

I introduced also the system of the gradual withdrawal of the federal government from the two major fields of direct taxation, mainly personal income tax and the corporation income tax, in order that the provinces should be at liberty if they so chose to enter those fields to the extent that we were vacating them. Our assistance to the provinces developed on an enormous scale, and this is one of the major reasons that we incurred deficits. Our credit was very much stronger than the provinces.

I think, some day, somebody should write an authentic study on the fiscal position of the provinces when we came into office in 1957. I don't want to use too strong a term, but that position gave cause for great deal of concern. This was not a problem that could be resolved in a day, but we moved very swiftly. Virtually every budget that I introduced provided further assistance to the provinces. Without that assistance, I think there would have been a very different story told of development in this country in those years.

GRATTAN O'LEARY

I remember that when the Bill of Rights first came in, I used to have talks with Davie Fulton about it. The provinces hadn't all accepted the damned thing. People thought that the courts wouldn't accept it. As a matter of fact, I have talked to Supreme Court judges who downgraded the Bill of Rights. But apparently now it is taking a place in the country. So you could say this was something he did.

DAVIE FULTON

I don't think there is any question but that John Diefenbaker greatly broadened the base of the Conservative party. In a sense, that is a political achievement rather than a governmental one. In the over-all concept of politics this was an important thing, as I am a great believer in a strong, broadly based party of the right. I don't mean a right-wing party, but a broadly based Conservative party. I think it is healthy and essential to maintain the over-all political balance of the country, and John Diefenbaker's contribution in restoring that, and certainly broadening the base, is to my mind one of his major achievements. Some of us I think would be justified in claiming to have played a part in it.

In the sense of what did the government do, I think of the improvement of the economy of the prairies, as far as it is dependent upon farming. I am thinking of the policy on advance payments for farm-stored grain, which greatly helped to level out the peaks and valleys of prairie farming income. Then there is the concept of the development of the North and the initial steps that were taken in that direction. Amongst other achievements, I would mention the Bill of Rights, to which I attached very great importance, not only as a symbol and as an embodiment, if you like, of philosophy, but as an important piece of legislation. It is only just beginning to come into its own.

When Davie Fulton first entered Parliament in 1945 he was twenty-nine years old, a clean-cut young officer fresh from the battlefields of Europe. He had been nominated by the Kamloops Conservative Association while serving in Italy, had agreed to stand, but had said that he would not come home to campaign until the war ended. VE day was 8 May 1945, and on 14 May he was flown home with some twenty-eight other 'khaki' candidates for seats in the federal election of 11 June and the Ontario provincial election which was held a week earlier.

Edmund Davie Fulton came from a prominent British Columbia family. He was the fourth son of Frederick John Fulton, who had been a minister in the provincial government of Sir Richard McBride between 1901 and 1909 and a Conservative Unionist MP for Cariboo between 1917 and 1921. On his mother's side, his grandfather, A.E.B. Davie, and his great uncle, Theodore Davie, had been premiers of British Columbia in the late nineteenth century.

He was born on 10 March 1916 in Kamloops. He studied at the University of British Columbia and, from 1937 to 1939 at Oxford University as a Rhodes scholar. He had little time to practise law; the year after leaving Oxford he was back in England with the Seaforth Highlanders of Canada.

DAVIE FULTON

I was directly concerned with the Columbia River treaty as a treaty. This was a unique concept. It was the first time it had been done anywhere in the world – two nations agreeing on the joint development of an international river for their mutual benefit. Some of the subsequent developments, with respect to the handling of the benefits in Canada, and the controversy with the government of British Columbia as to whether they would be sold for cash or used here, threw away a great deal of what Canada otherwise would have realized. But the treaty itself, the basis of the treaty and the potential benefit, was in my view a major achievement, a near success.

For the first time we got near-unanimity of Parliament on a formula to make it possible to amend Canada's constitution at home. We came within an ace of agreement. We didn't quite succeed and so I don't know whether you call that a success or a failure. It is still there as a valid basis for future discussion upon which we might be able to build. It became known as the Fulton-Favreau formula when [Liberal Justice Minister Guy] Favreau took it up and again came within an ace of success. There are some things you can do if the political climate is right, and we faced the same thing as Favreau and the Pearson government ultimately faced – a particular development in the political climate that made it impossible to achieve that final step of ten provinces, as well as the federal government, agreeing. Again it was the government of Quebec which, because of the political atmosphere that was developing at home, felt it was impossible to agree in the last analysis.

As justice minister, Davie Fulton was in charge of the Royal Canadian Mounted Police. In the winter of 1958–9, he was faced with a crisis over the dispatch of RCMP *reinforcements to Newfoundland, where an ugly labour dispute was under way.*

DAVIE FULTON

The background was the IWA [International Woodworkers of America] strike in Newfoundland, and Premier Smallwood's obvious determination to have a confrontation at almost any cost and drive the IWA, as a union, out of Newfoundland. Rioting developed. The RCM Police, as a provincial police force under the contract system, the division in Newfoundland being under the authority of the attorney general of the province, stripped down nearly all their other detachments to concentrate at the small village of Badger. That was the area of the most violence and most direct confrontation.

Eventually, the attorney general of Newfoundland [Leslie Roy Curtis] called upon me as minister of justice for Canada, and minister responsible for the RCM Police, to send in reinforcements. The agreements, by which the RCM Police performed the functions which would otherwise be performed by the provincial police forces in the provinces, do have a provision that if the attorney general of the province calls upon the attorney general of Canada to send reinforcements, then they *will* be sent provided that in the judgment – that is the word, 'judgment' – of the attorney general of Canada they can be sent without prejudice or detriment to the other interests and responsibilities of the force.

When the call was made I discussed it first with the commissioner [L.H. Nicholson], and he said, 'I am getting ready to send them; I am ordering planes to stand by.' I said, 'I think you had better make sure that nothing is done, that the planes don't take off, because this is a matter having obvious political and intergovernmental implications and I have to discuss it with cabinet and get clearance before a move of this major proportion is made.' I did so and the cabinet felt that we should not send the reinforcements. The prime minister was, perhaps, the most outspoken. He remembered the Regina riots and the Winnipeg riots, and other matters of that sort, and he felt that the RCM Police themselves, as a force, could not stand another such confrontation.

I want to be very clear. I'm not in any sense backing away from the obligation of the police to maintain law and order in the ordinary sense. But this was the basis of the position: in circumstances where the confrontation had been almost provoked by the government, then you couldn't cast the RCMP in the role of strikebreakers and become an instrument in driving a union out of the province. That was the decision of cabinet. It did concern me. I don't want to hide that. But, on thinking it over at that time, not just since, I came to the conclusion that the position was right, that it was sound. I supported it. I have never made any attempt to fix the blame on John Diefenbaker because I accepted the decision and made it my own. It was not one where I might, had it not been for those discussions, have followed a different course. It wasn't a case where I said, 'Okay, if you insist, well, perhaps, I should have resigned but you know, I will carry it out, but against my better judgment.' It was a case where I was convinced by the force of argument, and after reflection and looking at what the contract said.

I asked Commissioner Nicholson: 'Can you maintain order in your opinion with the present strength of the force in Newfoundland, the resources presently at your disposal and at the disposal of the officer in command down there?'

He said, 'Yes, I believe we can.'

I asked him a further question, 'Can you do so without endangering the lives and safety of the members of your force? Do you consider that unless we send reinforcements that there may be an outbreak of such a nature that you will be so unable to handle it that we would be putting the lives and safety of the men who are there now in danger?'

He thought that over very carefully and very fairly and I admired him for this. He said, 'No, I do not. I consider that we can maintain the position, but it is dicey and the strain on my men is terrific.'

I reported those answers to cabinet and cabinet confirmed this decision. I so acquainted the commissioner that the reinforcements were not, without my further order, to be moved. He said, 'Very well, sir. You will have my resignation in the morning.'

We made every effort to persuade him that he should not resign, because the decision was not a decision of the commissioner which had been overruled by the minister; the decision, under the terms of the contract, very clearly was a decision of the minister. At worst there might have been a recommendation and advice from the comissioner which was not followed. But it wasn't a case of the commissioner's authority being undermined or a decision within his power being reversed.

He said, however, that in his view the basic arrangement was such that he felt that the honour of the force was at stake and that it would be undermined by the decision not to send the reinforcements. He could not conscientiously carry on as commissioner, although he never went back on his statement that it was not necessary in the interests either of maintaining order or preserving the life of his men who were there at the time. I pointed out to him the considerations arising under the larger implications for the force in the long run of being cast in the role of strikebreakers and of being a political instrument of the government of Newfoundland in effect to ensure the breaking of the strike. I think that carried some weight with him, but not enough weight. In any event, I asked him to reconsider it overnight. The next day he said, 'No, I am sorry. I confirm my decision to resign.'

While I questioned the commissioner's judgment – I think he made a wrong judgment to resign on the wrong basis – I certainly respected his integrity and his motives. As for the situation: there was no more violence, there were no further outbreaks. It did not prove necessary in the strict sense to send the reinforcements. It was a difficult decision, but I think that the event proves it to have been a correct one, not to send them.

There was not complete agreement among his opponents about Diefenbaker's accomplishments. But T.C. Douglas, as well as Conservatives, agreed that the government's social welfare programs represented an advance.

J.W. PICKERSGILL

I've said over and over again in Parliament, I challenged them to tell me anything they ever did – and not between '57 and '58 when they were just providing a few earnests for an election. I always said, apart from the Atlantic Province Grants that they gave, name me one achievement after the election of '58. I've yet to have any of my buddies tell me a single thing. The nearest thing was perhaps ARDA, whether it was good, bad, or indifferent. There is a lot of argument about it, but it was basically a good idea. But I don't know anything else. Diefenbaker never even abolished closure, which he promised to do and which I challenged him to do over and over again. I said we would vote for it. It took him four years to get his Bill of Rights through, not that we were going to oppose it, but he just couldn't seem to bring himself to do it. It just seemed to me that they never got anything done. I think that's the real reason they collapsed.

There was the South Saskatchewan Dam, and there was a dam in New Brunswick called Beechwood. They did that too. In fact you might say that the only thing they did was two dams.

I don't see why I shouldn't say now what I said many times before, that Mr Diefenbaker is one of those people who is a merchant of words and when he says something he thinks he has done something. Now, I attribute this to his long period in opposition, to the fact that he was a courtroom lawyer where when you say something and it is effective you have done something. I also attribute it to another thing: that he was a loner. He never learned how to work cooperatively. Moreover, I don't think that his cabinet was run in such fashion as to have any real program.

I think Mr Diefenbaker wanted to be prime minister. That's not an unworthy ambition and I'm not disparaging it. But Mr St Laurent didn't particularly want to be prime minister. He wanted to do things that he couldn't do unless he was prime minister. Again, apart from the Bill of Rights, which is also largely words, I could never see anything that Mr Diefenbaker really wanted to do. He had been a *frondeur*, a destroyer; you know, a hell-raiser in opposition. He had done all these things with great skill but, you know, that was his skill. It's the kind of skill that isn't very helpful in running a government.

ALLISTER GROSART

In the time that Mr Diefenbaker was prime minister, the total payments on social justice accounts doubled. In other words, in the ninety years of Confederation they reached X and by the time Mr Diefenbaker's government was defeated it was double X. This was a tremendous achievement and perhaps could only have been brought about by a government that had a very strong majority.

PIERRE SÉVIGNY

I think that Diefenbaker between the years 1957 and 1963 did more for Canada in more fields of endeavour than had been done by the previous government in twenty-two years of power.

Diefenbaker gave a new life to farming in Canada. Where the farmers before had pretty dismal prospects because of various laws, their well-being, their welfare, their chances to succeed on their farms were vastly increased. That was due mainly to Mr Diefenbaker himself, who always took a great interest in farming, to a very good minister, Doug Harkness, in Agriculture, and to a man of great imaginative power, Alvin Hamilton.

Unfortunately we didn't do enough for Quebec farmers, for the eastern farmers. That was something that was in the program, but we didn't have the time to do it.

T.C. DOUGLAS

I will always feel Mr Diefenbaker deserves a special mention for the hospital insurance plan. I don't know why this has been played down.

The story is very simple. Saskatchewan was the first province in Canada to set up a government-sponsored universal hospital insurance plan. We began planning it as soon as we took office in 1944. We began immediately, within six months of taking office, providing complete health services to what we called category groups: old-age pensioners, mothers' allowance cases, widows and children, deserted wives, blind people, the physically handi- capped, and so on. They were given a blue card starting January 1, 1945. We had taken office on July 10, 1944, and they were entitled to comprehensive health services – everything: surgery, dental care, optometric care, glasses, prescription drugs, physicians' services, surgery, and so on. But we couldn't do this on a provincial scale. We hadn't the facilities. So we started in to build the hospitals, and we gave grants to local communities, long before the federal government came in. We recognized that we couldn't talk about hospital insurance unless we had five or six beds per 1000 of population: otherwise you were taking people's money for services you couldn't render.

I had legislation passed in 1946 to begin hospital insurance on January 1, 1947, and I came down to see Paul Martin, who was the minister of health and welfare in the King government, and went over our plans with him and Paul was very enthusiastic. Paul said, 'This is exactly what we have got to do.' This was in line, by the way, with the Green Book proposals which Mackenzie King and Mr Ilsley had put before the Federal–Provincial Con- ference in August 1945, just after the European war was over.

Paul said, 'This is completely in line with the Green Book proposals. You are a bit ahead of schedule, but you go ahead with this and you can be sure that within a year or two we will be in picking up part of the cost. If you can carry it for a year or two we will be in.'

We knew there was no choice but to carry on. We were committed to it. We knew unless somebody started on it, it would never be started. So we began on January 1, 1947, and it was eleven years before the federal govern- ment came in.

What makes me a little annoyed is that people like Peter Newman keep saying that the federal hospital insurance program was introduced by Paul Martin and the St Laurent government and they brought it in. That would have been in 1955 or 1956, probably 1956. But it had a joker in it, and the joker said that the federal government would contribute 50 per cent of the cost of hospital insurance in any province that had a hospital insurance plan, providing 50 per cent of the provinces representing at least 50 per cent of the population of Canada had entered the plan. They knew perfectly well that both the premier of Ontario and premier of Quebec were adamantly opposed to hospital insurance and there was no chance of having to pay 50 per cent. To Mr Diefenbaker's credit, he pounced on this in the House of Commons and pointed out that the thing was a farce and that this was mak- ing a gift without it costing anything. He said it was an empty gesture.

One of the first things Mr Diefenbaker did when he came into office was remove this provision, with the result that British Columbia, which had also, after Saskatchewan, introduced a provincial hospital insurance plan, and ourselves, for the first time got federal assistance. When we got federal assistance, the other provinces very quickly decided that they had better get into the act too, and they came in.

I am convinced that if Mr Diefenbaker hadn't taken that clause out, it isn't likely that we would have had hospital insurance for many years, if ever.

14
The Coyne catastrophe

In the spring and early summer of 1961, the Canadian public was entertained by the spectacle of the governor of the Bank of Canada challenging a government backed by the greatest parliamentary majority in Canadian history. James E. Coyne not only refused to resign, but carried on an open campaign, by means of speeches and pamphlets, against the government's economic policy. He attacked the attempts that were being made to get the country out of the recession and to reduce unemployment by deficit spending; he advocated instead a policy of restriction, of tight money, increased taxation, and lowered imports, and he insisted on pressing this policy regardless of the circumstances.

There had never been such serious trouble since the Bank of Canada had been set up as the country's central bank by Prime Minister R.B. Bennett in the thirties, and perhaps this was due to the political awareness of the first governor, Graham Towers. Personalities were involved in the Coyne dispute. From the beginning, the Bank had been given the responsibility for monetary policy, that is, the control of the money supply; but Walter Harris, when he was the Liberal finance minister, had suggested that the governor was in fact completely independent as far as monetary policy was concerned and not subject to the will of the government. Harris had adopted this interpretation largely to escape blame for the tight money policy in effect at the time – no politician wants to be held accountable for restricting the country's credit and thereby increasing unemployment, even if it is necessary to combat inflation. In the view of Merril Menzies, this created 'two sovereignties,' with monetary policy – the supply of money – entirely separate from fiscal or *financial policy – spending and the budget. It was an impossible situation, as it put an appointed official, James Coyne, on an equal standing with the elected government and meant that his tight money policy would cancel out the expansionary benefits of deficit financing. Yet, at first, Donald Fleming went along with the Harris view, and told Parliament that the governor was in charge of monetary policy and that the government could not interefere. In the end, it was because Coyne raised his own pension to $25,000 a year, which was really an irrelevant issue, that Fleming finally demanded his resignation.*

The conflict was so badly handled by the Conservatives that, in the view of some of them, it led to their reverse at the polls the following year.

MERRIL MENZIES

The governor of the Bank of Canada held that inflation was a problem at that time [1959] which it wasn't. The Consumer Price Index was so flat you could hardly see any bumps in it. He was carrying on a very restrictive monetary policy at this time, even though the government and Diefenbaker would get concerned and try to inject in various budgets some expansionary fiscal measures. But this meant that monetary policy was working in one direction and fiscal policy in another.

The prime minister had to force these expansionary fiscal measures against Mr Fleming's predilections, because Mr Fleming and his advisers saw as one on policy. This was very unfortunate.

Either late in '56 or early '57 I had written Mr Diefenbaker about the so-called Harris doctrine which became the basis for the so-called two sovereignties, with monetary policy entirely separate from having any responsibility to government. I found this not only unconstitutional, but economic and political nonsense. I don't think Mr Diefenbaker saw the whole point I was making. He did see some of it, and he used a bit of it in a speech in late January '57 or early in February, very effectively against Mr Harris. But he could not have understood the real implications, because in that short summer session of '57, Mr Fleming's first fiscal financial statement to the House – it wasn't a budget but a financial statement – re-asserted, re-instituted the Harris doctrine in full. I was in the Official Gallery, and I almost collapsed. I was struck with a deep sense of foreboding from there on that the government was divided within itself, which it was.

I could not expect Mr Diefenbaker to understand all the implications of this, and it would take time before they became evident, but it was quite clear that Mr Fleming had handed Mr Coyne gratuitously an enormous weapon to be used against the government. When the government finally did decide that they had to push strongly in the direction of expansionist policies, Mr Coyne maintained a very stubborn restrictive monetary policy right to the end.

ALVIN HAMILTON
The turning point came in the September '59 budget when Donald Fleming got up and said there is improvement in the economy, inflation is all about us, we have to tighten up here and tighten up there. It was a tight money budget. If there were two Irishmen in the cabinet before the budget, I can tell you the next day there were ten or twelve Irishmen, in other words over half the cabinet. They said, 'Who runs this country? These fellows [the civil servants] who write this stuff, or those of us who are elected?'

Diefenbaker's response was typical. He said, 'I think we should have a committee and you fellows talk to these civil servants who advise the minister of finance.' He deliberately kept Donald Fleming off the committee because Donald was always defending them.

We spent all that fall from September right through until Christmas talking to these chaps – [Ken] Taylor and [Simon] Reisman and [James] Coyne, who was the big one, as well as Bob Bryce, all the top civil servants. It was very clear by the spring of 1960 that you couldn't change Coyne. The other fellows would argue but wouldn't resist. But Coyne used to weep about how we couldn't see his point, that you had to restrict. He was advocating a 25 per cent increase in taxes, he was advocating that we arbitrarily stop 25 per cent of the goods coming across the border from the United States, that we tighten up monetary and fiscal spending. Then, in fifteen or eighteen or twenty years, we would be poor but we would be honest.

This man was very sincere and dedicated. He was very unstable when it came to anything like his views being crossed.

Two or three times I have seen him weep, just in frustration that we were so dense that we couldn't see his way, which was to restrict the economy. We were just amateurs! Some amateurs – when I think of Dick Bell and David Walker and Nowlan and Gordon Churchill and Mike Starr; we were all there.

His instability by this time had become well known. In the summer of 1960, he began to speak against us in public. We couldn't go out and answer him because our cabinet oath kept us quiet, but he thought that his duty was to go out and tell the public that this bunch of nit-wits was going to ruin the country by expanding the economy.

One of the key issues was to get the dollar down to its real value. That dollar value was artificial. You could take a look at our trade balances. We should have had our dollar way down below par with the United States. We were behind the eight ball in trade in those days. But we couldn't get Donald to agree. He was a great Christian gentleman. He fought for Coyne all that fall in 1960.

Then, what turned the tide was that Donald came in and told us one day that he found out, when he was sick for a couple of weeks, that the directors of the Bank of Canada, whom he had appointed, had voted Coyne a pension of $25,000 a year, raised from $15,000 a year. 'This is a terrible thing,' and he said to the prime minister, 'I failed you.' You never heard such a *mea culpa* in all your life.

MERRIL MENZIES

I think that Mr Fleming was only converted basically to the government position either in late '60 or '61 when he became aware of the pension increase to Mr Coyne, which was really not the essential issue. The essential issue was that Mr Coyne was following policies which maintained a grossly overvalued Canadian dollar with all the implications that had for the economy, for unemployment. Mr Fleming was a man of honour and rectitude and he just, I feel, thought that that this [pension increase] was immoral. Consequently, he came finally to oppose Mr Coyne's policies, but not, originally, on the grounds that those policies were wrong.

GORDON CHURCHILL

I had been disturbed by the high value of the Canadian dollar. It was limiting our export trade. It was running $1.05 against the American $1.00. At some time or other, it seemed to me that Coyne favoured keeping the dollar where it was. I remember speaking to Mr Fleming about it and he brushed me aside. I remember saying to him once in the House of Commons, when the opposition were attacking Mr Coyne, 'Don't defend him; I'm not happy about Mr Coyne.'

I think he was responsible for the tight money policy of 1959 and I date the decline of our government from September 1959, when the tight money policy was announced. Mr Diefenbaker was persuaded to go on the air to tell the people about it, and Don Fleming the same. That was the watershed and we started down the slope. It put many small businesses out of business and I didn't like it. So I said to Don Fleming, 'Don't defend Mr Coyne in the House.' But he wouldn't pay attention. Then, finally the crisis came with Mr Coyne, who was doing what no civil servant should do, and was making public policy statements across this country to the embarrassment of the minister of finance and the government. So something had to happen to Mr Coyne.

HOWARD GREEN

Mr Coyne was very arrogant. I never met a more arrogant Canadian in my experience. If I'd been the minister of finance I would have fired him about six months earlier. I think Mr Fleming was most patient with him. For example, when the president of Argentina came here, he brought a lot of leading businessmen with him, and I remember one of these men telling me – he was in a senior government position in the finance field – that he had been receiving literature from Mr Coyne criticizing the Canadian government. He just couldn't understand how this could possibly happen.

PAUL MARTIN

Pickersgill and I had carried on a campaign against the government for its handling of unemployment insurance – this would have been in 1959. Unemployment was at a very high level at this time. The unemployment insurance fund had been depleted. There was a deficit of something like $550 million, and we asked that an examination in a parliamentary committee be provided.

I spent a lot of time questioning Coyne on this because Coyne was a member of the investment committee of the unemployment insurance fund, as is every governor of the bank. And we criticized Coyne, we went after Coyne. The government should have come to his defence, you know. They left him alone there. This was about a year and a half before the question of his resignation came up. They had an opportunity of defending Coyne, because we were attacking him.

Coyne was a great friend of Jack Pickersgill's. Jack didn't altogether approve of these tactics, although later he joined in them for other reasons. But Coyne was defending the government at every point. I never could understand why Diefenbaker and Starr and Donald Fleming didn't join in attacking us for our attack on Coyne. It would have strengthened their position with Coyne later on.

Coyne's later campaign of speaking against government expenditures was an irresponsible thing for the governor to do. The governor has no right to pit himself against the government that he serves. Perhaps he would not have done this if he had earlier been defended by the administration.

J.W. PICKERSGILL

Jim Coyne did not need any advice from me. Anybody who knows Jim Coyne knows that he is not a very easy person to advise. He's got a tremendous intelligence and a tremendous will. But I was his friend.

Once – I think Mr Diefenbaker would probably have never believed that – I had almost no association with Jim Coyne, except on a purely social basis. We never discussed political questions at all during the period until this incident arose.

I know he did his utmost to help the government. He went to great lengths to help them with the program, far beyond the call of duty, but unsuccessfully. It wouldn't have helped us much if his advice had been taken because most of it was very good. If it had been taken, the Conservatives would have avoided a lot of trouble they got into. I think he behaved as a proper public servant in all this business.

The only question in my mind was the question of his public speeches, and he knew I didn't entirely agree with what he was doing. But once it had become a political issue, once it was clear that in my opinion he was being done the grossest injustice, I saw no reason whatever for concealing my support of him and going to see him and talk to him. There was nothing improper about it. I had a perfect right to do it.

Despite his salary of $50,000 a year as governor of the Bank of Canada [$13,000 more than the prime minister then received], James Coyne had a reputation as a penny pincher. He lived in a modest clapboard house in Manor Park, an inexpensive Ottawa suburb. A later business associate described him as 'security obsessed.' When he was governor, his private approach to finance found public expression in an insistence on keeping the Canadian dollar over-valued, in an extreme concern over the dangers of inflation. He wanted tight money to restrict borrowing. He was convinced that the Diefenbaker government's 'economic excesses' – the deficit spending made necessary by recession and unemployment – threatened Canadian survival. Nobody ever doubted his sincerity.

James Elliott Coyne was born in Winnipeg on 17 July 1910. His father, J.B. Coyne, a judge of the Manitoba Appeal Court, was a Liberal and a friend of John W. Dafoe, the editor of the Winnipeg Free Press. *In 1931 Jim Coyne, with honours in history and mathematics from the University of Manitoba, was awarded a Rhodes scholarship, and went to Oxford to study law. When he returned to Winnipeg, he joined his father's law firm. In 1936, he toured the West as assistant to Col. J.L. Ralston, who was counsel to the Turgeon Royal Commission investigating wheat-marketing. At the same time, a Bank of Canada research team was making a survey of the depression-ridden prairies, and Coyne got to know them and became so intrigued with what they said about the economic problems of Canada that he decided to join them. The following year, he gave up his increasingly lucrative law practise to become a $150-a-month clerk in the Bank of Canada's research department.*

During the Second World War, he was assistant to Donald Gordon and later deputy chairman of the Wartime Prices and Trade Board, which froze prices and was effectively in control of the economy. Even in those days he was such an austere figure, who kept himself apart from the general public, that Ottawa reporters used to refer to him as Jesus E. Coyne. After a short stint in the RCAF, where he topped his pilot's class but at thirty-four was ruled too old for combat, he returned to the staff of the Bank of Canada. He was appointed deputy governor in 1950 and governor in 1955.

DONALD FLEMING

Mr Coyne had been appointed governor of the Bank by the previous government for a seven-year term. There were questions at the time, in the minds of many people, as to whether he was the most suitable person from among the senior officers of the Bank of Canada. Many people wondered why Mr Louis Rasminsky had been passed over in favour of Mr Coyne. Rasminsky had a great reputation throughout Canada and particularly abroad. He was widely known among the governors of central banks, ministers of finance, and international financial organizations, and most highly respected. However Mr Coyne, for reasons only the previous government knows, was appointed.

I have been told various stories about this from what I thought were authentic sources. I was told that Mr St Laurent took the view that Quebec would not accept the appointment of a Jew as governor of the Bank. Another version that came from high sources was that he took the view that the banks would not accept, or view with favour, the appointment of a Jew as governor of the Bank. Another view that I got from one of my predecessors as minister of finance was that the decision was actually made by the governors, or the board of directors, of the Bank itself and that the government didn't interfere in their choice. Be this as it may, the view was widely held – and I must say that I was one of those who from the very beginning held this view – that the appointment of Mr Coyne instead of Mr Rasminsky was inexplicable.

When I became minister of finance, I knew Mr Coyne slightly. He met with me. Our initial meeting was pleasant enough. I was quite prepared to work in the fullest cooperation with him because it is absolutely essential that there should be a good working relationship between the minister of finance and the governor of the Bank of Canada if the utmost benefit is to be secured, as long as neither surrenders his point of view lightly. There is an independence expected of the governor of the Bank in discharge of his duties and also in advising the minister of finance. I always respected this independence and think it is essential.

The first trouble that we had took the form of complaints from the banks to me – that is to say the chartered banks – of lack of communication on the part of Mr Coyne. This was a matter of complaint all the time I was minister of finance right up till the crisis with Mr Coyne in 1961. Coyne handled his relations with the chartered banks very badly.

The next element however came out in the open in the election campaign in the early part of 1958. Mr Coyne wrote his annual report as governor and submitted it to me. The tight money policy of the previous regime was an issue in that campaign as it had been in 1957. There was a shortage of credit for needed commercial enterprises. Nevertheless, Mr Coyne chose, in the face of that political fact, to insert in his report a statement that there had been no tight money policy! I was faced with the necessity of making a decision as to whether to release that report or to delay publication of it. This was when the election campaign was reaching its climax in March 1958. I chose to follow the regular practice and not to sit on that report until after the election. I allowed it to be released.

I knew what would happen. I knew that Mr Pearson would take it up and say that this was vindication of the stand that he had taken, that there had been on the part of the previous government no tight policy money. I knew that this had all the possibilities of injecting the Bank of Canada into the arena of political conflict as early as 1958. However, I considered that it was my duty to make that report public and let the Canadian people form their own conclusions.

What I expected happened. Mr Pearson, within an hour or two of the publication of the report, picked up this point and tried to make an issue out of it. We, as the government, were obliged to say that, notwithstanding what the governor of the Bank was saying, there certainly had been a tight policy, and everybody else in the country knew it. That was an unhappy episode. Naturally, the press were looking for opportunities to get to the bottom of this and I was interviewed and asked if I was going to seek Mr Coyne's resignation. At the time, I said no, I would respect the independence of his office and do my best to work with him.

Time went on. His public relations were lamentably bad. He was getting me into trouble constantly. Every time he opened his mouth he gave offence to the provincial governments or others and I took it in hand to urge on him that he make a serious effort to improve his public relations, particularly his communications with provincial governments, with the banks, and others. He seemed to take this in. He went up to Queen's Park [the Ontario Legislature] and had a meeting with [Premier] Frost. The result was less than happy. He declined to discuss the very questions that Mr Frost was most interested in discussing.

Frankly, while I was ready to take advice from Mr Coyne in matters in which it was normal for the governor to advise the minister and there were numerous meetings, I was all too well aware that he was an arrogant man and a most difficult person to deal with. This was widely known. As a matter of fact, I have been told on very good authority that the Liberal government, particularly C.D. Howe, had concluded they would have to get rid of Mr Coyne.

At first Dick Bell, who was parliamentary assistant to the minister of finance, did not recognize the seriousness of the dispute. He told me that it could have been settled over a drink, 'if you had not had two very inflexible men involved' – not that Donald Fleming ever took a drink. Bell did try to bring the two men together in the hope that they could work out a settlement.

R.A. BELL

I really felt at the time that there was common ground that could be found. But, instead of an attempt being made to find the common ground, the divergence was emphasized. There was no doubt that Coyne was infuriating Diefenbaker. Diefenbaker was saying something had to be done to discipline him and other senior members of the cabinet were very irritated.

I don't give Ken Taylor, then deputy minister of finance, too high marks in this respect. I don't want to sound critical of civil servants. I think we had absolute loyalty from the civil service in the Department of Finance and, indeed, in all other departments, contrary to the views Gordon Churchill takes, which are totally false – any difficulties he had were of his own making with his Department of Trade and Commerce. But I don't think the liaison which was supposed to be between the executive committee of the Bank and the minister of finance through the deputy minister, was anything like as adequate as it should be. I think Ken Taylor was getting tired. He was getting older than his years at this stage and he was not reporting with the clarity and the depth that he ought to have been doing.

I tried some time late in 1960 to do something about this. I kept urging a meeting between senior officials of Finance and senior officials of the Bank: 'Let's work out an agreed formula on both what the Bank's role is and what the minister of finance's role is in this.' I talked to Fleming on two or three occasions.

Finally, it was decided that, through Taylor, a meeting would be set up either for Thursday or Friday. Coyne was expecting that. The Saturday was

Grey Cup day in Vancouver and the Grey Cup time in Ottawa was 4:30 in the afternoon.

No contact was made between Fleming or Taylor and Coyne on Thursday or Friday, so Friday afternoon Coyne left for the Seigniory Club to make a speech at a meeting there Friday night. When he had finished his speech, he drove on to Montreal to stay with friends where he was going to watch the Grey Cup.

At 11:30 Friday night, Ken Taylor located him in Montreal and suggested he return for a meeting at 2 o'clock in the afternoon. Coyne just said, no, he couldn't some back, the arrangements were made. He would have [J.R.] Beattie and Rasminsky attend the meeting.

So, on Saturday afternoon at 2 o'clock, in the House of Commons office of the minister of finance, there occurred a meeting between: the minister of finance, Fleming; his parliamentary assistant, Bell; his deputy minister, Taylor, and two of his assistant deputy ministers, [A.F.W.] Plumptre and [C.M.] Isbister; and on the other side, the deputy governor, Beattie, and Rasminsky, the number three man. There was no particular lack of sympathy between the Department of Finance and Beattie and Rasminsky. We talked for two hours about the situation, but we talked without the one person who needed to be talked to in the situation. We all missed the Grey Cup parade anyhow. At 4:15 the meeting broke up. Plumptre drove Fleming home, so he could see the Grey Cup. The rest of us couldn't get to our homes in fifteen minutes, and we missed the first part of the game.

I can only say that it was just the worst mishandling of what I had been trying to do – to get everybody together and talk it out. There never was another meeting between the elements of the quarrel. Never another meeting between Coyne and Fleming.

DONALD FLEMING

It was in 1960, amid the difficulties of the fiscal position that was developing in the country at that time, that Mr Coyne, without any consultation with me and for reasons that were understood only by him, decided to go out on a program of making speeches. He lined up a total of thirteen engagements in different parts of the country. The theme of these speeches was that everything was right with monetary policy and the Bank of Canada was responsible for monetary policy, but all the economic ills of the country were the result of bad fiscal policies and the government was responsible for fiscal policy.

This was interpreted, of course, as an attack on the government, indeed a series of attacks. He didn't content himself with that position but went on to advocate programs of fiscal policy. These were pretty wild policies. They were stiffly protectionist, they were virtually isolationist, they were entirely unacceptable, and they were put forward publicly without any consultation with myself or with the government.

R.A. BELL

He was advocating tighter money and also advocating a form of economic nationalism and control of foreign ownership. Perhaps some of his speeches would sound a little more moderate today than they sounded at the particular time.

DONALD FLEMING

The speeches created a supreme embarrassment. I was plied with questions in the House of Commons by the Liberals, day in and day out. Every time a speech was made, an attempt was made to associate the government with the speech, and make it appear that Mr Coyne was expounding fiscal policy. He was not doing so. He never consulted me about any of these speeches. I didn't even know in advance when or where the next one was coming

The dissatisfaction with Mr Coyne's whole conduct of his office – and he had in effect, as it was interpreted, declared war on the government – made my position in the cabinet virtually impossible. I had been trying to keep the cabinet at arms' length from involvement with the Bank of Canada. I was looked upon within the cabinet as having protected Mr Coyne, as having defended him in the face of attack. A majority of my colleagues in the cabinet were openly advocating an action to dispose of Mr Coyne. I resisted them, until the situation became intolerable.

I was finally convinced that the situation could no longer be left to follow its own course – that Mr Coyne could not be left in his office until the expiry of his term, which had another year to run – when, following these speeches, we were devising fiscal programs to meet the economic conditions of 1960. These [conditions] were taking a disappointing turn. We were framing new policies to meet them and we had meetings between officials of the departments of Finance, Trade and Commerce, and the Bank of Canada, and in these meetings open and angry breaches developed between Mr Coyne on the one hand and officials of the Department of Finance on the other. I had always assumed that my senior officials in the department looked on Mr Coyne with respect, but I was brought down to earth as a result of these experiences. I learned that a very low opinion of Mr Coyne was entertained by some of my senior officials. This, to me, was the last straw. I was convinced that it was impossible for us to concert the fiscal policies that were required as long as Mr Coyne was in a position to damn our fiscal policies and put forward his own wildly unacceptable fiscal policies and, at the same time, not cooperate with us adequately in monetary policies.

It was just about this time that I learned to my consternation also that, without any consultation with myself, the board [of the Bank of Canada] had, at the request of, and with the full participation of, Mr Coyne, voted him a substantial increase in his pension. In the event of his not being reappointed he would have acquired – he was then about fifty years of age – a pension of $25,000 a year for life.

This had not been reported to me. I was never furnished with copies of the minutes of the Board of Governors of the Bank. This decision was not published in the *Gazette* as I thought, on review of the Bank of Canada Act, it was required to be. When I took this matter up with Mr Coyne I was anything but satisfied with the attempt to convince me that this was a matter exclusively for the Bank board and not for the minister of finance. I made it crystal clear that it was only at this point that I had heard about it. It surprised many people, and it surprised me.

My deputy minister [Ken Taylor] was a member of the board of the Bank and of its executive committee. He knew about this but hadn't reported it to me. At a later time, when the matter burst in Parliament, he came to me and apologized very completely for his failure to report; he even offered me his resignation at the time because of his role in not acquainting me with this action, which I thought was intolerable. I declined it. I thought that I shouldn't accept or ask for his resignation simply over one matter of that kind. I had a high regard for Ken Taylor as a conscientious and dedicated public official. There were some reasons that might have been extenuating under the circumstances. He himself was not actually present at the meeting of the board where this pension had been voted to Mr Coyne. He had sent a substitute. He was away at a funeral that day, and the matter had not come as directly to his mind then as it might under ordinary circumstances. I felt that Mr Taylor shouldn't be called upon to pay the price of his office which he was serving very capably.

I took the matter to the cabinet. I told them that I was at last convinced that it was no longer possible to reconcile Mr Coyne's tenure and the policies that he was following and the fiscal policies that he was advocating with the responsibilities of the government. As long as Mr Coyne was there and pursued his programs and his speeches, they would in effect inhibit any effective use of government fiscal policy to assist the economy at that time. I therefore accepted the view that a number of my colleagues had been pressing for some time that Mr Coyne had to go. The cabinet gave quick approval to this.

My thought was that the matter would be quietly handled in a way that would embarrass Mr Coyne just as little as possible. I had no wish to pillory him. I invited him to my office one day, with Mr Taylor, my deputy minister, and told him in a friendly way the reasons why the government had come to the conclusion that it was not possible to reconcile his policies and his speeches and attitude with the efforts of the government to improve the economic situation. For that reason, I said, it was the view of the government that his term should not be allowed to proceed to its conclusion, and that we were asking for his resignation.

This was all done in the secrecy of my office. When Mr Coyne parted, he shook hands, telling me he would think it over and get in touch with me. He never got in touch with me except through the medium of public statements after that. He went to certain people in the Liberal party and apparently was persuaded that a major issue could be made out of this regardless of the harm it might do to the Bank of Canada. Meanwhile, I acquainted the board of directors of the Bank or their representatives with what had happened in order that they would be aware of this. Mr Coyne came to their meeting, which was in Quebec city, and appeared before them in a very truculent mood. I received a telephone call to tell me that Mr Coyne had intimated that if he were allowed to complete his term he would address himself largely to administrative problems, but that he would in effect resist the request for his resignation. I told the spokesman, Bruce Hill of St Catharines, Ontario, who was a member of the board calling me at the request of the board, that the government had taken its decision on this matter and was not prepared to change.

The board endorsed the government's request for his resignation with only one dissenting voice. Mr Coyne stormed out, came back to Ottawa, called a press conference, and launched a bitter attack on the government and on myself. This developed into what became known as the Coyne–Fleming controversy.

It's one of the anomalies and mockeries of public life that I became involved in this personally, although I was the one member of the cabinet who had protected Mr Coyne against the attacks that were made on him constantly by reason of the conduct of his office up to that time. However, I had my duty to do as minister of finance, and I did it.

R.A. BELL

The pension made more of an impact, as I understand it – and here I can't speak directly – it had more of an impression upon Diefenbaker than upon anybody else. 'Twenty-five thousand dollars a year!' This was Diefenbaker speaking and he said this in caucus: 'Here am I prime minister of Canada, a lifetime of public service, not a dollar of pension for me – and this fellow with $25,000.'

DONALD FLEMING

The matter got into the House of Commons as the result of Mr Coyne's announcement of a public nature to the press, his use – and I have nothing but condemnation of him for this – his use of the facilities of the Bank of Canada at the expense of the Bank of Canada to carry his attacks on the government, not only throughout this country but around the world. He sent his version of the request for resignation to all the central banks throughout the world, creating a consternation there – a most irresponsible action and all done at the expense of the Bank. He kept this up all the way through and operated in the closest collusion with some of the leading figures in the Liberal party in the House.

Now, I want to make it very clear that at no time did I act individually in this matter. I realized the perils of the situation, and I made a point of keeping this matter before cabinet at every meeting in this period. I was very, very particular about this because I wasn't going to go one step farther than I was sure of having the support of the cabinet. Once Mr Coyne had started on this campaign of attacks on the government, which I regarded as utterly shameful, there was no telling how far it would go in collusion with the Liberal leaders in the House. Mr Pickersgill was the principal one, but there were others. Whatever was done in this situation, whatever happened or was done or was not done, was the result of the conscious decision of cabinet at every stage. At no point did I act without full authority and full consultation with the cabinet. I want to make that abundantly clear.

The matter of course led to statements in the House and replies to questions that were asked there and to debate. The government in the end, in view of the defiance of Mr Coyne, brought in a bill to declare the office vacant and, as a result of the debates that occurred there, the bill passed the House. It went to the Senate. It was in the Senate that the Liberal party staged its play, tried to make a drama out of this, and used the facilities of the committee of the Senate to act as a sounding board for Mr Coyne's statements.

I can only say this of many of the statements that were made by Mr Coyne, that they were untruthful. He tried to create impressions there that I had been aware of the voting of the board of that pension to him. This was absolutely untrue. I have already indicated what the facts were, but he sought to leave an entirely different impression with his hearers. Everything was magnified. The services of a large advertising agency were employed at the time to give the widest possible circulation and the utmost effects to the evidence that Mr Coyne was giving to that committee.

Should I have gone to that committee and appeared as a witness before it? The government decided I should not. Earlier, when Mr Pearson asked for a committee hearing on the bill in the House of Commons, it was the government that decided against that procedure.

The fact that the government would not allow Coyne to be brought before a House of Commons committee was just part of the extraordinary mishandling of this issue which was to prove to be so costly for the Conservatives. In retrospect, some of the members of the Diefenbaker government were to point an accusing finger at Donald Fleming, but the finance minister indignantly denied that it was his fault; it was the decision of the cabinet as a whole, he said.

Donald Methuen Fleming had been a Conservative from a young age. At sixteen, when he was in university, he was elected secretary of the Conservative Student Club; at twenty-one, he was campaigning for the Tories in the 1926 federal election, and he never stopped campaigning until he left public life. He was elected as a member for Eglinton (Toronto) in 1945 after half a dozen years in municipal politics.

Born 23 May 1905 at Exeter, Ontario, he was educated at Galt schools and the University of Toronto and Osgoode Hall law school. Some of his colleagues, like his friend, George Hees, felt that he took himself too seriously. Others scorned him as a 'typical do-gooder': he was active in the United Church, the YMCA, and the Masons. However, not even those members of the cabinet who were irritated by him, could dislike him.

One fault he did have, according to some, was that he was too much given to detail. In a sense, he was a good counterpoint to Prime Minister Diefenbaker, and Paul Martineau said that he was the administrator for the government: 'He was the man who could present almost any problem or any question in a most thorough manner, analysing all the pros and cons, bringing out all the details.'

ALVIN HAMILTON

The issue was, how should we get rid of him [Coyne]. There were half a dozen approaches, Gordon Churchill put one forward, Davie Fulton put one forward, and I put one forward.

My approach was to call a budget right off the bat, and say: We want to expand the economy; one of the techniques is going to be to devalue the dollar; this will give more jobs and higher prices on the export side, and so on; this is how we can do it. Then say one man stands in the way of all these increased jobs and increased wealth: he is the head of the Bank of Canada, so we are serving notice that we are going to dismiss him by motion in Parliament. That was my proposal.

Another proposal was that we dismiss him and bring in the motion to have hearings in the House of Commons. Dick Bell and David Walker and a couple of others who were pretty good help at any time were keen to get Coyne to repeat before a committee of the House what he had told us in private because he could really believe that stuff. Then he would have destroyed himself. But Donald said, 'Oh no, we can't do that to Coyne. He is a good Christian gentleman and a great Canadian. We can't hurt him.' So Donald's solution carried the day. The solution was to give him six months' warning that we are going to fire him so he would have time to sneak around and get a job lined up before the announcement came out.

What happened? He immediately told his old friend, Pickersgill. Now, that mind knows what to do with that type of information. Bring in this MacLaren advertising agency. Write out a scenario and get it into the Senate. Then, when he comes out of the Senate meeting, wipe a tear off here, go another three steps, another camera picks him up, he is grabbing his wife and waving good-bye – you have never seen such a tear-jerker.

GEORGE HEES

What undid us on the Coyne affair was that Paul Martin, very cleverly, one day in the House of Commons asked, in a very sneering way, Donald Fleming that he didn't suppose the minister of finance would have the decency to allow Mr Coyne to be heard before the Commons Banking and Commerce Committee. Now, if Don Fleming had said, 'Yes,' Coyne would have been just done for, because we had the majority on that committee and we had some very clever people who would have made a monkey out of Mr Coyne. Don Fleming rose to the bait, snapped it up, and said, 'No, he was not going to.'

Why? I don't know.

So Coyne wasn't called before that committee, and was invited before the Senate Banking and Commerce committee where they had a predominance of Liberals, very able lawyers, who made Mr Coyne look like God, and were absolutely able to murder us; whereas on the other committee, we would have murdered him. This is political tactics; this is one of the things that hurt us.

DONALD FLEMING

It was not my decision [to dismiss Coyne]. It came about in this way. The bill [to dismiss him] was introduced, and I made my speech in the morning.

I went to Mr Diefenbaker's residence that day at noon to have lunch with the Japanese prime minister who was visiting Canada at the time. When I went back to the House, Mr Diefenbaker stayed on to entertain the Japanese prime minister at his home. Mr Pearson made his speech and asked for this committee. He asked that I give a point blank answer and offered to curtail the debate if there would be a committee. Following the decision of the government, I made the statement that it was the government's view that the matter should proceed in the House.

As soon as there was an opportunity to speak to Mr Diefenbaker about this, I did so and asked that the question should be made a matter of review by the cabinet because I didn't want to be in the position of having to make a point-blank answer in the House in the absence of the prime minister. I didn't want to take the responsibility for what could prove to be a very fateful decision. In this respect it was considered and the decision was taken that there should be no deviation from what had been announced.

Now, this was a mistake, this was a tactical mistake indeed, of serious proportions. I would call it a blunder. It would have been ever so much better if we had set up a committee of the Commons. We would have had voting control of the committee. We could have had people on that committee who could have torn Coyne to ribbons. Dave Walker could have gone on that committee, Noel Dorion, both men had made telling speeches in the House; they were skilled cross-examiners. I think Mr Coyne would have presented a very sorry spectacle. But this opportunity was passed up.

Then the Senate, which had a large Liberal majority, decided that it should give Mr Coyne his so-called day in court. I think the matter was not well handled before the Senate. The government's position was not handled nearly as effectively as it could have been by people in the House of Commons, who are much more familiar with it.

I am the first to say that a tactical mistake was made, that Coyne got much more publicity out of this and a far better interpretation of his role throughout than he could possibly have gotten if the whole facts had been adequately presented. I agree that it hurt the government at the time. It hurt the government in the election campaign in 1962. I don't think it was the determining factor. I think there were other factors, but undoubtedly it had hurt the government's image.

I think it hurt my own personal image very seriously. I have always felt deeply agrieved about this, first of all, because of the fact that I had in effect over the years protected Coyne from many attacks that were being made on him behind closed doors, and, secondly, I had tried to let him down gently in connection with his resignation, thinking that the thing could be handled very quietly in a way that wouldn't do him any personal hurt. Of all the ministers, I am the one who was singled out for blame. Yet, I was the one who came to a decision probably last that Coyne in the interests of the country had to go, and was quite willing to have a committee of the House of Commons to sit on this. We had discussed it over the lunch table at cabinet more than once.

Mr Diefenbaker felt that, where there was an issue on credibility – an issue as to what the facts were – a minister shouldn't be put in the same position as the governor of the Bank of Canada who had behaved, in the view of the government, so abominably. I think this must have been the prevailing factor in the situation. There were discussions about this at the cabinet table, and I made it quite clear then that I was quite ready to have a committee of the House. It wasn't my decision, and it wasn't my opposition to the idea that led to this course.

Coyne's resignation got the Senate off the hook in the end, because some of those Liberal senators would have had great difficulty in exculpating him. They had had their own feelings about Coyne and his arrogance in the past. However, when he had had his day in court and got all the publicity with the assistance of a large advertising agency, he resigned.

ALVIN HAMILTON
Diefenbaker took Donald's position. His respect for Donald was primarily because of Donald's complete 100 per cent unstinting loyalty. Poor old Donald was always being forced off his own positions by the cabinet. He never had a balanced budget. And he didn't want to be in that position. The cabinet forced him into that.

Diefenbaker just took his position, although his instinct should have told him that David Walker was right: 'Let's get him in that House of Commons and just tear the flesh right off him.' There could have been half a dozen of us make him repeat what he told us privately. I wasn't quite as ruthless as Davie Fulton and David Walker were. They really wanted to rip him apart. But Diefenbaker took that position, and he has to bear the responsibility of it.

Politically I just saw that Toronto, which had been luke-warm to us anyway after that Arrow, suddenly became violently, pathologically, opposed to Diefenbaker. I don't think there is any question that that was the destruction of the Diefenbaker government right then and there.

DOUGLAS HARKNESS
Personally I was very much opposed to the action which was taken at that time. Coyne was going to be out in six months anyway. It was very much better, we will say, to let the thing go over quietly for the period he was still going to be there. When his term was up, he's gone and that would have been

the end of it. To make the great to-do over firing him that did actually occur, and make him a martyr in the eyes of a great number of people, damaged the party and damaged its image very very considerably.

GORDON CHURCHILL

I disagreed completely with the action that was taken with that gentleman. I thought that he should have been given an extended holiday, a six months' holiday with pay because his term of office ran out at the end of that year. That's the way I would have dealt with the thing, instead of putting him on the carpet.

J.W. PICKERSGILL

It shouldn't have been handled at all. The whole point was that Jim Coyne's term was nearly up, and if they couldn't get along with him a wise government would have just sat it out.

I can't be neutral about Jim Coyne. He is my closest personal friend. But I did not really approve of his campaign of speech-making. He took the view that he had this independent position, that he was indispensable, that the interests of the country were being sacrificed, and it was his duty to do these things. I never said a word in support of that campaign. If the government had made a real issue of those speeches, I would have been hard put to know what position to take. But instead of doing that, the idea of trying to suggest that he was doing something improper and underhanded about his pension was so cheap and nasty and despicable that it just completely destroyed what case they had.

You know a lot of people would have said: they are the government, if they want to run our monetary system badly, well, we can turn them out in an election.

I think the original cause was a very debatable thing. But the way of dealing with it and an attempt at blackmail was just, well, I just think it was one – there is no doubt that of all the things that happened, I think that had the biggest effect on the public.

DAVIE FULTON

I think it would be fair to say that once the decision to join issue was made, then there was an overemphasis: 'To hell with the consequences, we have got to do it.' Nobody had thought that you have got to get Senate concurrence as well. We didn't have a majority in the Senate. I shouldn't say nobody, but if it was thought of, I think the frustration was such that, 'To hell with the Senate, we are going to do it, just go ahead and do it.'

At one stage, after it had become apparent that the Senate, if it went this way, was going to have its own committee to deal with the matter, I urged Donald Fleming to set up a joint Parliamentary committee on which he would have a majority. We would still have a very awkward time because we couldn't stop them saying what they wanted but at least we would have a chance to control the proceedings and the ultimate decision of the committee. Donald's reply as I recall it was, 'I wish that it were possible but it is too late now. We have committed ourselves to the other course.'

PAUL MARTIN
I asked Don Fleming this very question, 'When we wanted a committee to go into the whole Coyne affair, to examine the differences between Coyne on public expenditure and you and Diefenbaker, and so on, why didn't you let him go? Why didn't you give us our day in court?' He said, 'Why, that would've been foolish. We'd had one experience. You had gone after Coyne successfully on the unemployment insurance. You would have done the same thing here. You would have given him an opportunity to continue his public criticisms of the government, and this time you would have used him for your own advantage as if he turned Crown's witness.'

I think, perhaps, that he was right. Except that what the government failed to realize was that you had in the Senate some pretty able people, very able lawyers, who really befriended Coyne, as undoubtedly we likely would have befriended him in the committee.

DONALD FLEMING
Immediately after Coyne resigned, the directors of the Bank, with the full approval and, indeed, nomination of the government, appointed Mr Rasminsky as governor. A notable improvement in the functioning of the Bank of Canada resulted. This was one of the best things that a government, of which I was a member, ever did.

Lou Rasminsky has been an admirable public servant and his relations with banks, with the government, with the public, were a model. He and I had a good and close working relationship. We made it a point of meeting every Friday afternoon. He kept me acquainted with what was being done in the executive committee of the Bank and at meetings of the board of the Bank. We had the closest possible discussions of fiscal policy on the government side, and monetary policy on the side of the Bank – monetary control, as administered by the Bank. This was an admirable working relationship. If I had had that from 1957 on, believe me, the country would have been much the better for it. Perhaps, looking back, we should have made an issue with Mr Coyne in March 1958. The country would have been the better for it.

The ultimate sequel is what happened under a Liberal government. After they received the report of the Royal Commission on Finance, they introduced legislation which copies exactly what we had contended for, that in such matters the ultimate responsibility would rest with the government, and if a governor of the Bank found himself out of sympathy with government policy and unable in the last analysis to accept directives from the minister of finance, that he should resign. This is now the statute law of this country written on to the statute books by a Liberal government.

In that, I find absolutely complete vindication for the position which I took all the way through this most unhappy and discreditable episode. When I say discreditable I think of the way in which it was misrepresented and turned to the advantage of the Liberal party and the disadvantage of the Conservative government by tactics which I can only regard as reprehensible.

15

The disaster of an election devaluation

It was inevitable that the great expectations aroused by the fervour of the 1958 election campaign could not be realized, and by 1962 the country was becoming disillusioned with the Conservative government. The mishandling of the Coyne affair had shattered the myth of Conservative invincibility. Now, the Liberals had reason to hope. They could also count on the picture of government indecision which was magnified in the papers – so much proposed and so little done. Still, when Prime Minister Diefenbaker rose in the House of Commons on 18 April to announce that he would seek dissolution of Parliament the next day (the election was held on 18 June 1962) most people believed that the government would be returned, with at worst a reduced majority. The PC members tossed their order papers in the air and confidently predicted that they would be back.

In the midst of the campaign, the Canadian dollar was officially pegged at 92.5 cents US. The government took this step in response to pressure on the dollar, and to the extent that devaluation assisted export trade, and thus stimulated the economy, its effects were unquestionably beneficial. But the psychological impact on Canadians of having their dollar devalued like the once-mighty pound and the franc was to hurt the Tories. Perhaps more than any other single factor in the 1962 campaign, devaluation led to their losing ninety-two seats and being returned as a minority government. To some extent the move was welcomed in the west: devaluation led to higher prices for wheat and it increased exports of other natural resources. Elsewhere, it gave the Liberals an issue which they were quick to exploit – the 'Diefenbuck' which had seven and a half cents cut out of it. Nationalist pride was hurt;

Governor General Georges Vanier and Prime Minister Diefenbaker leave the Citadel after the dissolution of Parliament in 1962 *the Conservatives lost all but one of the seats bordering the United States. In retrospect, Mr Diefenbaker regretted that he had not stood his ground and had not heeded the recommendations of the civil servants. The border seats would have been enough to give him a majority.*

In 1957, when the government had come to power and Donald Fleming became minister of finance, the Canadian dollar was quoted at $1.0625 US. In the view of many economists, that level was too high and was hurting the economy, and Fleming was under constant pressure to do something about it.

DONALD FLEMING

We had made it public as a matter of policy that we thought the Canadian dollar was too high. We hoped that this might have some psychological effect in bringing down its value in terms of US and other currencies. The dollar did move in '61. We had introduced some tax measures in December 1960 that it was thought might contribute to this – a withholding tax on interest of the dividends and some other measures. By late 1961 the Canadian dollar was declining in terms of the US dollar. As a matter of fact it came down at one stage to about $1.03 US. Our hope was that it would go further, but it lodged itself there for some while. Canada, as a member of the International Monetary Fund, was under obligation to peg its dollar at a fixed relationship to the US dollar – and we were in default. We were having missions from the Fund coming up to see me and officials of the department, pressing for action toward fixing the value of our dollar. The view that had prevailed was that we were better off with the so-called floating dollar as long as the Monetary Fund would tolerate it. But the pressure was growing, and in my budget speech in the spring of 1962 a passage was inserted, literally at the last moment, which the officials and I thought was needed as a defence against the pressure from the International Monetary Fund. In those paragraphs, I was giving the reasons why Canada was not moving to peg the dollar. That was just a few days before the election campaign was called.

ALVIN HAMILTON

The dollar was devalued in 1961, but Mr Fleming made it very clear we didn't know where it would settle down. That was the start of the economic revival. If you look at the indicators, they started to move up in February 1961 largely because of the infusion of about $500 million extra from those wheat sales to China. But the real permanent impulse to the revival of the economy was the devaluing of the dollar, done deliberately by the government, going absolutely contrary to the advice of our advisers, in the June budget of 1961. This was a deliberate, logical, coherent act as part of a policy of expansion in trade, to get the country moving forward by using the efforts of the private sector of the economy.

In January and February of 1962, a raid on our dollar started. This raid was not by international speculators. This was a Canadian raid on our dollar by people from Toronto. Rightly or wrongly, the officials running the reserve fund decided to stop this raid by drawing on the reserve account. I think wrongly. We should have let the dollar float, and just let the passion for making money go out against the natural flow of other people buying the Canadian dollar and the dollar probably would have levelled off at about 92.5 cents US or thereabouts. However, we drained our reserve account at that time and we checked it at 95 cents US. In effect it was a pegged dollar by the use of our reserves.

I personally was opposed to the pegging of the dollar, on the grounds that it is in Canada's interest as we expand in world trade to keep our dollar at a realistic level vis-à-vis our trade. We have to pay off huge international obligations because of huge investments in this country and I knew that the balance between the tangible trade balance and the intangible, which comes from the investment returns, would mean that we would have to have a dollar, for about ten to twenty years, seven or eight points below the American dollar.

MERRIL MENZIES

The change of direction of government came too late. If it had happened in '58 or at the latest by mid '59 or the fall of '59, it might have been different. But having given away monetary policy, which Fleming did in '57, there was no way to get it back. They could develop expansionary fiscal policy, but if monetary policy was working against it, which it was, then it not only cancelled out but confounded the existing confusion. And so, certainly, Diefenbaker went to the country with many regions and groups and interests confused, some profoundly disenchanted, some extremely hostile.

PIERRE SÉVIGNY

This indecision of Diefenbaker is what cost him the real electoral merits of devaluing the dollar. The policy was developed back in January 1962. The boys who sat in Treasury Board, and I was one of them, wanted to boost the Canadian economy. To do that we had to devalue the dollar, because that meant more export sales, more dollars, more profits, more taxes, more employment, more everything. This was explained to Diefenbaker but he dilly-dallied and dilly-dallied and hesitated and hesitated and then he declared the election.

I have always been convinced of treachery, that some opposition forces got together and organized a run on the Canadian dollar. That was planned, that was systematic, that was organized, and I know by whom, but I can't prove it. So, right in the midst of the campaign, Don Fleming became alarmed and went to Diefenbaker and said, 'We have no choice, either we devalue or we are in bad, bad trouble.' It was done on the spur of the moment, and it was something that was finally decided at least six months after it should have been done.

It was the timing of the devaluation of the dollar which proved so harmful. If the move had been taken well before the election, there would have been time to explain; but, as George Hees said, 'it snuck up' in the midst of the campaign. That was not designed to inspire confidence in the way the Conservatives were running the country. The Liberals made hay with the 'Diefenbuck.' Yet why, with the growing fiscal pressures, was the election called when it was? There had been a move to have it earlier, and some losses might have been avoided if it had been held later.

GORDON CHURCHILL

I thought that the climate of opinion was such that we could ask for a renewed mandate in the fall of 1961. Some people would have said, 'Oh, well, you haven't been in office very long.' My argument was that we had been in office from 1957; that the interruption of the 1958 election was simply a run-off and had been brought about by the attitude of Mr Pearson and his party; and that we had put in four years of pretty solid accomplishment and could reasonably go to the country and ask for a renewed mandate. That suggestion of mine was not accepted. I put it forward in the summer of 1961. When you look back you can always see what should have been done, and, in looking back, that was a pretty good idea. But the election was postponed. It occurred in June of 1962, and we suffered very seriously for it.

ALVIN HAMILTON

Diefenbaker planned to have an election in the fall of 1961. But the Ontario government had put on a 2 per cent sales tax, and all the Ontario members of caucus cried out, 'Oh, don't call an election now! All the little businessmen – they have got to collect this sales tax – they're our main supporters and they are against us.' Against his better political judgment they talked him out of that fall election. It was too bad because we could have come back with 160, 180 members, I think. But even then I wasn't despondent. We had the awful business of the Arrow, and of Coyne, but things were getting better economically. I was watching those indicators like a hawk and repeating the figures to him.

ROY FAIBISH

If there was going to be an election, it should have been in late '61 – the prime minister was in favour of it – but the Ontario members said: 'No way! If we go into an election with Ontario having just put on a sales tax, we'll be wiped out.' They panicked. So there was no more talk about it.

Even in late '61 there was enough evidence – of pressure on the Canadian dollar, and the whole monetary situation – that there were going to be problems. But the cabinet wasn't mentally preparing for it. There were no speeches to get the people ready to face problems of devaluation, and talk about the external dollar and the internal dollar, and all the things that were thrown at them subsequently. So when '62 came the party was, in a sense, in disarray and the cabinet was in disarray. The prime minister reluctantly, as things got worse, as the economic and financial situation got worse, for no reason called an election! It's not explicable.

DONALD FLEMING

Consideration had been given to calling the election in the fall of 1961. Three and a half years had passed since the last general election. The feeling, however, was that the economic measures which we had introduced to stimulate the economy were working well by the fall of '61, but we would see much more result from them by the spring of '62, and this would be to the government's advantage. There was also a factor that in late '61 the Ontario government had introduced a sales tax. There was a good deal of resentment against this in Ontario, and we felt that this would be taken out at our expense, as the federal government, in the Ontario ridings, if we called an election then. So the decision was taken to go forward in 1962.

As things turned out, we would have been much better off to have waited until the fall of 1962. We did not foresee that a crisis would occur in the external value of the Canadian dollar when it did, in the spring of 1962.

ANGUS MACLEAN

Perhaps judgments were swayed by the fact that everyone assumed we were going to stay in power, and there was a tendency to just look on the '62 election as a formality that had to be gotten over with. I didn't feel that way about it. I thought there would be a strong tendency on the part of the public to reduce the majority, at least, of the government. I considered that a very dangerous situation, because the public wouldn't be doing it in concert. It is just as easy for a million people to change their minds as it is for one.

J.W. PICKERSGILL

I think they realized that time was running out for them and with 208 members or whatever it was – by that time there had been a little attrition – they figured they couldn't possibly lose their whole majority, that if they had an election in 1962 they would come back with a slim majority. Then they would have another four or five years. Which I think is not an unreasonable calculation. I don't think at the beginning of the campaign many of us [Liberals] were very sanguine about winning. About halfway through we were. Then at the end, it seemed to tail off a bit, but, of course, it was a disastrous defeat from a moral standpoint [for the Conservatives].

In 1961, Prime Minister Diefenbaker asked Alvin Hamilton to prepare a program for an election – another sign that he wanted to go to the country then. The agriculture minister set to work and came up with another, much greater 'vision.'

ALVIN HAMILTON

I worked very fast. I brought in fellows like Baldur Kristjanson and Roy Faibish and Merril Menzies, the old team from Agriculture. We had been asked to prepare a development program. We called it not the second stage of the previous development program, but the 'Rounding of Confederation.' We put together a program that was literally, physically and economically, ten, fifteen times more grandiose than the program that we worked out in '57 and '58 for the '58 election.

Diefenbaker knew that if he could get going on these proposals with all the costing worked out – and all were going to be self-liquidating – he would have a type of campaign that he would love to do. The glory of the Lord, the vision in the hills, and all the rest of it. Ten times more dramatic than the stuff in '58, and with all these figures to back it up. A speech was prepared for every section of the country, so wherever he went he always had a new version because there were so many things to describe.

There was the big transmission grid, where you bumped power from one side of Canada to the other. The costing was there – we had the committee that didn't actually report until the fall of '63 – but all that stuff was under way, and we had the tentative reports. Then the proposal to move natural gas into Quebec city from both sides of the St Lawrence. Liquified natural gas from Venezuela and from North Africa would be brought to supply these areas instead of building expensive pipelines into the Maritimes. The development of power in Quebec and the development of the North, taking my 'Roads to Resources' grid and building up the Arctic, and all the rest of it. That program just delighted him. Diefenbaker said, 'This will put them on the defensive.' He said that only two ministers were aware of that program, Gordon Churchill and myself, and he said, 'Keep your mouth shut, no one is going to speak about this thing.'

He wanted the speech for the opening of the '62 campaign. I never saw the final draft. I had written the thing in point form. Bunny Pound typed it out and Merril Menzies actually dictated it. Diefenbaker had it the way that he wanted it, and he took it down to the opening meeting in London, Ontario on May 6, 1962.

On the way down, he couldn't resist inviting some of the Toronto ministers to meet him in his private railway car, and he couldn't resist showing them what he was going to deliver that night: 'This will put the Grits on the defensive.' Donald Fleming almost had a heart attack. All this long list of things, ten times more grandiose than the one in '58. Donald Fleming was just outraged. He said that it would ruin the country.

Every point had been approved at one time or another by cabinet. You would sneak a point in here and sneak a point in there – 'I just want a person to study it and cost it.' Some of these big developments on the Fundy and things like that, I had tentative costings on. We have them now finally, but all these studies were being done.

George Hees was also there. One Toronto guy is dangerous, but two of them are suicide. They just scared the hell out of each other. The result was that Diefenbaker was so shaken by this that, when he got up to speak, he wouldn't mention anything in the speech, he would just mumble things and go on to something else and mumble something else. Merril Menzies and Bunny Pound sat in the audience that night with six thousand people, all to hear the glory of the Lord explained. He could have set the country on fire. They would have forgotten about the unemployment, which was disappearing anyway. He could have thrown the Grits on the defensive again in '62. He could have just swamped them in every part of the country. But he muffed that speech.

ALLISTER GROSART

That is one election where the start was very bad. Because the party fortunes were to some extent on the decline, some bright fellow got the idea that London had to be a fantastic success. They carted in scores, hundreds of people by bus. I wasn't there, but it was a fantastic flop, I remember.

It's a funny thing about elections. Winnipeg was a fantastic start to '58, and the feel carried right through the election. So did the feeling of that London flop carry through. One meeting at the start can colour the whole campaign. Why this is so I don't know. It's partly the press: naturally political commentators try to get down to cases and they are going to find a peg for a story, and a great success or a flop is a peg. They tend to carry on, to feed back, to relate back to this. If there are other successes, well, this is another Winnipeg; if it's a flop, this is another London.

Grosart did not believe in retrospect that the Conservatives conducted a bad campaign in 1962, but Dick Bell described it as 'the only poor campaign that John Diefenbaker ever ran.' He said the opening in London was one of the worst political meetings he had ever attended: the Armouries were jammed to the rafters, but Diefenbaker seemed to have no prepared speech, went on for ninety minutes, and lost a third of his audience. Ellen Fairclough felt nevertheless that the Conservatives would have won a majority in 1962 had it not been for the devaluation of the dollar: 'the scales were tipped' by that.

There was a second raid on the Canadian dollar after the election had been called at the end of April.

ALVIN HAMILTON

Diefenbaker knew the names of every person who raided the dollar. Every single one was Canadian, every single one was in Toronto. He would not divulge their names because he didn't think prime ministers and cabinet ministers should divulge this type of information, even though that was a deliberate political ploy in the middle of the election to destroy him.

DONALD FLEMING

Events moved very swiftly and, in the terms of the government's fortune, very unfavourably, just around the time that the election campaign was launched. Parliament was dissolved, the election called, and the issues drawn between the rival parties. We did not foresee, and I had no reason to think that we should have been expected to foresee, something that occurred quite suddenly. This was the run on the Canadian dollar. It was largely precipitated by speculators. This was the information that came to us from the markets. This was a raid by speculators on the Canadian dollar, and it had very severe consequences.

We started out with about $2 billion in the exchange fund. This was the cushion which could be resorted to, to defend the Canadian dollar against a too precipitous fall. Through Mr Rasminsky that fund was used, not to prevent *any* decline in the Canadian dollar at all, but to moderate because you couldn't use your resources all up in a day or two. In a crisis like this, no one knows in advance how far it will go or how long it will last.

As I said, when the election was called we did not foresee that speculative run on the Canadian dollar. It started suddenly. It was very intense for several days. In consultation with Mr Rasminsky and our officials in the department, I was led to the conclusion that the time had come, regardless of the immediate political consequences, when in the interests of the country the Canadian dollar must be pegged. I called a major conference of the officials of the Finance Department and of the Bank of Canada, and I must tell you that I couldn't get a consensus on what value we should seek for the Canadian dollar. There was a consensus that the time had come when we must devalue and peg the dollar in terms of the articles of the International Monetary Fund, but there was no consensus on how far we should go. I had those officials, including Mr Rasminsky, sitting around in a circle in my big office in the Department of Finance. After a lengthy discussion, and with full knowledge of the gravity of the decision, I went around the circle and polled every man as to his ideas. Consensus was not possible and it was my personal decision that we should seek a 92.5 cents US value for the Canadian dollar. I thought this was realistic. Under all the circumstances it would be extremely helpful to the Canadian economy if we could get it. It was in line with what leading Liberals like Walter Gordon and Paul Martin had been urging and advocating publicly. I took that decision.

I authorized Mr Rasminsky and Mr Plumptre to make preparations to go to Washington to meet there with the executive board of the International Monetary Fund and I took the matter to cabinet. The decision was acceped by cabinet without difficulty It's true that some of the ministers were not in Ottawa at the time, but we had a strong nucleus of the cabinet there. Mr Diefenbaker, of course, was there.

Then Mr Rasminsky and Mr Plumptre went to Washington. They had communicated in advance with Mr Per Jacobsson, the managing director of the International Monetary Fund, so he was aware of what the mission would be. He summoned a meeting of the executive boad of the Fund for six o'clock on May 2nd, 1962. No intimation was given to members of that board in advance as to the agenda of the meeting. I arranged that Plumptre and Rasminsky would leave that morning for Washington and would keep out of sight.

Mr Diefenbaker had left Ottawa, but I talked to him. He had been thinking it over since the day before and had developed fears that this change in the value of the dollar would hurt us in the election campaign. I said to him, 'John' – this was in our telephone conversation – 'whether it hurts us or not in this election campaign, I believe we must do this and must do it today in the interests of Canada.' I said, 'Already these two officials are on their way to the airport. I can call them back, but I will resist doing so.' In the end he reluctantly acquiesced, saying this could cost us the election.

My own personal situation was greatly complicated by the fact that I had to go up to Toronto that day to face my own nomination convention in my own riding, so you can imagine what kind of a day I put in on the 2nd day of May, 1962.

Our two emissaries went to Washington. They kept out of sight all day. I was in touch with them from time to time by telephone and watched the course of the Canadian dollar because the speculative pressure was very strong. These two men met the executive board of the International Monetary Fund at six o'clock that night, and by eight o'clock a decision had been taken giving unanimous approval to the request of the Canadian government to fix the value of the Canadian dollar at 92.5 cents US.

When I went on the platform that night at my convention, I hadn't been told the result but arrangements had been made that an official of the Bank of Canada would meet me, if not during the course of the evening, at the conclusion of the meeting. I made my speech, made no reference to the subject of exchange control, and, at the conclusion, the official of the Bank was there to tell me that approval had been given. The timing for publication was 11:15 PM, to be exactly halfway between the closing of the markets in North America and the opening of the markets the following morning in Europe. That is the story of the devaluation of the dollar.

The sequel is that I held a press conference the next day to explain what had happened. It was held in Toronto, and the Liberals seized on this. I have to say, with regret, that the Liberal campaign in relation to the devaluation of the Canadian dollar was, in my opinion, an utterly dishonest one. It was effective. I don't doubt that this issue hurt us, partly because the Canadian people didn't fully understand it or what had led up to it. They didn't fully understand the beneficial consequences which would ensue, and they were misled deliberately by the leading figures in the Liberal party, who exploited this, who confused the people, who misled the people to what I think is their everlasting shame.

The other feature of the sequel is that the Canadian economy derived enormous benefit from the devaluation of the dollar. It helped to boost our exports to have a cheaper currency, yet made it more difficult for exporters [in other countries] to take advantage of the Canadian market. It helped our tourist trade enormously.

ALVIN HAMILTON

I have always been a firm defender of devaluation because I played a large part in it. I point out that my instructions to the cabinet ministers who were present at that meeting when we pegged the dollar was that the minute the news was to be announced each one of us should phone every person in public opinion – the television stations and the radio stations and newspapers – to say that the dollar was pegged and these are the reasons for doing it, so that our story would be there. If you look at the *Free Press* of Winnipeg, the

Star Phoenix of Saskatoon, the *Leader Post* [of Regina], all through the West, every paper came through beautifully because they got the reasons – particularly the *Free Press*. I remember seeing the headlines, 'Dollar pegged at 92.5 cents, wheat prices up six cents, beef prices up so and so, pork prices up so and so.' Every farmer, every businessman knew that it was in his interest to support that expansionary step. But this was not done by anybody but myself. We failed miserably in BC, which was one of the great beneficiaries of that program, in western Ontario, and in the manufacturing areas, because they turned out to be the chief beneficiaries of that program – there was a great rise in manufacturing after that for another ten years.

This is the story that the economic historian will eventually get from looking at the records, and will know that it was the right move, but even to this day you find a reluctance on the part of a Conservative candidate to talk on any monetary or fiscal matter because (*a*) he doesn't understand it apparently, and (*b*) he remembers the hostility to our step in 1961 and '62.

> *Roy Faibish, Alvin Hamilton's executive assistant, was seconded to Prime Minister Diefenbaker's staff for the 1962 election campaign. He was working with Merril Menzies and John Fisher in the days before devaluation was announced.*

ROY FAIBISH

It was apparent to Dr Menzies and myself, just from the demeanour of the prime minister and his comportment, that he was deeply preoccupied and worried about something. But he didn't share it. I remember we were in Chicoutimi – the campaign train was there.

We went to bed. Menzies and I were sharing a room, down a couple of doors from the prime minister's suite. The phone rang at three, four o'clock in the morning. To this day, I don't know how the prime minister communicated with the French Canadian switchboard girl to find out where I was. But he did. He said, 'Would you come down?' I was puzzled why he didn't ask Menzies. That would have been the normal thing to do. So I jumped out of bed and said to Menzies, 'Should I shave? Should I take off my pyjamas, or should I just get down there?' He said, 'Better slip a pair of trousers over your pyjamas and get down there.'

I went into the suite. I hadn't been in the suite prior to that. It was dark. There were six or seven rooms, and the doors were mostly closed. The breakfast table had been set for breakfast. I listened, and I couldn't hear a thing. I didn't know where he was and I didn't want to wake up Mrs Diefenbaker. I slowly opened one door. Empty. Opened another. It was empty. Opened a third one, and there was Mrs Diefenbaker sleeping. I got out of there like a shot. I didn't want to say, 'Prime Minister, are you here?' and wake her up. I coughed and stammered, and I heard water running. I went into the bathroom, and he's lying in the bath and there are papers all over the place.

He got up and he towelled himself, and sat down – it was just about dawn – and he said, 'It's very serious, it's very serious.' But I didn't know what was serious. He kept saying, 'Very serious, very serious. I can't tell you what it is.' I still didn't know why I was being asked to come there. Finally, he said, 'I've been in touch constantly the last five or six hours by telephone with Bryce, and with Geneva, and with Rasminsky. Very serious, very serious, very serious.' I listened. I couldn't say anything, I didn't know what it was.

He said, 'Here, get these ministers.' He gave me a list that started off 'O'Hurley, Balcer, Nowlan.' That didn't make much sense to me. I suspected it was financial. I said, 'Okay, Prime Minister. It's pretty early in the morning in the east.'

I got O'Hurley out of bed. He'd lost his voice, so he couldn't talk. The prime minister did all the talking. I stayed there. He explained that the devaluation was going to be announced at midnight, that Bryce was going to release something, that Alvin was in Ottawa. By coincidence, Alvin was acting prime minister that day, which was amusing, because he'd been fighting for devaluation at 90 cents in cabinet. Balcer I couldn't find. George Nowlan was not available.

After he'd talked to a couple of other ministers, he told me about the devaluation. He said, 'Now, we've got to start refocusing all the speeches towards that.' So the speeches started to shift, to explain the virtues of devaluation and also some of the penalties, to try to explain some of the terms and conditions that the International Monetary Fund had placed on Canada, and to try to draw some parallels to what had happened in 1948 when Doug Abbott had to do something similar. But very quickly the Liberals were on the attack. I think we went for about a week, sort of on the offensive, until, out of Toronto particularly, came the Liberal offensive, and we were on the defensive from that day on, between the 'Diefenbuck' and the panic stealing over the consumers that it would cost them more for fruit and vegetables. We tried to emphasize how it would help primary industry, but we were essentially on the defensive from that day on.

Besides, Diefenbaker's press relations had deteriorated to the point that too much of his energy and time was spent sparring with the press. And so between a defensive campaign full of statistics, and fighting with the press over how many people were at Summerside and how many were at Windsor – it was just insane. It was totally inane and insane. It's funny now, but for those of us like Menzies and myself it was heartbreaking.

GORDON CHURCHILL

The devaluation of the Canadian dollar down to 92.5 cents US gave a great stimulus to our export trade, and the benefit of all that was reaped by the Pearson government in '64, '65, and '66, when things were really going very well. But at the time it was misunderstood and misinterpreted and effectively sabotaged by skilful Grit propaganda.

The cartoon that Kuch of the Winnipeg *Free Press* drew was reproduced in thousands and passed out as bogus money right across Canada. That cartoon depicted a Canadian dollar, with the prime minister's image on it, worth 92.5 cents. It looked as if the dollar had really declined so seriously as to effect everybody who had a dollar in his pocket. It was an extremely effective piece of political propaganda. I remember when I was campaigning in that election I would go into restaurants and I would find those bogus dollars lying on the counter. A combination of things brought about a weakening of confidence in the government, and that financial crisis, I think, capped it.

DONALD FLEMING

There was a further run on the Canadian dollar before the election was over. It was partly precipitated by a very foolish and improvident statement made by one of my colleagues in the cabinet [Alvin Hamilton], ten days before the election, that 92.5 cents US was just half way between 90 and 95 – it was just an obvious compromise.

His statement, which was in the papers Saturday, would have caused an enormous run on the Canadian dollar on Monday morning. I was speaking in Montreal that Sunday night, and I talked to Diefenbaker on the phone. I couldn't get him to come out and make a statement to correct this most unfortunate statement from Alvin from out in the West. But in the end he did ask me to make a statement to try to head off a run and to say that I made it with his full concurrence. I did that. That helped to stem what otherwise would have been an enormous run on the Canadian dollar one week before the general election.

ALVIN HAMILTON

We were on the defensive during the last month of the campaign on that issue. This made me very upset. I had gone into the hospital at St Michael's in Toronto to have an operation, and I just couldn't take it, lying in the hospital there, to find our party on the defensive when we should have been on the attack. This was an issue that was going to build up the jobs, it was going to increase the money for business and help our exporters, and so on. This is what we needed for the next ten, twenty years. This was the whole basis of the expansion program, expansion at home and expansion abroad in the form of export.

I left my hospital bed and went across the country, proposing a series of positive expansionist programs which caused another temporary raid on the dollar. Both Mr Fleming and Mr Diefenbaker said that there would be no change in the dollar yet: it was set – which I wasn't debating. However, my tough speeches on behalf of the devalued dollar and Canada's interest left the impression with a lot of people in Toronto and Montreal that we wanted to devalue again. So I took the political rap for that, I suppose, deservedly.

Actually, what I was doing was trying to point out the advantages in jobs in the manufacturing areas of Ontario and Quebec, as well as to the export industries. The greatest political and economic stroke of the Diefenbaker years was that decision to go for expansion, and we couldn't expand without getting the dollar down to a realistic value. If the whole party had fought on the offensive and attacked these people who wanted to restrict us and put us into a reservation concept, if we could have had the arguments of Coyne out in the public where they should have been, we should have come back with a very strong membership in the '62 election.

J. WALDO MONTEITH

Alvin Hamilton didn't help matters any by his statement out in Vancouver, when he said, 'You know, there were opinions of 95 cents, 90 cents, so we kind of sawed it off at 92.5 cents.' I recall being at a meeting just a day or so later, and Dief saying, 'Oh, I wish that Alvin would stay on his own dung heap.'

J.W. PICKERSGILL

The greatest campaign against the dollar was put on by Alvin Hamilton who announced publicly that he wanted to devalue it even more than it was devalued and they split the difference in the cabinet. Then he was ordered by Donald Fleming to shut up and never mention the dollar again. We didn't need to campaign against the dollar; they did a terrific job.

Devaluation in the midst of an election campaign was a blow to Diefenbaker personally. He was charged with having misled the Canadian people, of having said that things were improving when in fact the situation was perilous. The prime minister was jealous of his reputation as a man of absolute integrity, and the accusation stung. This may have been one reason why he seemed to be in a bad mood during much of the 1962 election campaign. He was often 'sullen and cranky,' according to Roy Faibish, who found him 'more difficult to work with in 1962 than he had been before or since.' For the first and only time, the Chief was not the happy warrior on the hustings.

He didn't seem to want the election that he had called, and he got into constant and unseemly rows with the press.

ROY FAIBISH

John Fisher no longer spent any time with Menzies and myself on speeches. His job was acting as a kind of interface between the prime minister and the press to keep peace. The atmosphere was very bad.

One of the best examples was after we had gone to Edmonton. We'd had a pretty good crowd – seven, eight thousand in the hockey arena there – but it was a big arena, and seats were empty. He had previously been there and had a much larger crowd. Unemployment was the problem in Edmonton, a lot of unemployment. He was well received, but not as well received as he had been in the past. Charlie King [Southam News Service correspondent] filed copy on it for his papers, one of which was the Edmonton *Journal*.

Our next stop was Trail. We were up on a cliff there, in those new motels. Diefenbaker and his wife were in the first room. Next to it was Fisher and Menzies, and then myself, and then the typists. There was only one telephone, and that was in the adjoining room between the prime minister and Fisher. Fisher was to screen all calls.

At quarter to eight Bert Herridge, the CCF member, called and he asked for a message to be passed to the prime minister as a personal favour: 'When you're en route down to the hockey arena, would you stop by the hotel where I'm having a banquet at eight o'clock for the Trail hockey players who are going to the Olympics? Would you stick your head in and say a non-partisan hello?' Dief agreed. He was happy to do that.

We were to leave at eight o'clock. The cars pulled up. At five minutes to eight Fisher momentarily had to leave his office. That left the telephone unguarded. Just five minutes before we were to get into the limousines to go downtown, the phone rang. It was Diefenbaker's 'old friend,' Mickey O'Brien, an old party worker from Vancouver. In his hand he's got the Edmonton *Journal* of the previous day, and he reads to Dief, five minutes before he's going to make a major speech, the headline that Charlie King didn't put on the article, but that some sub-editor did. It said, 'Diefenbubble bursts.'

Diefenbaker said to O'Brien, 'Well, who wrote it? Who wrote it?'

He said, 'Charlie King,' and he started to read it. All Charlie had said was that he'd had a meeting, it wasn't as good as the previous meeting there, it looks like he hasn't got the same amount of support this time. And the guy had put the headline 'Diefenbubble bursts.'

To give that kind of news to any leader before he goes to speak is not very good, but O'Brien had no political judgment at all. Diefenbaker was furious. We got in the limousine, went to the Bert Herridge thing, and then to the meeting. I'm sitting near the front with George Hogan. In the midst of his speech – he's got not a bad crowd listening – all of a sudden, to Diefenbaker's left, we see these white figures emerging. The ladies – they were Doukhobors – had decided to make a demonstration and disrobe. Dief handled it beautifully. He referred to his days up at Rosthern, where Ed Nasserden came from, and said, 'I guess they want to hear the naked truth.' They weren't obstreperous or obnoxious. Embarrassing to some people, because as I recall somewhat vividly, three of them were matronly and one of them was maidenly.

Diefenbaker was always at his best when he had a foil, something to go against. He never made his great speeches when the audience was with him. His greatest speeches were when he had a mixed audience – some with him, some against him, some neutral that he was swinging over, and some heckling. That's when he rose.

At the end of the speech he was on a little dais – and Hogan and I surged forward with two or three reporters who had managed to move very quickly in front of us, led by Charlie King. They wanted to get a reaction about the Doukhobors.

I was right behind Charlie. Diefenbaker stood there looking down, but all Diefenbaker had in his mind was what Mickey O'Brien had told him on the telephone. Charlie didn't know this. And I don't know whether Charlie at that time even knew what the heading was. Diefenbaker said, 'I don't have anything to do with you any more. I don't deal with you at all professionally.' I could see Charlie was stunned.

We immediately got out of the hall, went back to the motel, and there was a hell of an argument. Charlie King wasn't coming back on that aircraft. That's all there was to it. The next day, when we took off, he could go his own way. He wasn't coming back in the aircraft.

We argued with him: 'You can't do this. It's wrong.' And all the logical reasons why it was not in anybody's interest to do this sort of thing. This was midnight.

We had got word that if Charlie King wasn't going to be allowed, none of them would go on the plane. When we reached the airport the next morning, Mr and Mrs Diefenbaker got on the plane, the staff got on the plane, and John Fisher and I went forward. The press were on the plane, but Charlie King hadn't arrived. In the meantime, I'd found out that he'd been in touch with Charlie Lynch and others. Publishers were being involved, and there was a great curfuffle.

Fisher and I went forward to the prime minister and said, 'You've got to change your mind and make peace. He's got to come aboard.' No way. Mrs

Diefenbaker started to pacify him. But God bless Fisher. He said to the prime minister, 'Prime Minister, you're wrong. If he doesn't come aboard, I'm not coming aboard.' Fisher turned around, and walked out and went down on the tarmac and into the shack there, where there's a little cafeteria. He sat there. I thought to myself, 'Well, if Fisher's not going aboard, I guess I'm not going aboard.' So I stayed on the tarmac.

King arrived, and the aircraft propellers were turning. Down the gangway from the aircraft came Mrs Diefenbaker. She walked in to see John Fisher, and she said, 'Okay.' She had made the peace. But it was a highly tense, taut situation. We all came aboard and away we went. After we were airborne Mrs Diefenbaker came and sat with King and talked to him, trying to calm things down. But Dief wouldn't make his peace.

Other issues besides devaluation hurt the Conservatives in 1962. Unemployment was still high and led to some ugly scenes during the campaign. And indeed, shortly after coming to power, John Diefenbaker had told Merril Menzies that unemployment would be his nemesis. Both the dollar devaluation and unemployment had their effect in Quebec.

JACQUES FLYNN

We started rather well because we had a very strong argument – just compare our record with the Liberal record as far as Quebec's special aspirations were concerned. But then the Social Credit came from nowhere. In the last ten days it was just incredible what was happening.

At the beginning some people were telling us, 'Well, they may be dangerous.' We couldn't figure that too well. If we had realized that there was really a danger there, could we have done something? I doubt it. In retrospect – and I've been thinking about it for a long time – I doubt that we would have been able to do anything to prevent it, because Caouette's appeal – 'You have nothing to lose' – was getting a very strong response in the rural area.

The funny thing – when you look at the map of the 1962 elections in Quebec, you will find that all the Social Credit ridings are connected. There's not one which is isolated from the others – just like paint on a background. People were responding to this idea, 'You have nothing to lose.'

The pegging of the dollar during the campaign – I mean, if you play with money, that goes with the Social Credit idea. And the 'Diefendollar.' I mean, 'If you can do that, why can't you do what the Social Credit is preaching?' That helped.

In fact, I think all observers will tell you – and I'm not speaking only of Quebec – that the election was lost, really, when this decision had to be made during the campaign. They will tell you that Mr Diefenbaker was never the same as a campaigner during that campaign after this decision was made.

MICHAEL STARR

They were successful, the Four Horsemen [Pearson, Martin, Pickersgill, and Chevrier] in the continual pounding of unemployment until they imbedded it into the minds of the electorate. They just kept on and on and on and on, and they were saying that here is a government that created unemployment – as soon as they got in unemployment started – and they did nothing about it because we still have unemployment. For the sake of political reality, it's been proven that this hasn't been entirely our fault because ever since then we have had nothing but unemployment. For a period of time, with the action we took and the measures that we took, economic conditions improved and when the late Mr Pearson came in, he got the advantages of that.

In Vancouver, there was a near-riot.

ROY FAIBISH

We had heard the morning we arrived in Vancouver that there might be trouble. There were rumours that the Liberals or some others had hired some stevedores or longshoremen to bust up the meeting.

Menzies and I started to work on the Diefenbaker speech first thing in the morning. We worked harder on that speech than any that I could think of in the campaign because he had his best meetings in Vancouver in '57. We worked on it till right up to ten minutes to eight, and rushed it to Diefenbaker. We had gone through it with him a couple of times, but he really didn't get the finished copy until he was leaving.

We'd had breakfast but neither of us had had lunch or dinner. I said to Menzies, 'You go ahead with the prime minister, I'll get a taxi and I'll meet you at the arena.' There was a little delicatessen around the corner. I saw a big long pepperoni stick, about twelve inches long, and I said, 'Wrap it up.' He wrapped it up in white paper, which later became significant. I didn't have time in the taxi to eat it.

I got in [to the meeting], got myself settled, right beside Blair Fraser, right in the front row. We had a cameraman hired full-time to cover this because we were shipping film material back to eastern Canada. It was being edited in Toronto and being used for promotion material.

Within the first ten minutes, all hell broke out. And confusion. First, the chanting to drown him out, and then the physical violence. Sitting on the dais with him were his BC ministers, plus the key Vancouver members – six or seven of them. With the exception of Howard Green, they were frozen. Green was his normal self. This tremendous chant – trying to block him out so that the audience couldn't hear him. It was obviously an organized attempt to prevent him from speaking. I could see Diefenbaker – the perspiration coming down – I could see he was going to fight. But he was getting no encouragement from any of them – the cabinet ministers, the members beside him, just sat there like Buddhas. Just nothing, nothing to keep him going. They were stones.

I could see that he needed something and, as the cameraman was the highest – he was on a riser – I got up in front of him with my twelve-inch pepperoni stick, and I was yelling as loud as I could, telling him to keep going, to keep going. He later wrote me a most moving letter. He said I looked like the Statute of Liberty with the torch in her hand. But most people thought it was a club. Didn't know that it was just twelve inches of pepperoni.

I was swinging this thing over my head and urging him at the top of my voice to give them hell, keep going, don't give up, keep going. And he was looking me straight in the eye. I did this for forty minutes. The sweat was just pouring off me.

At that time, the physical violence started. I looked over my shoulder and I saw a tremendous sized man who had just about reached the little stairwell leading onto the dais, and I figured they were coming forward. I saw [J.A.] Macaulay, who was the executive assistant to Davie Fulton – he's a lawyer now in Vancouver – I saw, out of the corner of my eye, Macaulay backing up. He was being pushed. Nobody else doing a thing. This tremendous sized man hit Macaulay. Macaulay didn't go down. He's tougher than I thought. He looked like a typical English soccer player who didn't really have much stuff to him, but he had a lot of stuff. Macaulay turned around and he hit this guy, who was about 210 pounds, and he just floored him. Blood all over the place. I'll never forget it because as far as I could see, he was the only brave guy in that whole crowd of 8000 people. He was really fighting until they knocked him down.

By this time they're right up to the dais, and I'm swinging this thing, which looks like a club. So people weren't coming that close to me. I was as scared as I could be.

All of a sudden they were surging forward. I looked to my right, and I saw Harry Stevens, who must have been 84 years old. He had a black Malacca cane, and here he was swinging that cane and keeping them away from getting up on the dais.

On my left, out of nowhere – I think he'd been to a mess dinner because I have some recollection of him having his miniature medals on – was Col. Cec Merritt, vc. I remember him saying, 'It's just like Dieppe. Let's give 'em hell.'

So here was this 84-year-old man with a cane, and myself, a feather-weight if I added another 20 pounds to myself, with a pepperoni stick, and Cec Merritt, who was a distinguished soldier. We were blocking the little narrow entrance to these guys, holding them off. In the end they didn't get on the dais, but they came awfully close. But by then the police arrived.

All of this took sixty-five, seventy minutes, with this chanting to drown him out, and Dief fighting, and his hairlock was down and the sweat was pouring off him. He was going to go down fighting. And this image of those ministers there, just frozen. It was indescribable to someone who wasn't emotionally involved and who wasn't there.

I thought that his performance was tremendous. All on film, which we subsequently sent back to eastern Canada. However, Allister Grosart panicked and thought, 'We must try to suppress this event as if it never happened.' People were shouting him down and it would be interpreted that Dief was unpopular. So he wouldn't allow it to be edited and go on the air. It was a totally wrong decision in my view. It's never seen the light of day.

Another example of the extraordinary courage of the man happened at Chelmsford, near Sudbury. He was speaking in a small schoolhouse. There was a lot of unemployment among the miners. There had been an inter-jurisdictional fight between the two unions in that area, and the leader of one of the unions, [Don] Gillis, I believe, was the Conservative candidate. That was kind of unusual, for a strong labour man to be a Conservative candidate. Feelings were running very high.

A lot of supporters of the Liberal candidate, [Osias J.] Godin, had sur-rounded the small schoolhouse with placards. When Diefenbaker finished his speech, people came in from the outside saying that they were rocking the cars, and there was going to be trouble. There was only a small detach-ment of Ontario Provincial Police available. I remember him going to the inner door with Mrs. Diefenbaker, George Hogan and I following him, when Hogan suddenly whipped around and faced him with his arms up against the door. He said, 'Prime Minister, it's not wise for you to go out there at this time.' The prime minister gently pushed George aside, and he said, 'I'm the prime minister, and I'm going out there, and that's all there is to it.' A group of people had assembled with signs and with clubs, and they were rocking the cars and making a lot of noise. They were lined up pretty close to the door. I vividly recall one guy there with a Godin sign on him. He had a great pot belly. A heavy-set fellow. I'd never seen Mrs Diefenbaker ever do anything like this before, but as the prime minister went by – there was a bit of shuffling and pushing and shoving – I saw her left elbow whip out and she just drove it into this guy's stomach as far as she could drive it. He doubled over, and that left a massive hole in the line, so to speak, and everybody popped through.

We got the Diefenbakers in the car, but they started to rock the car. Gillis, the candidate, was supposed to get in the car as well, but instead he got up on the back, and sat on the trunk of the car, I guess to try to ward off people who were hitting and rocking the car. Everybody was telling him, 'Get off the car.' He was vulnerable. He was sitting on a smooth trunk, slippery, with no way to hold on. Just a tiny shove, and off he'd go. It was not a very bright thing to do. They were hitting him over the head with the cardboard parts of these signs. He put his hands up to defend himself, the car was slowly pulling away, and he was falling off the trunk. There were two policemen there, and they eventually got him inside the car, but not until after he'd taken a lambasting around his head and shoulders.

But the two coolest people there were Mr and Mrs Diefenbaker. His eyes were blazing like two lasers. Nobody touched him. It was like the Red Sea parting. They didn't touch him, but they were awfully close.

By any measure, the 1962 election was a disaster for the Progressive Conservatives. From the greatest majority of all times, they were reduced to a minority government with 116 seats. The Liberals had 100; Social Credit had 30 (26 of them formerly Conservatives seats in Quebec); the NDP had 19.

Tory majorities were eliminated or cut to pieces, especially in Toronto. Donald Fleming, who had had a plurality of 19,097 votes in 1958, just saved his Eglinton seat by 760 votes. George Hees' plurality was down to 1200. He had knocked on doors in the Cabbagetown end of his Toronto Broadview riding and found that the people there felt the 'government would sooner play politics than look after the affairs of the country.' The city folk, the consumers, had been scared by the Liberals into believing the cost-of-living would go up.

Still it was an 'absolute miracle,' in the view of Merril Menzies, that Diefenbaker should have been able to save his government in the face of unemployment, the Coyne affair, devaluation, and the deep divisions within his cabinet and party. Despite the losses, John G. Diefenbaker returned to Ottawa in 1962 as the first Conservative leader since his hero, Sir John A. Macdonald, to win three Canadian general elections.

Index

Abbott, Douglas 262
Adenauer, Konrad 162
Aitken, Margaret 70
Allison, Carlyle 19
Anderson-Thompson, John 116
Argue, Senator Hazen 96, 102
Aseltine, Senator W.M. 188

Balcer, Léon 5, 12, 15, 16, 17, 19, 54, 185, 187, 196, 197, 198, 262
– biography 196
– excerpts 18–19, 21, 32, 67–8, 185, 188, 193, 194, 196–7, 201, 202–3
Baldwin, Gerald 16
– excerpts 49–50, 105, 114–16
Barette, Antonio 57, 200, 201
Bawden, Peter 113
Beattie, J.R. 238
Beatty, Sir Edward 115
Beaubien, Senator Louis Philippe 57
Beaudoin, L. René 5
Bedson, Derek 181
Bell, Richard A. 12, 15, 29, 37, 43, 45, 231, 237, 238, 244, 258

– excerpts 12, 15–16, 28–9, 30, 30–1, 43–4, 45, 77, 103, 192, 197–8, 206, 213–14, 237–8, 239, 241–2
Bennett, R.B. 12, 19, 61, 78, 115, 179, 203, 207, 209, 210, 211, 214, 229
Bennett, W.A.C. 114, 179
Bennett, W.O. 148
Blair, Dr William Gourlay 62, 69
Booth, C.S. 146
Borden, Sir Robert 35, 78, 98, 194, 207
Bracken, John 13, 28, 29, 30
Brooks, Senator Alfred J. 67, 72
Brown, Clément
– excerpts 195–6, 201–2, 203, 204
Brown, Chief Justice J.T. 24
Brunt, Senator William 8, 31, 32, 61, 62, 66, 156, 183
Bryce, Robert 144, 145, 181, 231, 262
Buchanan, Senator John A. 115, 116
Burns, Art 57

Campeau, Robert 212
Caouette, Réal 267

Cardin, P.J.A. 194
Casselman, Arza Clair 74
Champagne, Gilbert 182, 183
Chevrier, Lionel 58, 74, 75, 76, 81,
   184, 211, 212, 268
– excerpts 58, 81–2, 83, 88, 99, 105,
   187
Churchill, Gordon 9, 13, 16, 20, 36,
   44, 58, 67, 125, 134, 137, 149, 150,
   151, 152, 180, 185, 214, 231, 237,
   243, 256
– biography 40–1
– excerpts 9–11, 17–18, 21, 41–3, 44–
   5, 46, 66–7, 73, 79, 93–4, 137–8,
   146–7, 152–5, 204, 215, 219, 232,
   247, 254, 263
Churchill, Sir Winston 72
Clark, Clifford 148
Coldwell, M.J. 53, 76, 77, 95, 99, 128,
   134
Comtois, Paul 187, 196, 199
Courtemanche, Henri 197
Coyne, James 118, 124, 229–49, 251,
   254, 264, 271
– biography 234–5
Curtis, Leslie Roy 222

De Gaulle, Charles 162, 170
Dempson, Peter 63
Dexter, Grant 152
Diefenbaker, Edna Brower 27, 33
Diefenbaker, Elmer 23, 27, 161, 162
Diefenbaker, John George passim
– biography 23–33
Diefenbaker, Mary Florence 23
Diefenbaker, Olive 10, 50, 56, 66, 158,
   161, 261, 265, 266, 267, 270, 271
Diefenbaker, William Thomas 23, 24
Dinsdale, Walter 41, 112
– excerpts 112–14, 147, 185

Donnelly, Alan 161
Dorion, Noel 187, 188, 198, 245
Douglas, T.C. 25, 127, 128, 130, 224
– biography 128–9
– excerpts 25, 95–6, 104–5, 127–8,
   129–30, 132, 194, 225–7
Drew, Fiorenza 6, 7, 69
Drew, George 4, 5, 6, 7, 8, 9, 10, 12,
   16, 28, 31, 32, 33, 35, 36, 40, 45, 58,
   62, 69, 70, 71, 93, 146, 182
Drouin, Senator Marc 55
Duplessis, Maurice 54, 55, 56, 57, 58,
   77, 100, 101, 191, 195, 196, 199,
   200, 203, 204, 205

Eisenhower, Dwight D. 171
English, John 73

Faibish, Roy 144, 256, 264
– excerpts 145, 149–50, 172, 177–8,
   211, 255, 261–2, 265–7, 268–71
Fairclough, Ellen 6, 28, 64, 185, 258
– biography 69
– excerpts 6, 69–71, 158, 180, 218
Favreau, Guy 221
Ferguson, George 155
Fines, Clarence 130
Firestone, O.J. 211
Fisher, Douglas 155
Fisher, John 171, 181, 261, 265, 266,
   267
– excerpts 171–2, 172–3, 182–3,
   183–4
Fleming, Donald M. 4, 5, 8, 9, 11, 12,
   13, 14, 15, 16, 21, 31, 37, 38, 70, 77,
   115, 118, 124, 125, 128, 129, 155,
   165, 180, 188, 198, 200, 230, 231,
   232, 233, 237, 238, 244, 248, 252,
   253, 254, 257, 264, 271
– biography 243

– excerpts 5, 14–15, 21, 29–30, 31–2,
  68, 78–9, 179, 200–1, 210–11, 212–
  13, 219–20, 235–7, 238–9, 239–41,
  242–3, 244–6, 248–9, 252, 255,
  258–60, 263
Flemming, Hugh John 16, 17, 18, 150,
  192
– excerpts 20–1, 52–3, 192
Flynn, Senator Jacques 16
– biography 199
– excerpts 16–17, 100, 187–8, 195,
  199–200, 205, 218, 267–8
Forsey, Senator Eugene 38, 141, 142
– excerpts 39, 40, 142, 143, 150, 206,
  215–17
Forsyth-Smith, C.M. (Max) 134, 137,
  138
Foulkes, General Charles 74
Fraser, Blair 152, 177, 268
Frost, Leslie M. 12, 62, 93, 188, 236,
  237
Fulton, Davie 13, 14, 16, 21, 26, 28,
  33, 38, 62, 70, 89, 115, 125, 168,
  188, 198, 209, 220, 221, 243, 246,
  269
– excerpts 14, 26, 68–9, 178–9, 204,
  209–10, 220, 221, 222–4, 247–8

Gagnon,Onésime 57
Gainer, W.D. 116
Gallagher, Jack 113
Gardiner, James G. 25, 26, 27, 61, 75,
  77, 95, 127
Garson, Stuart S. 82, 117
Gillis, Donald 270, 271
Godin, Osias J. 270
Goldberg, A.I. 154, 155
Goodman, Eddie 51, 52
Gordon, Crawford 121
Gordon, Donald 235

Gordon, Walter 39, 112, 259
Granger, Charles 58, 59
Graydon, Gordon 29, 30
Green, Dr Glen 110
Green, Howard 3, 4, 30, 62, 115, 125,
  146, 161, 164, 168, 169, 170, 180,
  185, 203, 268
– biography 168–9
– excerpts 103, 138, 168, 169, 175–6,
  179, 217, 233
Green, Senator R.F. 168
Griffiths, William 65
Grosart, Senator Allister 7, 8, 10, 11,
  13, 18, 20, 35, 37, 45, 63, 64, 66, 91,
  92, 94, 141, 150, 151, 159, 182,
  258, 270
– biography 92–3
– excerpts 8, 11–12, 13, 19, 35–7, 38,
  45–6, 48–9, 50–1, 59, 91–2, 93, 94–
  5, 96–7, 101–2, 103–4, 150–1, 165–
  6, 225, 257
Guest, Gowan 142, 143, 144, 161,
  171, 181, 184
– excerpts 144, 163, 181–2

Hackett, Senator John Thomas 42
Hall, Mr Justice Emmett 24
– excerpts 24, 25, 27, 28
Hamilton, Alvin 16, 72, 112, 114,
  115, 116, 125, 127, 132, 149, 150,
  185, 198, 225, 256, 262, 263, 264
– biography 134
– excerpts 16, 32, 72, 78, 98–9, 111–
  12, 130, 133–4, 134–7, 138–9, 163–
  4, 175, 179, 214–15, 231–2, 243–4,
  246, 252–3, 254, 256–7, 258, 260–1,
  263–4
Hamilton, William M. 54, 64
– excerpts 38, 64–6, 94, 100–1, 122–
  3, 164–5, 193, 197, 198, 202, 204

Hanson, Richard B. 30
Harkness, Douglas 16, 62, 72, 115, 128, 129, 130, 133, 178, 225
– excerpts 16, 104, 122, 131, 176–7, 246–7
Harnois, Berthe 196
Harris, J.H. 30
Harris, Walter 59, 82, 83, 229, 230
Hawrelak, William 62
Hees, George 4, 10, 13, 16, 36, 46, 66, 121, 165, 166, 214, 215, 219, 243, 254, 257, 271
– excerpts 4, 18, 47–8, 67, 74–7, 96, 102–3, 146, 166–7, 180–1, 244
Hellyer, Paul 59
Herridge, H.W. 265
Hill, Bruce 241
Hodgson, Clayton W. 10
Hogan, George 266, 270
Howe, C.D. 26, 59, 67, 68, 73, 75, 77, 95, 108, 109, 148, 149, 150, 166, 237

Ilsley, James L. 226
Isbister, C.M. 238

Jack, Mel 36
Jacobsson, Per 259
Jodoin, Claude 142, 216
Johnson, Daniel 203
Johnson, George 156
Johnston, Fred 26
Jorgenson, Warner 133
Juba, Steven 62

Kearns, Kate 35, 37
Kennedy, D.M. 115
Kennedy, John F. 111, 139, 171, 172, 173
Khruschev, Nikita 146
King, Charles 265, 266, 267

King, W.L. Mackenzie 25, 27, 73, 85, 103, 144, 151, 179, 194, 201, 204, 226
Knowles, Stanley 99
Kristjanson, Baldur 256
Kuch 263

Ladner, Leon J. 168
Lafontaine, Paul 17, 194
Lamb, Kaye 171
Lapointe, Ernest 194
Lapointe, Hugues 59
Laurier, Sir Wilfrid 98, 99
Lawrence, Allan F. 13, 14
Leblanc, Jean 157
Lesage, Jean 204, 205
Lévesque, René 112
Longchamps, Don 161
Lougheed, Peter 98
Lougheed, Senator 98
Low, Solon 53
Lynch, Charles 158, 266
Macaulay, J.A. 269
MacDonald, Donald 142
Macdonald, Sir John A. 23, 75, 99, 179, 207, 271
MacDonald, Ramsay 216
Macdonnell, James M. 5, 6, 7, 12, 30, 68
McIvor, George 148
Mackenzie, Ian 74
Mackenzie, M.W. 110
Mackie, Victor J. 33, 156
– excerpts 33, 156–8, 158–9
MacLean, Angus 4, 44, 125
– excerpts 4, 38, 79, 179, 205, 255
Macmillan, Harold 162, 164, 165, 173
McNamara, Senator W.C. 135, 136
MacPherson, Murdo 180
Manning, M.E. 116

Marler, George C. 74
Martin, Paul 51, 83, 170, 184, 211, 212, 214, 226, 244, 259, 268
– biography 83
– excerpts 53–4, 71–2, 82, 84–5, 88–9, 145, 164, 169–70, 170–1, 194–5, 217–18, 233, 248
Martineau, Paul 184, 192, 198, 243
– excerpts 184, 191–2, 197, 218–19
Matthews, Bev 47
Meighen, Arthur 194, 196
Menzies, Merril 51, 98, 107, 110, 111, 123, 127, 229, 256, 257, 261, 262, 265, 267, 268, 271
– biography 116–17
– excerpts 51, 107–10, 110–11, 111, 117 19, 119–21, 123–5, 125, 131–2, 182, 230–1, 232, 253
Merritt, Lt Col C.C.I. 269, 270
Méthot, Léon 30
Michener, Roland 187, 214
Miller, Air Marshall Frank 74
Milner, H.R. 28, 29
Monteith, J. Waldo
– excerpts 103, 264
Moon, Robert 180
Munro, Ross 19

Nasserden, Ed 266
Nehru, Jawaharlal 162, 164
Nelson, James 102, 157, 161, 163, 181
– excerpts 102, 162–3
Neville, William 161
Newman, Peter 226
Nicholson, L.H. 222, 223, 224
Nickle, Carl 155
Nollet, I.C. 129
Normand, Dr Louis-Philippe 196
Nowlan, George 5, 12, 66, 122, 158, 159, 198, 231, 262

O'Brien, Mickey 265, 266
O'Hurley, Raymond 197, 198, 199, 262
O'Leary, Senator Grattan 3, 6, 7, 12, 173, 175
– excerpts 3, 5, 12, 13, 78, 121–2, 145–6, 148, 173, 207, 220

Pallett, John 62, 63, 153
Patterson, Donald D. 52
Pearkes, George 16, 17, 18, 20, 39, 61, 65, 66, 73, 120, 125
– excerpts 18, 61–2, 74
Pearson, L.B. 81, 82, 83, 84, 85, 86, 87, 88, 89, 92, 99, 142, 144, 147, 149, 154, 164, 171, 177, 179, 184, 194, 200, 206, 210, 211, 212, 221, 236, 243, 245, 254, 263, 268
Petrie, Richard 150
Pickersgill, J.W. 39, 49, 58, 89, 115, 165, 184, 211, 212, 233, 242, 244, 268
– biography 85
– excerpts 53, 58–9, 82–3, 85–8, 89, 96, 99, 147–8, 205–6, 224–5, 233–4, 255–6, 264
Plumptre, A.F.W. 238, 259
Porter, Dana H. 39
Pound, M. 146, 172, 257
Power, Senator C.G. 151, 194

Quirin, G. David 113

Ralston, Colonel J.L. 234
Rasminsky, Louis 235, 238, 248, 258, 259, 262
Reisman, Simon 214, 231
Riddel, W. 135
Rivard, Antoine 57, 201
Roberts, James 146

Robertson, Gordon 114, 115, 116
Robertson, Norman 145
Robinson, Basil 144, 161
Robinson, Judith 42, 152
Roblin, Duff 9, 10, 181
Roosevelt, F.D. 194
Rostow, Walt 173
Rowe, Earl 5, 6, 7, 10, 12, 35, 61
Rowe, William 6, 7, 35
Rynard, Dr P.B. 161

Sabourin, Ivan 17, 194
St Laurent, Louis 36, 41, 49, 51, 52
53, 54, 58, 59, 61, 72, 77, 79, 81, 82,
83, 85, 87, 89, 95, 107, 119, 129,
141, 144, 147, 165, 169, 177, 181,
195, 200, 201, 203, 204, 218, 225,
226, 234
St Laurent, Reynaud 81, 82
Samson, Dr Mathieu 81
Sauvé, Paul 57, 191, 200, 201, 202,
203, 204, 205
Sévigny, Pierre 16, 17, 18, 54, 56, 94,
198, 199
– excerpts 19, 20, 44, 54–8, 77–8,
97–8, 177, 189, 198–9, 225, 253–4
Sharp, Mitchell 73, 148, 149, 150, 152
– biography 148–9
Sissons, Jack 115
Small, C. John 134, 137
Smallwood, Joseph R. 85, 222

Smith, Sidney 12, 73, 161
Spooner, J. Wilfred 112
Starr, Michael 7, 8, 66, 125, 153, 211,
214, 215, 216, 231, 233
– biography 62
– excerpts 7, 62–4, 73, 95, 186–7,
211–12, 268
Stevens, H.H. 269
Stevenson, Adlai 84
Stirling Grote 30

Talbot, Antonio 57, 201
Taylor, Fred W. (Cyclone) 48
Taylor, Kenneth 231, 237, 238, 240,
241
Taylor, John 48
Towers, Graham 229
Tustin, George J. 11

Underhill, Frank 110

Vanier, Georges 19, 192, 195, 199

Wagner, Marion 161, 172
Walker, Senator David J. 8, 13, 28,
125, 185, 187, 231, 244, 245, 246
Warren, J.H. 153, 154
Whitehead, William 32
Willis, Senator Harry 47, 48, 51, 52
Winter, Jed 96
Winters, Robert 59